A Romance with the Exotic Madrona, Alias of the Arbutus

Roy W. Martin Ph.D.

To order additional copies of this book, contact:
Xlibris
844-714-8691
www.Xlibris.com
Orders@Xlibris.com

ISBN: Softcover 978-1-6698-0523-6
Hardcover 978-1-6698-0524-3
EBook 978-1-6698-0522-9

Library of Congress Control Number: 2022900176

Print information available on the last page

Rev. date: 02/19/2022

All the prepared material is by the author unless
stated otherwise. It is a non-fiction book.

Photographs

All photographs in the book have been taken by the author unless stated otherwise. The photographs from the cover through the Part One Introduction are of the Madrona (i.e. Pacific Madrone, *arbutus menziesii*). The locations where the of the pictures have been taken are at various places during our travels in the Salish Sea.

Ode to the Madrona

I hear your call,
I walk the rocky trail,
Each turn a befall,
Of delight - a fairytale
Of serpentine form,
And changing detail,
Like wind and storm.

You twist and turn,
Is it the sun you yearn?
Or is there another secret,
That we can't discern?

You shed your thin peel,
To reveal new skin,
Satin to the feel,
Florid from within.

You reach out from the rocks,
Over the cascading waves,
Sandstone pocks,
And cliffs with enclaves.

You love the wind shaking your leaves,
The mist mixing with the sun,
The freshness of the breeze.
Intrigue - you have spun.
You are the exotic of the trees!

Aloof, hiding, peeking,
Bending around other trunks.
Silent - except rustling, creaking,
Spiritual like pilgrimaging monks.

Enrapture has just begun,
Amplifying your persona,
In the sinking sun.
I see your corona,
Of leaves and branches.
Oh Madrona! Oh Madrona!
Your exposed skin enhances
The glow of the red light,
As it glistens and dances
And so I too frolic - with delight!

A Romance with the Exotic Madrona – Alias of the *Arbutus*

Contents

Part One Introduction: The Arbutus Artesian of Cortes Island

The air was dripping with moisture that morning in the summer of 2015 as I nudged *The Sea Overture* into Tiber Bay in Desolation Sound, British Columbia, Canada. Ripples receded from her hull, rocking several skiffs tied to an ancient dock, otherwise a perfect stillness prevailed. Uncertain whether this was the correct cove, I telephoned Ron. "Yes," he reassured me. "You're in the right spot. Just follow the path around the bay and go up the road to the second driveway."

I released our anchor and the chain clanged out. Reversing the propeller, the boat backed until the chain tightened, and we were secured in eighteen feet of water. Taking my camera Darlene, my wife, and I disembarked. Circling the dock in our dingy, we looked for a space to bump into. Once we found one, we grasped the tie plank, stabilized the boat, and struggled out and up onto the dock. After fastening the dingy, we were ready. We jiggled and swayed across a weathered walkway to the rocky shore, my camera dangling from my shoulder and bouncing against my hip. We were welcomed by a hybrid path of boards, rock, and moss along the shore. Each step was greeted with a mixture of damp shoreline, stable yet slippery surfaces, and the fruits of the occasional bygone traveler's pains to beat a passable trail, this culminating finally in a path flanked by tall grass beyond which loomed several houses, that were well adjusted to the moisture of the sea and their position along the bay. (Figure PI 1B & C) A road leading back into the woods emerged as we came abreast one of the houses. I impulsively decided this must be it

Stepping onto the long-ago graveled road, I noticed that the grass grew high between the tire paths. This sounded an alarm in the back of my brain somewhere, but I promptly if unwisely ignored it. The road – or perhaps just tire pathways, with some well-worn rocks occasionally protruding from the road surface – wound itself up an incline and out of sight into the woods. Trees that guarded the road on either side reached out and blocked the arc of the sun. Sword ferns populated the understory, penetrating and being lifted by a blanket of moss.

Looking for the driveway, we finally passed an impression of a road, perhaps so infrequently traveled to be of the endangered variety; nevertheless, it meandered off into the forest. "Something is wrong," Darlene, said to me, but I was reluctant to admit it. Nevertheless, I dialed Ron again. After some discussion, I was asked to describe what was around us.

"Well," I said, "a rough and rocky road… lots of tall trees, rocks, and ferns…" I trailed off, realizing the futility of the task.

"That's not very helpful," our would-be host replied, "as that could describe anywhere around here. Go up the road a little farther and tell me what you see." We proceeded as directed but saw nothing particularly identifying until I noticed short sections of concrete in the ridged tire paths. These had been poured to provide traction for vehicles with drivers intrepid enough to brave the steep incline. When I relayed this information to Ron, he said: "Stay there. I think I know where you are and I will come and find you." Darlene, having heard only one side of the conservation, was anxious to continue up the road, but we stayed close.

Presently I heard a voice call from the woods. "Roy!" I answered back with relief in my voice, and soon a slim man with wavy hair, glasses, knee-high boots, and a big smile appeared through the misty foliage. This was how we first met Ron Bazar. I had been anxious to meet him ever since discovering his informative website

(ArbutusArts.com), with intriguing photos and lively discussions of the *Arbutus* tree – and, of course, the sundry items he famously fashioned from its wood.

After we shook hands, he guided us along a deer trail, thoughtfully assisting Darlene as we went, she was wearing nothing on her feet but flip-flops, as we wove our way through a colony of large rocks and *Arbutus* trees. Some of these latter snaked toward the sky; some shared space with conifers, and still others lay defunct upon the forest floor, fallen by the strong winds of a recent storm. Ron remarked that this was one of the areas where he routinely harvested wood for his work.

As the woods thinned several cabins appeared, each nestled into its own space in the trees, retreats which Ron himself had built and his friends sometimes made use of. He guided us to his cottage, and we entered, over a suspended walkway elevated at least ten feet above the ground, onto his front porch. We stopped, transfixed by the panoramic view before us (Figure PI 1A). We were perched at least five hundred feet above the waters of Desolation Sound on a series of rolling and descending hilltops dressed in rocks, *Arbutus*, and evergreens. The whole world seemed to lie at our feet. The open waters extended all the way to the horizon, east across the sound and up through Homfray Channel, to Forbes Bay with its backdrop of huge, snow-covered mountains accented by Mount Denman, which Ron called the Canadian Matterhorn. To our southeast lay the Malaspina and Gifford Peninsulas, tendrils of the mainland boasting such popular hideaways as Tenedos Bay and Prideaux Haven. Northeast of us, the Lewis Channel butted against West Redonda Island, home to Refuge Cove, the smaller Martin Islands mere specks below it. And finally, in the more immediate forefront, Kinghorn Island shadowed by Mink Island summoned our eyes.

Eventually, after some difficulty tearing ourselves away from the view, we sat and listened as Ron described how he got started carving *Arbutus* wood. He had for fun carved a letter opener and had sent it to his mother as a gift. As all good mothers would, she had encouraged him to make some more and see if he could sell them. He now sells and distributes his creations through his website, numerous galleries, and stores in British Columbia, and at the Friday Market at Manson Hall on Cortes Island in the summers.

After a while, Ron brought out several baskets of his salad *hands* which were like salad forks but without tines, all of which he had carved himself. Each was astonishingly beautiful and unique. The patterns of the grains varied and mixed with the colors in the wood in distinctive blends, recording the struggles and successes of each tree during its life. The richness of the colors captivated us, and caressing each piece, we discovered that the utensils' surfaces were silken to the touch, the result of hours of labor-intensive sanding with increasingly finer grit and various oils.

We just had to have some of these, but which? Each piece seemed more attractive than the last but wait, no, that earlier one was more exquisite still. Back and forth we went. Darlene asked: "What do you think?" "Which one do you like best?"

I liked them all. Eventually we settled on a pair for ourselves and a pair as a gift. Two of these salad hands now decorate a bowl in our living room. I don't think they will ever touch salad, as they are art. (Figure PI 2B)

After a bit more socializing, we reluctantly bade Ron farewell. He showed us the correct way to return to our boat, whereupon the rain decided to baptize us. We hurried down the hill, past the house, and around the cove, peering as best we could from beneath our hoods. Slipping here and there, we finally wobbled across to the dock and to our dingy. Soon we were safely back in our boat, shaking off the water and turning on the heat. Once we had the engine running and our anchor up, we headed out of the cove. We were just remarking to each other what a fun visit we'd had when something rather extraordinary happened.

Off the starboard side of our boat, a large triangular fin suddenly appeared, followed by a smaller second fin and even a third small fin. I immediately pulled back to neutral, shut off the engine and the depth sounder, and coasted the boat to a stop. Three Orcas whales were rising, submerging, rising again, and cutting through the glassy water. They were coming in our direction (Figure PI 3)!

We held our breath and I grabbed my camera. The whales kept coming closer, closer, periodically blasting water from their blowholes, shocking our ears with the explosive sound the action produced. Their sleek black sides slipped effortlessly through the water, creating only the subtlest of wakes. Each time one of the majestic beasts emerged from the water, it seemed to reach higher than the last – when, suddenly, one of them did a quick spy-hop. Having snapped a ream of photographs in rapid succession, I hoped at least one of them had captured the stunt. At some point Darlene cried, "I think they're going to go under our boat!" And, indeed, just then the larger one headed directly toward us, its fin a black dagger jutting prominently from its broad, slick back. It turned just in time to avoid our boat, exposing its dorsal regions now in broadside. The fin had a slight hook indicative of the female of the species. We were ecstatic. What magnificent creatures they were.

We remained spellbound until they faded from our view on their journey north. Darlene and I looked at each other. Something clicked. We were retired. We could do as we pleased. Thoughts of a grand adventure began to materialize in my mind.

Figure PI 1 Cortes Island: A. *Upper* View over Desolation Sound, B. *Lower Left* Darlene on the trail, C. *Lower Right* Trail along the shore.

Figure Pl 2 A. *Upper* Ron Bazar's workshop, B. *Lower* Salad Hands.

Figure PL 3 Orcas whales east of Cortes Island. Upper right photo Orca *Spy Hops*.

Budding of My Romance

It was in another bay and another time, fog hung low over the water, dew weeping from its mist, collecting in droplets on the waxen leaves of the evergreen trees along the shoreline. Each tree had its own distinct posture, its own unique contortions, but all of them inclined toward the water. All of them, as if in carefully choreographed unison, leaning out over a sliver of rocky beach, bathing in the milky light of the fog-laden morn. The chlorophyll in the green leaves, though eager to go to work, patiently waited.

These trees in question have the alias name "Madrona," more formally the Pacific Madrone – or, in the botanical lexicon, *Arbutus menziesii* (pronounced are-BEW-tus men-ZEEZ-ee-eye), followed by the word Pursh. (To me, a more fitting name might simply be "Gorgeous.") I dipped my paddle deep into the water, jockeying the kayak to get a better camera view of another luxurious, peeling trunk. (Figure PL 4 & 5)

"What are you going to do with all those pictures of that tree?" Darlene would later ask me.

"What indeed?" I would wonder.

This thought was undeniably the start of my romance. The answer ultimately took the form of geographical, botanical, and archival treks on which I had no previous plans to embark. Although I had darkened the halls of many engineering and medical libraries over the years, and devoured a large swath of the literature, stepping into the world of Botany, was a wholly new adventure for me. Soon I encountered botanical words I'd never seen before; Latin words as to whose meanings at I could merely guess; and sections of libraries, I had never previously explored. For example, I don't recall that Latin was a prerequisite of any of the engineering classes I took in college or graduate school, or even a subject with which many engineering students especially sought to familiarize themselves.

Fortunately, thanks to the Internet, the process of data gathering, and assimilation had been rendered far easier and more efficient than in my days as a student and subsequently, a college professor. Although my education had begun with file cards and punch cards, now I could sit at my kitchen table and access information from all over the world just by clicking a mouse. Digesting and collating this information, however, still required the same diligence and scrutiny as always.

Many a college romance has begun in a classroom, a library, or perhaps a student union building. However, one spark of my romance began with curiosity about the name of these beautiful trees I was photographing. We called them Madrona, but the British Columbia people called them Arbutus. I soon learned Arbutus was actually part of its scientific name and should be italicized. In further exploration I encountered the two words *Arbutus* Linneaus. This is the title Paul Sørensen gives in his definitive 1995 monogram about these trees.[1] What is this word, "Linnaeus", and why is it tacked onto "*Arbutus*"? This is an excellent place to start.

Linnaeus, Carl Linnaeus, is a pillar in Botany and is the Father of Taxonomy, a system for scientifically classifying organism. He was born in 1707 in Uppsala, Sweden and died there in 1778. Uppsala is a beautiful inland city, surrounded by a picturesque natural environment. Located at the fifty-ninth parallel, with its short daylight of six hours in the winter and long summer daylight of up to eighteen hours, the city's geographical position likely had an impact on Linnaeus' work schedule, mooring him to his desk during the dark, cold months and enticing him outdoors in the spring and summer. For whatever reason(s), Linnaeus was very prolific professionally.

His contribution of binomial nomenclature, which describes a specimen with two words, remains the standard to this day. The first word is the genus, a taxonomic category of the specimen, in this case *Arbutus*. The second word is the species, in this case, *menziesii*. This word identifies which of perhaps several species the organism is, bearing characteristics different from the others but still enough similarity to fall under the same genus classification. The name of a species itself typically arises from that of a person involved in its discovery, the location where it is first or most often found, or, in a few cases, entirely from the imagination or whim of the person(s) tasked with classifying it. The third word is not always included. In the case of *Arbutus menziesii*

Pursh. Pursh is the last name of the individual who first scientifically reported the species. It is a great honor for a botanist to discover and name a new species; botanists as a group are therefore quite competitive with their peers in this venture, feeling a great deal of pressure to claim that honor, and much exuberance when they do.

Returning to the words "*Arbutus* Linnaeus," here Sørensen has given the credit to Linnaeus for reporting and naming the entire genus in one of his famous writings, Species Planarum 1753.[2] I can clearly picture Linnaeus sitting at his desk, penning "*caule erecto, foliis glabris serratis, baccis polyspermis*" after the word "*Arbutus*". According to the Google translation of Latin to English, this phrase means: "stiff stems, leaves smooth, jagged, red berries, polyspermis." "Polyspermis" implying "multiple seeds."

To the right of Linnaeus' disclosure one finds the word "Unedo," and he supplies "Europe" as its habitat. Certainly, he had never been to America, so it would have been the Eastern Hemisphere *Arbutus* tree, *unedo*, upon which he based this revelation. There are three other species included in his diction, but the other three are ruled out according to Sørensen, as they belong to a different genus. Linnaeus' report thus bestows upon him the credit, not only for describing the genus *Arbutus*, but also for describing one of the species itself, *Arbutus unedo*, a species elaborated on later.

Returning to *Arbutus menziesii* Pursh, my favorite tree, grows in the western coast of the North America, ranging from southern California all the way north into the Salish sea in British Columbia, Canada, with still more growing in a certain area on the western side of Vancouver Island. However, the question remains: exactly where does the species name *menziesii* come from, and how did the *Arbutus* tree come to bear, in part, Pursh's name?

Frederick T. Pursh (1774-1820) became well known through his 1814 publication of: *A Systematic Arrangement and Descriptions of the Plants of North America*, which was his crowning achievement after many years of work in the United States and England. He apparently did not travel to the western United States, and probably never saw an *Arbutus menziesii* himself alive. He did, however, credit Captain Lewis for many specimens in the book which were gathered on the Lewis and Clark Expedition (1803-1806). [3] He also frequented herbariums in the United States, traveled across mountains along the East Coast, and ultimately found the specimen of interest in the Banksian Herbarium in England. This herbarium was formed from the collections of Sir Joseph Banks. Included in this herbarium were many specimens collected by Archibald Menzies throughout his travels to North America as a surgeon, first as part of a fur-trading trip and later as a naturalist on Captain George Vancouver's voyage to the Pacific Northwest and various other places (1791-1795). Pursh, in the preface, describes receiving permission from Menzies to use some of his specimens in his (Pursh's) book; in exchange, Pursh assigned the name *menziesii* as the species designation for a number of specimens, including most notably the *Arbutus menziesii*.

I have used the name "Madrona" in the title of the book. What are the origins of that name? To answer this question, we must travel a little farther. But first, I am going to put the *Arbutus* genus in scientific perspective with regards to the classification it falls under, starting with the Kingdom: **Plantae** (all plants). After that, the listing goes, in order from most general to most specific: **Angiosperms** (flowering plants which produce seeds enclosed in fruit (eight groups)); **Eudicots** (these have special flower components of approximately 175,000 different types); and **Asterids**. Next comes the Order: **Ericales** (a family of flowering plants); and then the Family: **Eriicaceae** (composed of over one hundred genere, including about twenty-five in the U.S.); and, finally, the **Genus**, (*Arbutus*) which comprises various species the names of which are italicized as a matter of convention.[4] In this case there are three major species of *Arbutus* in the Eastern Hemisphere and eight species in the Western Hemisphere (see below Table 1). [1,3][5]

Table 1
Arbutus Species

Species	Common Name	General Location
Eastern Hemisphere		
unedo	Strawberry Tree *	Mediterranean Area Greece, Turkey
andrachne	Greek Strawberry Tree	
canariensis	Canary Madrone*	Canary Islands
Western Hemisphere		
arizonica	Arizona Madrone	AZ, NM, and Mexico
bicolor		Central Mexico
madrensis		Western Mexico
menziesii	Pacific Madrone*, Arbutus	Pacific West
molis		Mexico
peninsularis	Baja Madrone*	Baja Peninsula, Mexico
tessellata		Mexico
xalapensis	Texas Madrone, Lady Legs	Texas, NM, Mexico

Madrono - Spanish name with accent on the n. *

The key to the origin of the name of Madrona involves the common name of the *Arbutus unedo* indigenous to the Mediterranean area. There it is generally referred to as the "Strawberry Tree" (see the table), so-called because the ripe berries are red and as large as garden-variety strawberries. The tree's Spanish name is *madroño* or sometimes *madroña*, these two different spellings reflect the Spanish the gender of the word. The first ending in "o" is masculine and ending in "a" is feminine. Which version is used may depend on the character of the writer and his or her outlook on the tree. Nevertheless, the Spanish meaning relates to describing the roundness of its fruit, *round tassel* according to Diana Wells, in her book: *Lives of the Trees: An Uncommon History*[6]. She contends, a Franciscan priest from Spain, Father Juan Crespi, was an early missionary to Baja California in 1767. In 1779 he traveled with an expedition through the San Diego area and as far north as Monterrey. He was the diarist for the trip, and in this capacity reported sightings of numerous *madroño* trees, noting that the berries were much smaller than those in Spain.

The name *madroño* or *madroña* seemed to stick, but losing its accent over time, and particularly the farther north one looks, the word has morphed into Madrone, pronounced like Madrona or Madron (the ending like the modern word drone) in California and Oregon, and just Madrona, in Washington. In the book of Willis Linn Jepson, a famous and early Botanist at the University of California Berkely he uses the spelling *madroña*. It seems that this version may be more responsible for the use of Madrona in Washington. However, contrary to this line of thinking, in British Columbia, Canada, the term "*Arbutus*" is used – and just "*Arbutus*" alone, rather than the full scientific name. Perhaps this reflects the British influence and original immigration history. The more formal common name found in many publications is Pacific Madrone, most likely due to the difficult pronunciation of *menziesii*. However, I must smile regarding the Spanish words with their masculine or feminine ending and how perhaps this factor may have influenced how the word morphed to describe the tree. When looking at the tree does it seem masculine or feminine to you? The author being of male gender looks on this beautiful graceful curved exotic tree and thinks of it as definitely feminine even though of course the tree is of both sexes with regards to reproduction.

Other less formal names are The Refrigerator Tree and (incorrectly) The Strawberry Tree. The expression Refrigerator Tree presumably arose because of the coolness of the feel of the exfoliated trunk, which some think derives from the water that passes up the tree to the leaves. Lastly, a brief note to the reader so as to prevent confusion later: as a long-time resident of Washington, I often slip into the regional vernacular and use the term Madrona (Ma- drone-nah), but also sometimes use, instead, the more widely recognized name Pacific Madrone or just Madrone when referring to our local species *menziesii*.

Recalling that morning in Desolation Sound, after our visit with Ron Bazar, along with the astonishing encounter with the orcas, complemented by a sizeable amount of photo events and encounters later with the tree I decided I wanted to write about it. Further, considering the eleven species of *Arbutus* genus located around the world. I wanted to see them all. In fact, I did see most of them, traveling to the east as far as Israel, to the Canary Islands, and physically and virtually to Ireland, Portugal, and Greece, then in the North America to Texas, Arizona, California, Baja California and of course the Pacific Coast. In addition, the Pacific Madrone trees can grow to immense size. I wanted to photograph these ancient, living monuments while I had a chance. I wanted to document their existence. I wanted to write the *Arbutus* story. I had a start; I had laid the groundwork for this book.

Now all I had I to do was break the news to Darlene.

Figure Pl 4 Madrona (*Arbutus menziesii*) trees posing on islands in the Salish Sea.

Figure PI 5 Madronas displaying their captivating form on three different islands.

Chapter One:

My Heroine - Pacific Madrone (*Arbutus menziesii*)

Hanging onto the side of a cliff; standing alone, spreading her arms; twisting around another tree, adorning the rocky enclaves of an island's shores; shedding her red bark and trimming the hillsides with radiant white blossoms; in the autumn, captivating passersby with clusters of red berries; and, in every season, standing proudly with varying colors: these are but a few of the many attributes that make the Madrona a favorite of nature-lovers and arboreal enthusiasts alike.

Each tree is as different from the next as one human being from another, a distinctly individual creature reflecting in varying measures a number of influences, for example: the variation of the seasons; the particular period within a given season; the history of its occupation; the surrounding trees and human presence; how far it has progressed in its life cycle; and the history of its ancestors. Although all *Arbutus* species boast their own special characteristics and unique beauty, to me the Pacific Madrone is the premier of them all – truly the "Exotica" of the *Arbutus* line.

Nevertheless, it is worth making a few general comments about trees before we delve into my favorite. Using an analogy to humans, at a distance, the first feature often noted is the person's hair, particularly long and well-maintained stylish hair. Similarly, the first feature in a tree that strikes the observer is its leaves. A tree with a full and a large crown of foliage attracts the eye. Further, the color of the leaves, bright green, signals health. Since the *Arbutus* tree is an evergreen it enlivens the landscape even in the winter. Unlike conifers the leaves are not needles but are shaped like a spear head, lanceolate, with a width of about one inch (2.5 cm) and length twice that. These lengths and widths vary on different parts of the tree, with the different species and with the environmental conditions. Although the leaves are quite complex their function is straight forward. They receive water from the roots, carbon dioxide from the air, and light from the sun. They use these to produce oxygen which they release to the atmosphere and carbohydrates they provide to the tree utilizing a photosynthesis process based on the chlorophyll in the leaves.

A prominent microscopic feature particularly on the underside of the leaves are thousands of stomatal openings or pores which regulate gas flow to and from the leaves as well as controlling transpiration (water exiting through the leaves). The average length of the collapsed stomatal is 17 microns (one millionth of a meter) and in the Pacific Madrone there are at a density of about 7800/cm^2. To obtain a perspective consider each stomatal representing a golf hole or cup on a golf course each cup 4.25" (10.8 cm) in diameter. Based on the stomatal density that would mean each cup was located about 28 inches (seven tenths of a meter) from each other. With that many cups on a golf course even I could get a *Hole in One* every time I tee off, or at least occasionally.

The second feature one often notices about a human from a distance is their body form or structure. Similarly for a tree it is the trunk, branches, and twigs. This structure supports the leaves and spreads and holds them out to the sun. The trunk with its bark also provides conduits (xylem) for water and minerals to be pulled up from the roots to the leaves, and also retuning conduits (phloem) for carbohydrates and nutrients manufactured in the leaves to be passed back to the rest of the tree.

It is hard to provide an analogous human feature comparable to the roots of a tree, although recent discussions by some researchers who seek to find a cognitive process in plants have felt if there is a central like nervous system, it would be in the roots. Nevertheless, the roots do anchor the tree and forage for water and minerals. In addition, recent evidence reveals the symbiotic relation of the roots with fungi which aid the tree in obtaining nutrients from the soil in exchange for carbohydrates from the tree and surprisingly provide a link to the roots of other trees for communication and exchange of resources [7]. These findings are eye openers and should captivate one's curiosity about this humble form of life, the fungi.

Returning to the of the Pacific Madrone, an interesting nature of it is, it is not an aggressive tree; it does not, as some trees do, grow rapidly in order to reach the upper stratosphere of the forest and thereby capture most of the available light at the expense of its neighbors. It is, rather, an uncommonly cordial tree, often contorting itself as necessary to find open spaces through which light falls naturally, as if to accommodate smaller trees it would otherwise effectively starve. It will follow those spaces as they shift over time, forever trying to keep its leaves in the light. This feature, I believe, is what gives the tree such interesting twists and turns in its trunks and branches.

Bear in mind that, when we observe a tree in its maturity, it already has a considerable history, including perhaps years of searching and following available light. This benevolent trait is present even in trees which are isolated in open, sunny spaces. The lower branches will reach far sideways, even farther than the upper branches, so as to absorb light. This long stretching allows strong, still-developing branches to support the cantilevered foliage, possibly contributing to the hardness of the wood. Even in the dark understory of a forest, where the only option is to grow up toward the sun, the trees tend to be long and skinny and yet also to exhibit various curvatures, evincing their struggle for light along the way. Overall, this trend toward cordiality means they will often survive by growing along shorelines, where they can reach out over the water to open light-spaces and avoid having to compete with other trees for a place in the upper canopy of the forest.

Another favorable location is on the south sides of hills or cliffs. The steeper the hill, the more light is available without the trees' having to grow to great heights. On steep, rocky cliffs, their presence may reflect a lack of herbivores such as deer on these cliffs. Herbivores when present often kill young seedlings by grazing all the leaves off. As mentioned, Madrones grow along the west coast, as far south as perhaps halfway between San Francisco and Santa Barbara, and as far north as British Columbia. They are found close to the sea in most cases but more inland in the Sonora County area in California. Why this is isn't entirely clear.

One hypothesis is that competition from the types of trees that grow inland may override the Madrona. For example, in the northwest, aggressive evergreen and deciduous trees are prevalent; however, in Sonora County, large oaks dominate the hillsides, leaving more open spaces for other trees. The climates of central California and northward of Oregon's southern border are quite different, after all, the former being much drier and sunnier and the latter wetter and cloudier. Marian Elliot observes in her dissertation that trees are found to grow on the north side of hills and in canyons in hot and dry climates, whereas the opposite is true in regions with greater rainfall and less sunlight.[8]

One of the most beautiful parts of the *Arbutus* is its exfoliating bark. The exfoliation process begins in late spring or early summer in the Pacific Madone, depending on the weather. The presence of warm to hot weather seems to trigger this phenomenon in the thin bark. It does usually occur in the mid-to-upper trunk and branches. A denser bark, sometimes several layers deep and tiled or scalloped in appearance (brown to gray in color), is often present on the lower portions of the tree, although sometimes it isn't present at all. The contrast between this dense bark and the thin exfoliating bark is quite remarkable.

I have observed that heavy bark seems to be preserved and, indeed, to have flourished, on trees growing in shaded areas. In fact, trees growing in the heavy forest have heavy bark growing all the way up the tree and one can easily walk past mistaking it for a deciduous tree. However, trees enjoying longer periods of direct sunlight will generally loose this bark. The heavy bark does peel off under various external conditions and generally when it does it comes off in chunks.

On the hill of Cap Sante in Anacortes, WA the wind often blows strong and the sunlight is varied due to the presence of non Madrona trees. Here one can find trees with the heavy bark in different locations and sizes. It almost looks like a battle occurred against it. Sometimes, there will be heavy bark on the one side over a region and on the other side, none. Occasionally the bark will be hanging in strips or strands. Conversely, all the giant Madrones (discussed later) were found to have dense bark growing some distance up the tree.

Returning to the thin bark that exfoliates, one of the most unusual and intriguing features of it are the vibrant shades of colors: green, yellowish-green, chartreuse, copper, red, cinnamon-red, terra cotta, brown, light tan, and even white. The colors vary depending on the season, the location of the tree, its size, the section(s) of the trunk under scrutiny, which side of the tree faces the sun, the light conditions, and possibly the gender of the observer. This last is a factor because, according to studies, eight percent of men are colorblind compared to just half of one percent of women.[1]

The seasonal progression is interesting, and I have photographically documented it in one tree (Figure 1.1) In the fall, as the weather cools and rain become more frequent, the exfoliated trunk begins to take on a cinnamon-red hue. In some cases, the tree continues to redden into spring. The color change may be due in part to a thickening of the bark. By summer or late spring, the bark undergoes the actual process of exfoliation. Just under the outermost layer of bark that peels, a new bark appears which is bright yellowish-green. Fairly quickly with regards to the normal cycle of change in the tree, this exposed bark begins to turn a tan (or "biscuit") color. The rate at which this occurs seems to be strongly correlated with the number of cumulative hours of unobstructed sunlight received by that region of the tree. The longer and more direct this exposure, the more the bark seems to "bleach out." The term "sun-scald" is a term which has been used in the literature to describe extreme overexposure. I have observed Madrona trees on the south side of steep hills in late August which were bleached almost to the color of bone. As mentioned, there is a great deal of variation in the coloring and exfoliating but perhaps the most consistent findings can be derived by observing either the entire tree in its relative infancy or, alternately, at its most recent growth, which occurs at the tip of its branches. The history of the progression of the bark in one tree during one season is shown in Figure 1.1.

As winter weather yields to the more hospitable conditions of spring, sprouts and new growth first appear at the tips of the branches. These nascent branches then commence to elongate beyond the existing leaves. A length of thirteen inches (33 cm) is typical in healthy trees. Whereupon multiple buds appear toward the distal end of the new growth. It's almost as if the tree were "up to something." And, in a manner of speaking, indeed it is; namely, it is preparing for the inflorescence (blooming) that will come later. (See Figure 1.2) When these blossoms finally appear, they are white, bell-like, inclined to droop, and form clusters along individual twigs, emerging at various points and angles along the distal branch at the peripheries of the tree.

This inflorescence appears as splashes on a green background when observed from a distance. In fact, looking over a hillside during the blooming season, one can easily distinguish Madrona trees from all the other species. (Figure 1.4). Traveling along the I5 Freeway south of Seattle during the blooming season I was amazed to see endless Madrona trees growing along the top edge of the embankment for miles and miles. Clearly these trees had seeded themselves since the excavation and road work were initially performed. I had never noticed them before because when they are not blooming, they look like any other tree from a distance.

Continuing with the metamorphosis progression, toward the end of the blooming season, new leaves also manifest along the branches, but more proximately than the blossoms themselves. The old leaves will soon begin to fall off, sometimes taking on a reddish tinge beforehand. All the old leaves will be gone by early summer. The blossoms themselves, when pollinated, will turn into berry-carrying seeds during the summer. They are green in color initially, but as they ripen in the autumn, they turn red (see Figure 1.3)

Finally, it is worth noting that the living cycle of a tree is seasonal, there may be periods of apparent dormancy but overall it continues to grow. In contrast to mammals, the tree doesn't just grow to a mature size

1 As it happens, this writer is part of that eight percent, so when I describe something in a specific color, it should be interpreted with caution. - Incidentally, my optometrist prefers the term "color-confused" to "colorblind," since colorblind people can detect colors; but their brains register them in a different color category than those not suffering from this problem.

in a linear fashion until eventually it stops growing altogether. Rather, it keeps growing each year in a cyclical manner until the tree itself dies due to external forces such as weather, human intervention, etc. or internal forces from disease. This will become more apparent in Part Two of this book which is dedicated to my romance with Giant Madrona trees which in many cases have grown for hundreds of years.

Importantly, one must consider reproduction a necessity for the tree to propagate and survive. The blossoms are the natural step in the process which provide pollen, means for pollination and a host for the ovary where seeds are produced if pollinated. I have provided many photographs which reveal their beauty and in Appendix A microscopic exploration of them, divulging in more detail their anatomy. Overall, each blossom results in one berry which can contain perhaps ten seeds on the average. In nature, after the berries ripen they fall to the ground, or may be eaten by birds, herbivores, and rodents. The seeds in the fallen berries may sprout if conditions are right. Further, seeds in eaten berries may survive the digestive system and be evicted in various places. Nevertheless, once seeds sprout and grow they now must survive predators. Slugs, snails and herbivores are these main enemies. Consequently, although yearly thousands of berries may be produced on a single tree and hundreds of thousands on several trees it is difficult to find small saplings of Madrona trees growing in the wild. Clearly, it happens or there would not be the Madrona trees growing in nature. In recent years, I have looked for small saplings in my travels and I have had the most success on Sucia Island, in the San Juan Islands in Washington. I later learned that there are no deer on this island as it is too far to swim from other islands. I contribute this an important factor for the growth and survival of some of these small trees.

As we all know humans are the worst predators of anything that is good to eat or look at and they are the biggest transplantors and propagators of such items. However, the propagation of Madrona trees has remained a challenge over the years. There are now several websites and publications describing techniques for reproducing them. Nursing stock is also now available in some places (http://natnursery.com/contact-us). I have had limited experience with a couple of them. The first try failed miserably with the tree dying in the spring. The second tree I took more care to ensure the soil drained well and it survived. During the late summer it really began to grow rapidly reaching about three feet (0.9 m) in a couple of months. However, then suddenly the leaves turned brown and the tree died. I was shattered as I was just starting to get confident.

In the last couple of years I have tried to grow trees from berries and I have met with some success. A key to inducing seeds from trees to sprout is stratification. This means to expose the seeds to cold temperature for some length of time. Presumably this sets their internal clock in a way that they sense winter is over and spring is here, and it is time to come to life. The first year I tried it I was disorganized about the effort and had not researched it properly. I put some berries in the freezer, some in a small refrigerator I have in my shop which was so cold that they froze, and then fortunately some in a regular refrigerator. In the latter case I sneaked them into Darlene's refrigerator hiding them behind some jars of olives and jam we rarely used. That worked well for about a month until she was reorganizing her refrigerator one day and she ran across them. She looked at me holding my bag of berries in her hand and said: "What is this?".

I then had to negotiate with her to let them stay for several months. Fortunately, these were only chilled and didn't freeze and indeed some of them sprouted in the spring under a growing light. None of the frozen ones sprouted. I had mashed the berries, separated the seeds and then soaked them. After they had been submerged for two days I removed them and planted only seeds that had settled to the bottom as sinking is an indication of viability. I planted 10 seeds per paper pot. The ones that did sprout and developed leaves, grew very slowly and were only about 1 inch tall with two or more leaves by the end of the summer. I had moved them outside from late spring and elevated them above the ground to keep the slugs and snails away. In the spring of the next year, they seemed to wake up and really started growing competitively. You may say competitive with what? The answer is competitive to weeds or anything else that started growing in the pot. By late fall the largest was eleven inches tall.

Figure 1.1 The same Madrona during the season: A. & B. View of total tree, C.-E. Views of the trunk from same perspective, F. Close up view of peeling trunk, G. Later view of peeled trunk.

Figure 1.2 The same Madrona as Figure 1.1 illustrating the blooming process during the season, G. at this time point the outer shells of the blossoms containing the male part have fallen off leaving the female ovaries to develop into berries.

Figure 1.3 The same Madrona as Figures 1.1 & 2 but illustrating the berry maturation during the season. D. The berries have ripened, G. Completion of the cycle with the ripened berries blown off by the wind.

The second year I only used a refrigerator for striation and left the berries for about three months then planted them in the same way but maintained the temperature 58° F under growing lights. In fourteen days the first sprouts appeared. I gradually increased the temperature to 70° F over the following weeks. Ultimately, only a few survived till summer partly due to fungus killing them and my failure to always keep them watered properly.

Although growing saplings is a lot of fun, perhaps the most rewarding exercise is a walk amongst nature, where one can observe the results of time, multiplicity of trials, and the successes (and sometimes failures) of various foliage. All up and down the Pacific Coast from the latitude of mid Vancouver Island BC to south of San Francisco this has happened and continues to happen. (Initial pictures in book, Figures, PI 4 &5, and 1.5 & 6)

I provide here a few places of interest around my hometown of Anacortes, Washington: Washington Park; Tommy Thompson Trail (N 48° 28' 52.649", W 122° 35' 13.817"); Cap Sante Park (just off the main street in the downtown area); and a grove near the old railroad depot at 6th St. and R Ave. (also the location of the Saturday Farmers Market in the summertime); and, perhaps most picturesque of all, Deception Pass Bridge along Highway 20 (which connects Fidalgo and Whidbey Islands) (Figure 1.4)

Darlene and I have been fortunate to make yearly cruises in our boat "Sea Overture" throughout the San Juan Islands [9] (US), Gulf Islands (British Columbia) [10] and north as far as Desolation Sound [11]. There we have observed and photographed numerous beautiful trees. Almost all of the islands in these areas are richly populated with fantastic *Arbutus menziesii,* hence destinations for 'Madrona Romance' - perhaps, one even grows right by you, but you just haven't noticed it yet - let your romance start! Mine has and it has continued to grow as I began to learn about other *Arbutus* species as depicted in the chapters ahead.

Figure 1.4 Madorna trees blooming. *Upper Left* Deception Pass over the secondary channel, *Upper Right* Cap Sante Hill, *Lower*: Looking out over bay at Deception Pass. The white blossoms identify the Madrona trees.

Figure 1.5 A Madrona tree displaying its exposed branches in August along the Salish Sea.

Figure 1.6 A Madrona tree growing on a hill side with its roots clinging to the soil that hasn't slipped away.

Chapter Two:

A Maturing Romance – The Strawberry Tree (*Arbutus unedo*) Rooted in History and Mystery

My personal experience with the *unedo* was like an explorer discovering a crack in a glacier along a bay. Following initial inspection, subsequent observations showed it rapidly spreading into a full-blown fissure. Then in a cascading effect the massive formation splintered throughout, calving into the ocean in a terrific avalanche, jagged hunks of ice tumbling into the water setting up huge waves that ricocheted off the walls of the bay.

Similarly, my investigation and discovery of the *unedo* started slow but then cascaded rapidly surprising me and rocking my "boat" along the way.

However, first some basic information about the species. The *unedo* is one of the most prevalent and best known of the Old World *Arbutus* species (i.e., those growing predominantly in the Eastern Hemisphere). It is broadly distributed along the shores of the Mediterranean Sea [12] in the south, from Morocco to Tunisia Kroumerie, and in the north from Spain all the way along the coastline to Italy, where it then continues eastward along the shores of the Adriatic and Aegean seas, extending at least as far as the seaboards of Turkey. On the western Atlantic side, it is found along the coast of Portugal, the sea border of northern Spain, and again near the sea in the southern part of France. There is a so-called "disjunct population"[2] in Ireland, most near Killarney National Park, and a small grouping in Sligo. The climate throughout these regions varies significantly from one area to the next but is buffered throughout by coastal conditions (wind, rain, and particularly moderation of the temperature).

My first *unedo* discovery happened in August 2016, when boating to Lopez Island Washington. Darlene and I anchored In the west side of the island in Fisherman Bay overnight, and the next day went ashore to explore the village. Among several interesting stores and cafés was a cooperative art gallery. We were delighted to find bowls made from Madrona wood by the artisan T. J. Anderson. We bought one, and later learned through conversation about a former nurseryman in the village. He had planted a number of *Arbutus unedo* bushes in the 1980s. It was thought that they were still there, even though the nursery was long gone. Sure enough, alongside what is now a real estate office, I found a row of *unedo* trees. Yes, they were right here not in the Mediterranean! There were several berries starting to mature on the trees. Not to be outdone a tall, truly beautiful Pacific Madrone grew there too.

A woman in the adjacent office said that the *unedo* trees were regularly pruned to avoid blocking the view. The bushes were about six feet tall at the time, but the bases of the bushes were several inches in diameter, indicating that they were older than their height suggested. The real estate lady was previously unaware that the trees were of a species native to Europe rather than Lopez Island; however, she didn't seem to be as excited about it as I (this hardly surprised my wife).

My "boat" so to speak was again rocked when I found an *unedo* tree growing in a yard about three blocks from my house. I know I had passed right by it several times during the year, but for some reason the large, bright red berries caught my eye this time. The tree not only had bright berries but had white blossoms on the bush as well. This clarified what had been confusing to me when reading about the tree. It can blossom in the

2 A distribution of organisms consisting of two or more groups which, though taxonomically related, are considerably separated from one another geographically.

fall at the same time as it has the mature berries, contrary to our spring blooming Madronas. Furthermore, the large, bright red berries were about inch in diameter (2.5 cm), indeed, they distinctly resembled strawberries. I could now clearly see why the tree had been given its common name: the Strawberry Tree.

My surprising observations continued: Strawberry Trees were growing all around the parking lot of the marina where we keep our boat. They lined a parking area by the entrance to the Tommy Thompson trail in Anacortes. There was also one across from my son's house in Seattle; they even grew near the Seattle campus of the University of Washington, alongside the Gilman-Burke trail, as well as a short distance north along University Way NE. Online, I had read descriptions of such trees growing in the San Francisco Bay area in California, and in Portland, Oregon.

It became apparent to me at this point that the Strawberry tree is different from the Pacific Madrone. It is not resistant to proliferation, as the Pacific Madrone tends to be, but in fact is easily propagated. This is precisely why the Strawberry Tree had leapt clear across the Atlantic, as it were, to populate the Pacific coast not by birds or ocean currents, but by people. This wide distribution makes sense given that *unedo* thrive in a mild climate, they are ornamentally attractive and fit well in landscaping schemes. Furthermore, there are some special alluring variants of the tree. For example, *Arbutus unedo f. rubra* has an eye-catching pink-reddish flower, while the *A. unedo* 'Compacta' and A. *unedo* 'Elfin King' are commercial cultivars (selected and propagated by humans for their 'dwarf' properties) which blend in nicely in gardens.

After a wide search of the internet and scientific literature for material on the *Arbutus unedo f. rubra*, a paper by Daniel Mount [13] ultimately proved the most valuable and informative. In Ireland (near Glengarriff, County Cork), there circulated a report in 1835 of a Strawberry Tree with pink-to-red flowers. Mount reveals that, in 1960, the Washington Park Arboretum (situated adjacent to the University of Washington in Seattle) came into possession of rooted cuttings acquired from this tree variant. Consequently, some *f. rubra* trees now grow in the arboretum. Darlene and I used to park our car near there in the fall and walk over to the stadium to watch the University of Washington Husky football team play but never noticed these trees. Based on Mount's information in the autumn of 2018, I went to see these trees when they were blooming. Furthermore, Mount had contacted me telling about some more he had observed in Medina, (near Bellevue) WA. I also visited all of these and found the ones in Medina very beautiful with not pink but very ruby colored blossoms. (Figure A1C). An advantage of this *f. rubra* tree, in contrast to the similarly flowering *Arbutus* 'Marina' (discussed later) that is being propagated in the San Francisco area, is that its Irish origin has given it a tolerance for colder temperatures.

I was starting to feel comfortable with my understanding of the *A. undeo* when my contentment was rocked by reading a very definitive paper on the wild *Arbutus unedo* trees in Ireland, written in 1949 by J. Robert Sealy, an associate of the Herbarium of the Royal Botanic Gardens, in Kew, England. [14] I had been basing my observations on the *undeo* trees that grow around our region, which had been planted primarily for landscaping purposes. As such, they grow in areas with limited competition from other trees, generally fertile soil, and locations affording abundant sunshine. Sealy's description of the trees growing naturally in the wild revealed characteristics much like the Pacific Madrone that I have seen here in the wild. They are often found on the edges of groves of other trees, along rocky shores, or among rocks, and they seem to a have a *geniality* like that of our own Madronas. They will reach out horizontally into open spaces, in an effort to absorb more sunlight, rather than attempt to outgrow their competitors vertically. In some regions the trees are more akin to shrubs but in other areas they can grow quite large if given sufficient sunlight, water, and nutrients. Also, by some accounts the bark itself seems to vary in terms of exfoliating, perhaps depending on the relative sunniness (or cloudiness) of the region but is reported in some narrations to peel. This stands in rather stark contrast to my observations of the local Strawberry Trees, whose bark tends to remain thicker and remain intact on the tree.

Sealy continues with a discussion of the necessity of trees' producing enough viable seeds to maintain a presence in a location. Over several years, he found that the production of berries was heavy, and each berry averaged about twenty-five seeds. Therefore, a huge number of seeds are produced each year. However, the blackbirds, thrushes, and some wood pigeons eagerly feast on them, and thus disperse the seeds in a wide smattering of geographical locations, not all of which are likely conducive to propagation. He estimated that only a small percentage ever find a suitable site. He also studied the germination of seeds under ideal conditions and found that just over half (56%) produce seedling, but that even in such cases the seedling is unlikely to grow much beyond infancy, particularly if aggravated by drought, cold weather, and/or shade. Sealy surmised, therefore, that a steady, annual production of seeds is required to maintain the survival of *unedo* trees in a wilderness area. I am quite sure that a similar situation exists with regards to the wild Pacific Madrone. On the positive side, Sealy notes that, once the trees reach the beginnings of maturity (two or three years, in most cases), they cling to life very aggressively, tolerate drought remarkably well, and prove themselves highly adaptive to their environment.

Finally, he provides beautiful illustrations of the presence of regions with swollen stems in the root structures, just below the soil surface. More recently these have been called lignotubers [15] and are known to be root areas that promote re-sprouting if the upper structure of the tree suffers trauma, such as from fire or cutting. The presence of stored starch and dormant buds facilitate this regeneration action. This is thought to be an important adaptive feature. In the Pacific Madrone these engorged regions are called burls and are similarly believed responsible for rapid recovery after a fire (or damage caused otherwise). They seem to give the *Arbutus* a reforesting head start over some of the other trees. [16] This has proven a source of some frustration for foresters, insofar as it has hampered their efforts to repopulate clear-cut or burnt regions with the more commercially attractive Douglas Fir.

One of the mysteries of the *unedo* is why is there such a wide distribution of the tree across quite different environments [14]. For example, how did this disjunct population arrive in Ireland? In his 1993 paper, Mitchel addresses this topic and further describes a separate population in Silago.[17] He suggests that fossil studies of pollen, place the earliest finding in Killarney at 4000 B.C.E. and at Sligo around the start of the second century A.D. In more recent times Sealy notes that, in the 1700s, the trees were more abundant than they are now because, in the centuries since, they have been widely used to make charcoal for the purpose of smelting silver and lead.

A comprehensive study of distributed *unedo* was recently conducted by a team of scientists who took leaves and seeds from nineteen sites around the Mediterranean Basin, the Atlantic side of the Iberian Peninsula, southwestern France, and Ireland. This team first performed a genetic analysis on the leaves, then on germinating seeds, and finally on raising seedlings which were later measured in various ways. In this way, the scientists discovered two clades[3] which split from each other sometime before the last glacial maximum, which occurred about 25,000 years ago. One clade occupied North Africa and west Iberia, while the other appears to have inhabited the remaining western Mediterranean region (e.g. France). Further, the eastern Mediterranean *unedo* were found to be the byproduct of a subsequent split from both of the former clades. Returning to the Irish population, it seemed to be linked to the Iberian Peninsula rather than to France, as some experts had previously held [18]. They also found adaptability in certain traits, which implies that the trees will adjust to changing environments in the future [12]. With regard to drought, the tree seems able to reduce growth and water consumption as necessary and to disperse sun radiation it no longer requires[19]. They also report several measures of certain pertinent characteristics of the trees they cultivated. Going forward, these measures may provide a useful baseline for comparison with the same attributes in other species (such as stomatal density; root and shoot biomass; photosynthesis; and efficiency of use of radiation).

Finally, there are at least five main features of the *unedo* which distinguish it importantly from "New World" *Arbutus* species. First, as mentioned previously, it blooms in the fall and its fruit ripen in the fall. The fruit grows for over a year after the blossoms have been pollinated. Second, the fruit is much bigger, often one inch (two- and one-half cm) in diameter, than that of the New World species, whose diameter averages 4 tenths of an inch or just one centimeter. Thirdly, the surface of the fruit is covered with hard, pyramid-shaped protuberances. These

3 Common ancestry

are what people report as causing a sensation of grittiness on their teeth when they taste the berries. Fourth, the branches and trunks of the *unedo* are smaller, and whether they exfoliate as beautifully or readily as the New World species appears to depend on the climate in which they grow. Fifth and finally, the leaves tend to be smaller. Figures 2.1 and 2.2 illustrate these features. Undeniably the tree is beautiful in the fall with its blossoms and berries.

Since the Strawberry Tree has existed so long in well populated areas of Europe, it has made an imprint on the history and customs there. I have already explained elsewhere how the name "Madroño" was imported to California and applied to the Pacific Madrona by Father Crespi. In Madrid, a most interesting statue stands in the main square (*Puerto del Sol*). This statue depicts a very muscular female bear standing on her hind legs with her head in the branches of a Madroño tree (see below). What is she doing? Considering the Strawberry Tree, with its delightfully large, bright red berries, and knowing how bears operate, it becomes clear that she is helping herself to a scrumptious feast. I have seen black bears devour berries along a river in British Columbia. Bears don't consume such meals in small, leisurely bites. Quite the opposite, in fact: they open their mouths wide, inhaling the berries leaves and all, crunching them down before spitting out the indigestible bits (twigs and leave), then go back again for another mouthful. This statue, I believe, illustrates similar dedication. Weighing in at about twenty-two tons and thirteen feet high, constructed from stone and bronze, it was sculptured by Antonio Navarro Santaf and introduced to the city in 1967. (The picture was taken by my grandson, Zandy Zender.) The statue is based on a similar image which appears on the crest of the city. There are various, somewhat conflicting accounts of how this came to be and what precisely the crest is supposed to signify, but the consensus seems to be that it commentates a compromise in a dispute over control of certain pastures and trees in the early years of its cityhood. [20]

A quite different historic use exists in Portugal for the Medronho, the Portuguese name for the Strawberry Tree. Jan Sandford has published a delightful tale in her book *Algarve – Medronho Story.* [21] Sandford had a home in the hills of Portugal for over ten years and witnessed how the locals harvested the Medronho berries in the fall and later converted them into a brandy called *Aguardente de Medronho.* This brandy is extremely powerful, with an ABV (alcohol-by-volume) of 50%, for comparison wine is about 11.5 %. This very high alcohol content is the result of a double-distilling process. Jan describes having had some trouble finding her way home after visiting the distillery and sampling the first crop of the year. Having attended a few *laboratory parties* where there was ready access to 100% ethanol and no scruples among the scientists mixing the punch for the night, I can relate to Sandford's experience very well.

Videos of the process of producing the brandy can be readily found on the internet. Commercially produced *Aguardente de Medronho* (or some form of it, anyway) can be found in select liquor stores throughout Portugal, but the locals much prefer the rough-and-ready, grassroots variety. I told a friend who planned to visit Portugal about this drink, and he brought home two bottles of the liqueur. We sampled one of these (see photo) and indeed did find it like fire water, with an interesting taste. We tried some with honey and lemon mixture and then with just honey mixture. The latter we found more satisfying.

There is another saga about liquor from the Strawberry Tree though likely little more than an old Irish yarn, it merits a brief recitation regardless of its historical accuracy. The events of the account take place between the death of Julius Caesar on

March 15, 44 BC, and the Roman invasion of the Britain Isles, circa 44 AD. Prior to the invasion, the Romans had traded routinely with Britain. However, according to the legend, merchants weren't finding much success in selling their wine, one of their common exports, in Britain because as an alternate domestic drink was more popular. The merchants soon discovered that the source of this preferred beverage lay in Ireland. Consequently, they enlisted two ships full of mercenaries to sail to Ireland and then allegedly up the river Boyne. In present-day Ireland, the mouth of this river is situated north of Dublin, beginning in County Kildare, the river itself about seventy miles from beginning to end. After reaching the end of the navigational region of the river, the mercenaries reputedly marched west to the coast of Ireland and found the villages where the offending drink was being fermented. As the legend has it, these soldiers of fortune thereupon destroyed all the trees in sight, along with, most likely, the brewers, their families, and the villages themselves. Since it was trees which the legend says were decimated, arm-chair historians have long assumed that they were *Arbutus unedo* trees and the drink was some concoction produced from their berries. Returning from their mission, the legionnaires collected their pay and, soon thereafter – wouldn't you know it? – the merchants began selling their wine successfully in Britain. One bit of historical evidence which tends to corroborate the contour of this account is the subsequent discovery, in the southern part of England, of large, clay amphora much like the vessels the Romans traditionally used for storing and transporting wine. Scientific tests performed on the vessels have shown them to likely predate the Roman invasion of the British Isles in 44 A.D.

Now, one might question whether the *Arbutus* product was really the culprit behind the lagging wine sales in Britain. An alcoholic drink called *mead*, with a very long history, is made from the fermentation of water and honey, and is known to have been exceedingly popular in early Ireland and elsewhere. There are various stories and ideas about mead, some amusing. According to one, the drink promotes a fruitful bonding with much fertility. The prevalence of this belief presumably contributed to the birth of the local custom whereby bridal couples are given a *moon's*, month's, worth of wine made from honey - hence the term *honeymoon*.

Continuing in the vein of Irish tales, Frank Delaney, in his novel about Ireland, describes a scene told by a "Story Teller", a main character in the book, in which a leprechaun is sitting under an *Arbutus* tree. [23] I find this interesting, but not exactly plausible in the context of a Pacific Madrone. I can more readily picture, for example, a mermaid stretching along the curved trunk, the surf breaking in the background, her sensuous arms wrapped around the tree, the image accented by the peeling red bark, green leaves, and hanging berries. I find this image to be evoked quite effectively in a painting by Melani Bishop, a British Columbia artist who has portrayed a similar scene. [24]

The wood of the *unedo* itself had early uses besides production of charcoal. Recently, a study of sunken boats in ancient Roman harbors identified wood used in the boats from the first through the third centuries A.D.[22] Three ships were dug up inland about five hundred meters from the current location of a Naples dock. The ships were covered by seven meters of silt which, as it happened, made for a well-preserved artifact and aided dating their age. A variety of wood were used in the boats, but one of the most interesting findings is the presence of wooden nails, tree nails, or pegs. Such nails were commonly applied in ancient boatbuilding. Wooden pegs were first shaped,size and taper and then driven into holes pre-drilled into the planking and frame to bind them together. Once the boat was put out to sea, the wood would absorb the water and expand in such a way as to promote additional binding. In the 2015 report of Sadori et al., *Arbutus unedo* was found to be the wood most often used for this purpose. The hardwood branches of the tree, already round and uniform for some distance, are naturally ideal for the task. I can easily picture these ancient boats weathering a stormy Mediterranean Sea, their holds creaking and straining, their timbers thankfully bound to one other by these strong, tree nails made from hard *unedo* branches.

Finally, a unique phenomenon currently manifesting itself among the *unedo* species is domestication for agriculture purposes. As mentioned previously, the berries are primarily used for making liquor but secondarily for jams. To this latter end, the Portuguese have contemplated growing entire orchards of *unedo*. Furthermore, several studies have pointed to chemicals found within the tree, or extracts from it, which may have medical applications.

Two other quite interesting utilizations have been indicated in the literature as well: first, the production of single-flower, monofloral, honey [25] as a specialty interest unlike most flowers, *unedo* blooms in the fall, so it may provide a restricted offering to bees at this time of year and thus perhaps aiding in off-season honey production; and, second, perhaps what is the most interesting of all these various possibilities, namely, the growing of truffles. One type of truffle (*Tuber borchii*) has been shown capable of developing a mycorrhizas relationship with the *Arbutus unedo*. Truffles are exceedingly popular in Italy, among other countries, and certain varieties of them are quite expensive. Therefore, orchards that could also produce truffles and berry products would be of enormous value to companies involved in the manufacture and distribution of these beloved delicacies and so might come to play an important role in the economies of those regions hospitable to the tree's growth. [26]

Finally, there are many other questions and mysteries associated with this tree. For example, was the fruit an important food for early humanoids? Where did the tree originate? How has climate changed it? Why is it so different from the other *Arbutus* trees? The first one poses opportunity for interesting speculation. There is evidence in the Gorham's cave of early presence of Neanderthals in Iberia.[27] Early humanoids were believed to be hunters and gatherers. Recent reports in Eastern Iberia found plants present at the Middle Paleolithic site of El Salt including seeds.[28] Although, no *Arbutus* presence was reported, one can easily visualize that the Strawberry Tree fruit would be very attractive to any primitive society that gathered food, if the Strawberry Tree existed in ancient times in the same manner it exists today. A few of the other questions will be also touched on later in the book and one attribute of the *Arbutus unedo* will be explored in depth.

Figure 2.1 *Arbutus undeo* A. Distant view of several trees blooming and with berries in the fall. B. Close up one trunk, C. Closer view of the trees of A.

Figure 2.2 Close up views of *Arbutus undeo* blooming and with berries. The berries in the lower photo are at several stages of maturity.

Chapter Three:

My Passion Goes International -The Greek Strawberry Tree (*Arbutus andrachne*)

Recently, while thinking back to the start of the new century, I found myself reflecting on the trip my Darlene and I took around that time. We stepped on the deck of the ferry and watched the small seaport of Acona, in the Marche region of central Italy, disappear into the impending night, anticipating the morning when we would arrive in Patras, Greece, at the northwestern shore of Peloponnese peninsula. This was the start of our trip through Greece, which was to culminate in a series of hops, by ferry, to a number of islands in route to western Turkey.

Disembarking that morning, we were on our way. Soon we traveled along the Gulf of Corinth, a body of water navigated by seafarers and traders for centuries. After visiting the ancient ruins of Corinth, we first passed over the man-made canal that links the Gulf of Corinth to the Aegean Sea, and then, shortly thereafter, entered into the sprawling city of Athens. There, antiquities hovered everywhere like the fog in the Pacific Northwest; residue of past centuries mixing with the unrestrained activity of a modern city.

All of this happened long before Darlene, had, asked me: "What are you going to do with all those Madrona pictures?"

At that time my passion was designing ultrasound systems, so I probably missed several opportunities to see the ancient *Arbutus andrachne*. Little did I know that two professors in Athens would answer an *Arbutus* question for me eighteen years later, in connection with trees that were just twenty-seven miles north of the city.

Nevertheless, we commenced our tour of Athens in earnest. We sauntered around the remains of the Temple of Olympian Zeus; sat in the marble chairs at the Theater of Dionysus and tried to imagine what famous people might have attended there; even sitting briefly upon the ornate, ceremonial chair reserved only for the elite leader of various eras. Sipping water and trying to ignore the heat, we climbed to the Acropolis. Exploring first the Parthenon, a former temple to the Goddess Athena, we later marveled at the architecture with its huge columns. Walking around the Erectheon, we viewed the six statues of the maidens, who have been tasked with holding up the ceiling, as it were, since about 400 B.C. Several hours later we ran out of energy and headed toward our hotel.

Along the way we encountered a festive gathering in a park. People were dancing it appeared to be a folkdance in a long, circular, rather snake-like formation, stepping and swaying to the captivating music of several enthusiastic musicians. As our toes tapped and hips began to undulate in rhythm, Darlene tugged at my hand, she wanted to join in. I tucked back reluctant, I enjoy dancing, but it is hard for me to get started in a new unfamiliar situation. Darlene has several names for this, one is *stick in the mud.* I later learned this is a famous Greek dance Kalamatianos, involving, at one point in the dance, fully ten steps counterclockwise; and, later, two steps clockwise, sometimes modified by the mood of the dancers, to step back and forth, without actually *going* anywhere, instead simply enjoying the feel of the music and the joy of it. [29] As I shall explore presently, this dance in many ways illustrates the history of the *Arbutus andrachne.*

The *andrachne* is a popular tree called the Greek or Eastern Strawberry Tree. It is distributed widely, from the shores of Croatia, across Greece, to the southwestern regions of Turkey, Lebanon, Israel, and Jordan. It is even present along the northern part of the Black Sea. Whether this distribution is entirely natural is difficult to decipher, because the tree is attractive, and its berries can be tasty; therefore, propagation through the berries as food may have been facilitated by people transporting them over wide regions. Bearing in mind, humans have occupied this territory for thousands, perhaps even tens of thousands of years. On the detrimental side, war has ravaged the area probably since the beginning of human presence, and modern warfare often leaves little behind. Further complicating the impact, is the need for humans to survive and make a living, often utilizing available resources even at potentially high long-term costs, especially to wildlife and even more particularly to trees of limited domestic value. However, in contrast, in more recent times there are nature enthusiasts, plant lovers, those who are driven to collect specimens of every sort imaginable – as well as those who, quite simply, delight in building beautiful gardens. Such folks often save species that might otherwise disappear, but in the process alter their natural distribution.

In terms of taxonomical characteristics, *Arbutus andrachne* differs in several ways from its western cousin, *Arbutus unedo*. First and foremost, the former blooms in spring, while the latter blooms in autumn. Moreover, *andrachne* often has a tortuous trunk comprising cinnamon-red bark which, when peeled, reveals a green outer cambium rather akin to that of the Pacific Madrone. Its inflorescence tends to be like that of the *A. unedo*: a drooping bell-shaped blossom, as opposed to the traditionally more skyward oriented of the Pacific Madrone and *Arbutus peninsularis*. Its berries in the fall average about one centimeter in diameter, smaller than the two-and a-half-centimeter diameter of the *A. unedo*'s. The tree itself is often reported to grow as high as five meters. Though arguably possible, whether it would ever reach the enormous stature that some Pacific Madrone have is doubtful, as its native region is generally less fertile and much dryer than the Madrone's.

Its leaves are fairly large and long, with an average area of 215.5 cm^2; length-to-width ratio of 1.5 cm; and length of 6.4 cm. [30] This is large compared to the corresponding dimensions of the *unedo*. It is a very hardy plant, re-sprouting aggressively after a fire. It is known to grow in poorly aerated soil, apparently relying on mycorrhiza fungi which has a symbiosis relationship with the roots of the tree to convert organic material into a form usable by it. [31] According to at least one report, it grows among shrubs and in the Turkish Pine forest, whose soil is composed of layers of volcanic-like rock and limestone[32]. Interestingly, Markovski reports that the *A. andrachne* withstands cooler temperatures than *A. unedo* and therefore can be found farther up gorges and river valleys along the coast of the Eastern Mediterranean. [33]. The author then goes on to say that the time for maturation of the *A. andrachne*'s berries is seven months, in contrast to twelve months for those of the *A. unedo*, with a more simultaneous and uniform ripening process. These features assist greatly in the commercial production of the *andrachne*'s berries, which historically are under exploited. The berries of both trees are known to be rich in anti-oxidants (e.g., Vitamin C and E, carotenoids, etc.) [34] and are tasty if eaten when very ripe, but, like most fruits, tend to have a fairly astringent taste if consumed at the wrong time.

A quite different study of uses of *A. andrachne* has emerged from the University of Jordan. Issa and colleagues have investigated the anti-tyrosinase impact of extracts from the leaves, stems, and berries of the tree. [35] The tree itself grows in the forest of Jordan. It is known traditionally to be usable for its de-pigmenting properties. Scientists have found that arbutin extracted from the tree and applied topically interferes with tyrosinase, an enzyme in the body important for melanin production. Melanin is responsible for darkening of the skin. Commercial development of such an agent would be of considerable value to the cosmetic industry. The laboratory investigation by Issa, et al identified the stems of *A. andrachne* as having the highest anti-tyrosinase ingredients compared to the other parts of the tree. This fact initially surprised me. But, given that the stem is the "transport lane" between the leaves and the branches, and that nutrients must pass through a small cross-section from the leaf, it makes sense that the concentration of anti-tyrosinase ingredients in the stem should indeed be quite high. Of five different extracts tested, nine milligrams of methanolic gave a 98% reduction of tyrosinase action, suggesting its potential for just this purpose.

In light of the increasing awareness of the usefulness of these plants, an informative study was conducted at the Agricultural University of Athens by Bertsouklis and Papafotiou, reporting the outcomes of storing *Arbutus andrachne* seeds under several conditions and later subjecting them to assorted germination temperatures. [36] Temperatures of: 10° C (50° F), 15° C (59° F), 20° C (68° F), and 25° C (77°F) were employed in each study group.

The optimal temperature found for maximal germination was 15° C (59° F), independent of any pre-treatment conditions. By contrast, the germination rate fell off remarkably at both higher and lower temperatures. The authors hypothesize that this temperature represents the time of year when the Mediterranean climate will be most conducive to the successful growth of young seedlings, well in advance of the region's characteristically dry, hot summer. Higher temperatures may *signal* the seeds that it is too late in the season to sprout and survive, while cooler temperatures communicate the reverse (i.e., that it is too early in the season). This premise receives some support from the climate records in Athens. The region's median temperature is roughly 15° C (59° F) from February through March. The precipitation is generally about forty-five millimeters per month at that same point in the year. July is the hottest month, with a median temperature of around 32° C (90° F), and June and July are the driest, with approximately five millimeters/month of precipitation on the average. It is only starting in October, when the rain level jumps to about fifty millimeters each month and lasting through peak levels of sixty-eight millimeters in December. Indeed, it seems as if the seeds are *programmed* to geminate at an optimal temperature.

The oldest reference I have found to *Arbutus andrachne* comes from the writings of De La Brocquire, in which he describes his travels between 1423 and 1433 C.E. [37] Around that time, he left Bursa, Turkey, traveling north across the plain, alongside a river which flows north into the sea of Marmara, the body of water linking the Aegean Sea to Istanbul. He describes unpleasant travels through mountain passes but along the way, he and his companions passed a tree with fruit slightly larger than the cherries he was familiar with, and which were shaped and tasted much like strawberries, only more acidic to the tongue. While emphasizing their appealing flavor, he also gave fair warning that eating too many of them could impair one's judgment through a kind of intoxication. The editor adds in a footnote that the tree appears from the description to have been an *Arbutus andrachne.*

There are reports of *Arbutus andrachne* from Israel, where the tree is called "Katlav." A famous *andrachne* stands isolated in a British Cemetery on Mount Scopus, Jerusalem. The grounds to the cemetery were initially given in 1917 to Britain in thanks for establishing a home in Palestine for people of Jewish heritage. There is a rich history associated with Mt. Scopus[38, 39], one of the earliest being it was the site from which the Roman, Titus, directed the siege of Jerusalem, during the first century B.C.E. The mountain rises to 834 meters above sea level and provides a commanding view of Jerusalem. The tree in the cemetery is said to have been preserved because its red bark symbolizes the copious bloodshed in numerous battles; for many of the fallen, this cemetery is their final resting place.

February 5, 2020, I had an opportunity to visit this tree, but it required some logistical maneuvering. Darlene and I were touring Israel on a Holy Land tour. Of course, the British Cemetery was not on the schedule of touring sites, since few people want to tour a cemetery. However, I did persuade the tour director to alter the driving course slightly on one of the trips to Jerusalem, to go by the cemetery. I thought if they could just stop for 10 minutes I could run out and snap a few pictures and that would not impose too much of a delay on the other 48 people on the tour. He agreed but as we approached the cemetery, we saw that there was road construction going on all around the entrance and no parking space for a big bus. He pointed out the tree to me and others confirmed the red color on it as we drove by. I snapped a couple of pictures through the window and at some distance. That evening when I reviewed my pictures, I saw the quick snapshots were far short of what a dedicated *Arbutu*s tree hunter wanted. I began plotting how I could somehow get to the cemetery. Darlene thought it was a dead issue (bad pun).

Fortunately, we were scheduled to spend some time at the Jerusalem Museum where among many other antiquities the Dead Sea Scrolls are kept. I would have loved to have seen them but decided to sacrifice my time to try to visit the cemetery instead. I asked the tour guide if I would have time to take a taxi to the cemetery and be back before the tour bus left. His answer was rather ambivalent; however, my next hurdle was convincing Darlene that I could do it and get back by 2:30 PM when the bus was scheduled to leave. Failure would impose considerable inconvenience on 48 other people if they had to wait. However, even worse would be if they left me. Suddenly, I would be by myself ten miles from the hotel in Bethlehem which is in the West Bank requiring passing through a military Israeli-Palestine check point where maybe or maybe not I had the proper credentials. This was certainly a challenge I didn't want.

"You better be here by then!" Darlene warned, with that look in her eye.

Leaving the museum I hurried to the taxi stand outside and spoke to the first driver in the line to learn first if he spoke English, second if he could take me to cemetery and wait, then bring me back by 2:30. Yes, was the answer to both questions and then I asked what it would cost but his answer was less definitive saying it depends on traffic. I should have been warned by that but in my anxiousness, I decided just to go. In order to get there faster, the driver took some short cuts which did provide exciting riding through areas of Jerusalem I would not otherwise had seen. Shortly we pulled up beside the entrance, there was no construction that day and I noticed an entrance was between two construction fences. As the driver waited, I hurried onto the cemetery lawn and made straight for the tree located centrally and towards the south western side of field.

I began taking pictures, circling the tree, and taking close ups of different aspects of it. The first surprise was there was only two main trunks rising and separating after a few feet above the ground (the outer separation being 34" or 86.4 cm at a height of 24" or 61 cm above the ground). (Figure 3.1) Each trunk digressing from each other by 60°, one to the northwest (circumference of 52" or 132 cm) and one to the southeast (circumference of 54" or 137.2 cm). Second, portions of each of these trunks were dead with only regions of viable red bark. This viability extended up the tree and supported clumps of green foliage growing near the tip of each of them. Third, there was a short, much smaller, but very healthy trunk full of foliage at the northern side of the collage, with buds starting to show for later flowering.(Figure 3.3 and 3.2D & E) This much smaller trunk seemed to be a more recent off shoot of the base of the tree maybe even a larger trunk that had been severed at the base. This surviving limited medley of tree structure surprised me because I had seen pictures on the internet which had shown at least four major trunks all green with foliage. I guessed these pictures had been taken a number of years ago and considerable deterioration had occurred requiring removing major trunks. Clearly, a western and an eastern trunk had been cut and removed and a major branch part way up the northwest trunk as well. I closely studied a leaf on the tree which had a length 6.8 cm, width 3.6 cm and length/width ratio of 1.9. Later comparing these measurements to the comprehensive findings of Bertsouklis and Papafotiou (2016) [40] it hinted that the tree might be a hybrid of *A. unedo* and *A. andrachne* the well-known *A. x andrachnoides* rather than to the stated *A. andrachne* [41]. In a subsequent email conversation with Dr. Bertsouklis he agreed with me but with only one leaf one could not be sure; it essentially aroused interest for further study but by then it was too late.

The tree was a form of a monument to all who were buried at the cemetery with as mentioned its red bark symbolizing their blood shed. I felt it especially memorialized three people marked by three tombstones adjacent to the tree. One was of Lieutenant William Jeffray Johnstone of the Fife and Forfar Yeomanry who died Dec. 12, 1917 at the age of 20. He was a son of William and Mary Lockhart Johnstone of Glasgow Scotland. The inscription on the tombstone was: "DULCE ET DECOURUM EST PRO PATRIA MORI" in Latin which means: *It is sweet and honorable to die for your country.* This unit was a calvary unit that fought under General Allenby who directed the effort in taking the region from the Suez Canal to Jerusalem from the Ottoman Empire. (You may read the horror that the soldiers went through in Professor Woodward's 2006 book: *Hell in the Holy Land* published by The University of Kentucky in Lexington.) It has also been historically noted that Lawrence of Arabia (TE Lawrence) also marched into Jerusalem with the General's officers at the climax of taking the city.[42]

The second adjacent buried solder was Private Joseph Abraham Robinson of the Somerset Light Infantry who died Dec. 27,1917 at the age of 37. He was the son of William and Hannah Robinson, and husband of Edith E. Robinson of Royal Terrace, Portishead, Somerset, UK. His tombstone carried the inscription: "WITH CHRIST WHICH IS FAR BETTER." Portishead is located near the Bristol Channel, about 10 miles west of Bristol and 127 miles west of London. This infantry group was part of the army mentioned above. Finally, slightly further away was a tombstone labeled only "A SOLDIER OF THE GREAT WAR", essentially an unknown soldier, even sadder as his sacrifice is unnoted by his name.

Time had transpired quickly so I hurried to the taxi. The driver returned us by driving on the freeway back which was relative open at that point because the traffic was flowing in the opposite direction. Exiting the freeway, we wound our way through the Israeli government buildings where the Prime Minister and Parliament preside. We arrived back at the museum with about 15 minutes to spare; however, when I asked him how much I owed him I learned I didn't have enough money even though it was about $80. He said there was an ATM machine near that we could go to and still get back in time. So off we went and found it and I extracted 600 shekels. The driver grumbled a bit but since that was equivalent to about $175, I thought that was more than enough. He redeposited me at the entrance to the museum at about 2:27 PM. I jumped out and dialed my wife while rapidly hustling towards where the bus was located. She was relieved to hear from me and even more so as I joined her in the line loading on to the bus. I must admit I smiled to myself, but silently said: "Whew!"

Much later as I was pondering the human activity that has been witnessed by the *Arbutus andrachne* over time: bloodshed; power struggles; evolving cultures and customs; changing governments; changing climates; the pains of childhood and anxieties of adolescence; the trials of adulthood and sorrows of old age; poverty and prosperity, death. All these have been witnessed by the *Arbutus andrachne* as the tree itself has struggled to survive across this diverse eastern Mediterranean area.

The Greek folkdance, Kalamatianos, comes to mind again. The steps may have been very slow when one looks back over, say, the last 300 million years. As cooling and warming of the earth occurred, the tendency of organisms to drift northward correlated predictably with warmer temperatures, and conversely vis-à-vis cooler weather. For example, the Last Glacial Maximum took place 15,000 to 20,000 years ago, followed by the Bølling-Allerød Interstadial period, in which a warming period induced migration of humans and flora northward until circa 10,500 to 13,000 B.C.E. [43] It then turned cold again during the Yonnger Dryas time period. forcing once more a southward exodus. The current inter-ice epoch, known widely as the Holocene period, started about 11,500 years and encouraged another northward passage. Since then, there have been a lot of *dance steps* forward and backward, influenced in part by other factors and more recently the vagaries of industry, commerce, and technology. We can only hope that sanity prevails and our impact on the environment is somehow squarely addressed – and soon.

Dancing aside, in a later section, (The Greek Love Triangle) some further interesting twists in the ever-winding tale of the *Arbutus andrachne* will be disclosed.

Figure 3.1 *Arbutus Andrachne* at the British Cemetery in Jerusalem.

Figure 3.2 Collage of views of the tree in Figure 3.1 showing different sections in more detail. D. and E. are close ups of leaves and buds that are preparing for blooming. February 5, 2020.

Figure 3.3 Another collage of views particularly showing the red bark. This bark is what the tree is famous for because it is a reminder of the blood the soldiers shed in the war before dying. The pictures in this Figure were taken near the base of the tree (see Figure 3.1) where there was new growth.

Chapter Four:

A Spanish Fling - Canary Island Indigenous Tree (*Arbutus canariensis*)

The rain was splattering against the skylight on a January morning in 2017 as I sat pondering the third Mediterranean *Arbutus* species the *canariesis*. This tree is indigenous to the Canary Islands. Indigenous, indeed, but how did it originally start there? Sipping my coffee I wondered in fact, where in the world are the Canary Islands? Clicking my computer, I saw that they are west of the northern tip of Africa and southwest of the Strait of Gibraltar. As I further read more of the limited information available about the tree one point stuck out, a comment about a yellowish color of the bark. What is this? I didn't know of any coloring like that on a Madrona tree. Further, searching the scientific literature a report popped up describing the *canariensis* crossing with an *Arbutus unedo*, the authors had given it the name *Arbutus x androsterilis* [53]. A hybrid, with the *unedo*, somehow this western Mediterranean tree had arrived at the island, but it must have been much later than the original *arbutus* that became indigenous. This *canariesis* tree did seem mysterious, an inner urge began to form in me, increasingly I knew I must go to the Canary Islands see it, but how?

It was another rainy and dark day in January, we have a lot of then in Anacortes, when Darlene said: "Let's travel somewhere we haven't been."

We opened a book of tours that had recently arrived and started browsing. Many of the places they offered we had been to but several were new to us. At one point Darlene paused turning the pages and pointed and said: "Ireland, I would like to go to see that."

Later when an associate heard about a possible trip to Ireland he said: "Hey, you can even kiss the Blarney Stone there."

"Whatever the Blarney Stone is and is it worth kissing?" I thought.

A week later as we were still pondering travel possibilities, my scheming mind began to work. Looking at the maps I could see that the Canary Islands were not so far from Ireland, certainly a lot closer than Anacortes. Maybe we could arrange a tour to Ireland then add on a side trip to the Canary Islands? This thought was enhanced when I learned that the Canary Islands to Europeans were like the Hawaiian Islands are to the west coast of North America, a tropical paradise to be visited. Ahh, this was useful information I could slip into my conversation with Darlene regarding our coming trip to Ireland, just a slight modification to our travel.

As plans matured, having received a positive response to my proposal to Darlene I booked two nights at a resort community not far from the airport at Tenerife, one of the main Canary Island with an international airport. The resort didn't seem far on the map, my first mistake.

So there we were on September 25th at 25,000 feet in a full plane from Dublin. I was still wondering why I had waited in a long line like millions of others to bend over backwards to kiss, what seemed like a wall of a castle, the Blarney Stone. "Oh well the sacrifice one must make." I thought.

I further chuckled to myself, recalling the earlier exhilaration I had felt when I read on the internet about an *Arbutus canariensis* in Victoria. [44] "Well, that is easy," I had thought to myself, since we live only a ferry ride and a short drive to Victoria. "We can go there to see the tree." Digging further to establish where to go in Victoria, I soon learned that the tree was to be found, not in Victoria, British Columbia, but rather in Victoria, *Australia* – a bit farther away from our home in the Pacific Northwest.

These thoughts were pushed from my mind by apprehension, uncertainty, and excitement as the plane began its descent to Tenerife. Is the *canariesis* waiting for us? Does it really have bark with a yellowing tint? Will we be able to find it? However, as the plane bumped onto the runway, I realized I needed to focus: find the baggage claim area, find our baggage, clear customs, and then locate the rental car office.

Three quarters of an hour later with the keys in my hand I pushed our hotel reservation across the desk and asked the agent where the hotel was. He pointed on a small map and gave directions, but we were quite tired by this time and I had some trouble remembering what he said. Outside it was getting dark, we got into the unfamiliar car. It had a stick shift and I fumbled around not knowing where all the controls were. In fact, I drove that night with the back-window wiper going the whole time. As we headed out, completely dark now, we really had no clue which way to go: Did we go right or left at the freeway? For that matter, where was the freeway? We programmed the hotel address into our "smart" phone's GPS. Unfortunately, the hotel had no street number, a problem which would plague us later. Nevertheless, off we went under the GPS' tentative *guidance*.

Soon on the freeway, finally headed in the right direction the GPS seemed much happier. After a while I saw a sign that said 11 KM to Los Christianos, the city that we were to stay in, or so I thought, anyway. Everything seemed to be going fine, until about 2 kilometers farther along, Siri, the voice from the GPS navigation system, started yapping about exiting in one-half kilometer. That didn't seem right, but Siri, must be obeyed, right? We reluctantly placed our trust in her directions, our second mistake. After a couple of exits later, she mercifully fell silent for a while. We zipped past apparently open fields as they were dark, some lighted hotels and restaurants, then into a residential area, around a few bends, and finally Siri awoke long enough to convey some heartening news: "You are almost there – turn to the left." Then, the words every driver longs to hear: "You have arrived at your destination." But where were we? It was a dead end on a residential street; clearly something was amiss.

It was now 11 p.m., dark as could be, we needed help. Soon we saw a tavern, stopping, I jumped out heading for the door hoping someone spoke English. The bar was buzzing, but I was able to get the bartender's attention and I showed him our reservation. He found his glasses and studied the paper. Fortunately, he spoke passable English. "Oh, you're in the wrong town!" he exclaimed, to my mild chagrin. "You must go to Los Christianos. You need to take the freeway to get there." Waving and pointing, he added, "It is a one-way street, so you have to continue on around it to the TF-1." Here we go again, I thought as we got back on the road. This time we watched for signs for the TF-1, the freeway, and followed them.

Returning to the multilane highway, we were reassured by a sign telling us we were only seven kilometers from Los Christianos. Fifty minutes later and two more stops for directions we were in front of a large, gaited resort complex. However, we didn't see a reception office anywhere. By this point my wife and I, both frazzled, were running very short on patience, so I didn't hesitate I went into an adjacent restaurant and a waiter took me outside and pointed up the hill, at two lights. After trudging up toward the lights, at last I came to what appeared, at least, to be a proper office. Indeed, it was, and – eureka! – they had our reservation on file. I hurried back to where we were parked and excitedly delivered the good news to an exhausted Darlene: "We won't have to sleep in the car, after all!" She eyed me but didn't comment on my attempt at humor.

Greeting us the receptionist soon called another attendant, who was kind enough to load our suitcases on a dolly and lead us up the rather steep hill. The poor fellow was almost panting by the time we finally arrived at our room. Hurray, I thought, at last we are here! It was about 12:30 AM, way past our bedtime.

We didn't look around the room or inspect the various amenities at that point. Instead, we just undressed, and melted into the bed with a joint sigh of weariness and relief. We had our fill of adventure for one night and I hoped we wouldn't have nearly so much trouble finding the *Arbutus canariensis* tree. Admittedly, our confidence had waned a bit over the course of our journey thus far.

The next morning, we awoke to a delightful view of the ocean from our balcony, with mist just beginning to rise from the water. A new day! After having toured Ireland for eleven days, we welcomed the warmth of the sunshine and happily broke out our shorts and sandals. Our plan was to hit the Play de Los Cristianos, a mostly tourist beach where the sand was not black because of the volcanic rock. It proved to be not white either like the Play de Las Teresitas which had been artificially formed. by bringing in tons of white sand from the Sahara Desert, apparently scorpions and red ants as well.

Smarting a little from our new exposure to the sun that evening, I began planning the route to find the *canariensis*. I opened my email notes from Sally Lamdin-Whymark, a visitor from the United Kingdom who had become so intrigued with Tenerife she moved there. Being an avid hiker, she published a book describing walks on the island.[45] Acquiring the book I pored over it, finding one trail where a group of *canariensis* grew. Before flying to Tenerife, I had sent her an e-mail, introducing myself and outlining my plan. To my delight, she had responded promptly which started a brief correspondence.[46] She seemed to sense that I preferred to drive to a location, rather than spending a half a day trekking through the mountains. She was kind enough to give me three suitable locations. These were all on the north side of the island. Studying the map, we decided to travel to Puerto de la Cruz, a good-sized city centrally situated to these destinations. We now had a plan of attack.

Tenerife is the largest and centermost of the seven Canary Islands. It is about 820 miles southwest of the Spanish side of the Strait of Gibraltar and about 250 miles due west of southwest Morocco. Lanzarote and Fuerteventura are the two Canary Islands closest to Africa, with Fuerteventura being 120 miles west on the average but at one point as close as 60 miles. The islands are from 1.8 to 20 million years old [47, 48]. They are volcanic but Tenerife has seen volcanic activity in 1704-1706, 1798, and 1909. It is the tallest island of the archipelago rising at least seven thousand meters (22,966 feet, or 4.35 miles) above the ocean floor, with Mount Teide, the highest mountain in Spain, reaching 3,718 meters (12,198 feet) above sea level.

Although the winds, called *los alisios*, and currents, Canaries Current, generally lie in the southerly direction, winds do blow westward briefly during the year, even carrying sand from the West Sahara onto the more easterly islands. Sally had told me that, even on Tenerife, dust and dry heat, called *Calima*, are seen and felt during this time.[45] One can speculate that primitive fishing craft, flora, and other debris may have been accidentally blown onto the islands in westerly storms, and debris from flooding rivers in Europe carrying *Arbutus* berries, which may have found their way to the island under the Canaries Current eons ago and started first trees with gradual adaptation to their current form.

Early sailors have played an important role in the islands. Lanzarote Marocello, from Genoa, sailing in 1336 A.D., discovered at least some of the Canary Islands and named Lanzarote after himself. Earlier excursions are rumored in history: 12th century B.C.E. - Phoenicians; 470 B.C.E. - Carthagianian Hanno; 40 B.C.E. - Juba II as reported by Pliny the Elder; and, in 150 A.D., Ptolemy from Egypt is reputed to have drawn an imaginary line through El Hierro, labeling it as the end of the known world. However, the sailor with whom the reader is most likely familiar with is Christopher Columbus, who left Spain on August 3, 1492 with his famous fleet of three ships: the *Nia*, the *Pinta*, and the *Santa Maria*. This was a foolish if courageous voyage; as most of us learned in grade school, many of his contemporaries feared that he and his crew would sail over the *edge* of the Earth. After disembarking at the Canary Islands, they had to repair the rudder of the Pinta and change the sails on the *Nina* from a set designed for coastal sailing to one made for the open sea. Reportedly, they were in the Canary Islands for about a month, taking on water and wood and other provisions, as they would during each of three subsequent voyages. Surprisingly he arrived a mere thirty-three days later, on October 12,1492, not at the end of the world but at an island in what is now called the Bahamas. This event has been celebrated yearly in most places in the United States as Columbus Day. [50] However, in 2021 an alternative name has arisen: Indigenous People's Day, which reflects in some ways the history that evolved from that event.

That history echoes the conquest and colonization, with all the positive and ill effects occurred early with Spain and Portugal as fierce rivals in this race, but in 1476, in the Treaty of Alcáçovas, Portgual agreed to give Spain control of the Canary Islands. [51] As a result, the islands are now a part of Spain, but they do have their local governments.

The land on the north and east side of Tenerife is very fertile due to the rain from the trade winds and the decomposed volcanic soil. Its volcano, Mount Teide, tends to determine the overall contour of the island: mountains in the central region and slopes going all the way to the sea on each side. The southern and western sections of the island are typically desert, heavily populated with volcanic rock and cacti. Much of the northern side is very steep, with slopes down to the sea and much of it heavily populated with laurel forests.

At ten o' clock, we were off on our adventure, heading northwest along the TF-1 freeway at 120 km/hr toward Puerto de la Cruz, which we had plugged into our phone's navigation system as the endpoint. Siri tried to redirect us along presumably a shorter route, but I was happy just cruising on the freeway. She then calculated the new route then mercifully kept her thoughts to herself. We climbed in elevation until, eventually, the freeway reached its terminus. Continuing onto a two-lane road, we began to see pine trees, then some agave plants. The agave looked like they were on steroids compared to some we had seen on a trip to Texas described later. They would be beautiful in the eyes of Tequila makers, although I had no idea whether there were any Tequila producers in Tenerife.

We were directed again by Siri, off what I thought was the main route but proved to be a delightful drive. At one point I saw an unusual gray covering over rock and stopped to get a closer look. It covered a whole side of the hill of lava from an ancient eruption. The gray layer was a type of lichen (*Sterocaulon vesuvianum*) (Figure 4.3). Its growth was probably stimulated by the mist coming from the sea. I thought, this maybe an example of what had been occurring for millions of years and had contributed to converting the rock into fertile soil [52].

Admiring the ever-changing landscape, we gasped in awe of the view as we came around a bend in the road. There, before us, was the blue sea at the north side of the island, contrasting picturesquely with the stark white, frothing, cresting breakers that rolled onto jutting cliffs, these cliffs protruding far out from the shore. Blue sea filled the space between these outcroppings. Green foliage rushed down the steep slopes to meet the cliff edges. In this manner we were introduced to the North Shore.

Not long after, we were weaving down a hill into Puerto de la Cruz, between a confusing array of high-rise hotels and resorts. Stopping at the first prospective hotel, we parked in a makeshift spot. I hurried inside to determine if accommodations could be procured. Luckily, they could, and presently we were rolling our suitcases past a swimming pool full of bathers enjoying the warm afternoon sun. We whizzed up to the fifth floor and entering our room, were delighted to find a balcony overlooking the sea. It was now about 12:30 in the afternoon, so we'd still have plenty of time to plan our first expedition to the *Arbutus canaresis*.

I had printed out a copy of Sally's e-mail, which provided quite a good explanation of how to find the first location. We programmed into my phone the last town of reasonable size along the route (Camino de Chasna). Sure enough, it appeared on the screen. Darlene pushed *directions* and *go* and Siri once again sprang into action to guide us. We crossed the freeway and headed into the mountains, through one roundabout after another, sometimes missing an exit I just continued around a second time. I think Siri got dizzy, and it took a little while for her to recalibrate. Incidentally, my wife thinks I have too close a relationship with Siri. I once asked Siri, in my wife's presence, if she was married. She answered: "Is that the way you always start a conversation?"

After she locates some information for me, I'll often say, "Thank you, Siri," to which she invariably and somewhat coyly replies: "I am here to serve."

I like that, but Darlene gives me that look and invariably a curt comment.

Back on the trail of the tree, we proceeded around bends, up and down hills, through narrow passages between buildings; despite occasional descents, on balance we continued to climb to higher and higher elevations, occasionally pulling over to let an oncoming car pass, an ever-expanding bevy of towns between us and the ocean below. We spied a few banana groves and even, at one point, a corn field, while the frequency of houses diminished. Finally, Siri said: "You have arrived at your destination." We pulled over to consult our notes, which said to turn right at a sign for Benijos then to go about five kilometers and look for a sign bearing the name Chanajiga or more fully the Spanish name: Chanajiga retkipaikka.

So off we sped toward this lovely-sounding name. A split-second after I saw the sign, we had already zipped past it. Quickly returning we followed this new course, heading up the mountain, houses became scarcer, the road getting narrower, the sea and port dropping farther and farther into the distance below us. Finally running out of tarmac, a sign said Chanajiga. It was a recreational park, for picnicking and perhaps camping. We bumped into the parking lot and came to a gate on the right which didn't seem to go anywhere, but the road continued.

What do we do, we wondered? Sally had said we should come to a T-junction and a gate and stop there.[46] But this didn't seem like much of a T-junction, and the gate was at the side of a parking lot. Uncertain, we continued down the dirt-rock road, watching as it slowly deteriorated further. After about a kilometer and a half, things didn't seem right, but being the brave, and stubborn fellow that I am, I said cautiously to my wife: "Let's go a little farther and maybe we'll find the T-junction." Reluctantly, she agreed.

The road became increasingly rocky. I kept swerving, uncertain where to place the wheels, straddling potholes. Darlene mumbled something – rather accurate, in hindsight – about our needing a jeep, not our little red Ford Escort. As I proceeded, I stole the occasional nervous glance on the right side of the road where the space was empty. Well not entirely empty, if one looked down where the bank descended hundreds of feet stippled with trees and shrubs. I could see increasingly Darlene squirming in her seat since that was her side of the car. On the left, my side, the mountain rose immediately up in a rocky cliff with some trees hanging on for their dear lives. The road was intended to be one lane only. Passing would be impossible. Stopping near a turn, we sat there pondering; proceeding seemed to offer only diminishing returns.

Suddenly, around the corner came an obviously very dedicated hiker wearing spandex, a headband, and earbuds, sweat pouring down his face. He appeared to be very fit and was clipping up the trail. I managed to get him to stop and tried to ask him where we were. He didn't speak English. I ran back to the car and fetched the book Sally had published and showed him the page where the little map outlined the trail. He instantly recognized what he was looking at and pointed back down the road we had come and indicated holding up 2 fingers the distance, I assumed two kilometers. Furthermore, pointing in the direction we were headed he waved is hand back and forth indicating, no, no, stop. "Okay," I said, smiling. "*Mucho Gracias*!" He put his earbuds back in and disappeared down the trail.

We drove forward to where the "road," thankfully, was a little wider. Darlene, got out of the car and guided me, saving me from bumping the cliff with the rear end and watching so I didn't drive off the edge of the road. Back and forth, putting the power steering to good use, we finally maneuvered the Escort out of its predicament and headed back the way we had come. Again, straddling rocks and holes, we soon reached a better road and shortly thereafter arrived back at the picnic tables and gate we had passed earlier. We looked at each other. *Now what?*

Then, unexpectedly, Darlene's face lit up as she pointed through the windshield. "There's the tree!" she blurted excitedly. Her eyes register color more accurately than mine, and in precisely the spot she was pointing to – Lo! There orange berries hung on the tree, waving at us (Figure 4.3).

We hopped out of the car. There were no blossoms, as I had anticipated there would be, but beautiful clusters of berries hung in many places on several trees. My impression was these berries were not quite as big as the *unedo* but approaching it perhaps 2 cm in diameter. Their trunks were gorgeous, smooth and twisting and climbing until they disappeared into the foliage. (Figure 4.1 & 4.2) Their leaves were bigger than I'd ever seen on the Pacific Madrone, and the trees themselves looked extremely healthy. Several trees grew nearby, along the hiking trail as described by Sally. All the trees seemed very vigorous, showing no sign of disease. Shreds of peeling bark still clung to some trunks, but, now at the start of autumn, they were clearly well past the shedding stage. These stripped trunks were smooth, slightly slippery, like the *Arbutus menziesii* where we lived. But there a was a yellow color imprinted in them in tinted vertical strips. (Figure 4.1) Almost like a painter had lightly applied a brush to a canvas. This feature was definitely not like the *menziesii* which in early stages is green to amber at this time of the year. (Contrast with Figure 1.1) This yellow color answered one of the mysteries that had intrigued me from the beginning, although why that color I still don't know. The elevation was 1.19 km and, the temperature warm but not so hot as it was farther down the mountain, perhaps 75° F.

I have to say I was delighted, taking pictures from every angle I could think of. After exhausting all the possibilities, including taking pictures of all the signs, we headed, I reluctantly, back down the mountain, weary but satisfied. After returning to our hotel we decided to extend our stay an extra day because it was so beautiful there.

The next morning, I walked out on the balcony while it was still dark, and from my vantage point I could watch as the sky slowly brightened. The waves on the barely discernible sea appeared as darkened lines morphing into heavier ones as they moved shoreward, finally peaking into white froth. Often just starting to break at one corner, they would pick up the rest of the wave and turn it over as it rushed onward. Small boats appeared as dots, with lights running parallel to the beach.

We had a full day available to us before we would have to head back toward the vicinity of the airport. I had been surprised at how small the island was. I began looking on the GPS for the location of the second possibility that Sally had provided. I saw that it was only fifteen kilometers from the hotel. In fact, it was just outside a wine museum called Casa del Vino de Tenerife. We decided to go after breakfast.

We pulled into the museum parking lot after having no difficulty finding it. *The reader is doubtless convinced by now that I get lost easily – not true*! The museum was quite interesting, with various informational displays of the history of winemaking on Tenerife. Evidently, they also hosted viticulture lectures there on occasion. The wine made in Tenerife was so good, according to one of the displays, that pirates would come ashore just to raid and pillage as much of it as would fit in their ships (Figure 4.5B). Other historically famous people: William Shakespeare, Walter Scott, Percy Shelley, Alexander Von Humboldt to name a few, were also connoisseurs of it according to the posters in the gallery at Museo Casa del Vino (House of Wine Museum).

Walking into the garden, we ran immediately into an *Arbutus canariensis* tree! Wonderful! (Figure 4.4) Many of the blossoms were mostly pink. They were drooping in clusters. A few berries also hung from the branches. The leaves were much smaller than the ones we had seen earlier, and the tree was much shorter, only about fifteen feet high, compared to 20'-30' trees we had seen the day before. The elevation here was about two hundred feet, and the climate drier than up on the mountain where the other trees grew. Up there the fog often persists for extended periods during the day, larger leaves were needed to capture more light for photosynthesis in this condition. It was also cooler and moister there. In contrast, smaller leaves are known to be a protective mechanism which many trees employ under drier conditions. Overall, the tree didn't look quite as healthy as the ones up on the mountains. There were a few dead branches, perhaps due to disease, I really don't know. Nevertheless, it was a noble tree and I was delighted to find one with blossoms still on it. After photographing it, we concluded our day's adventure by purchasing a bottle of wine fermented at one of the local vineyards.

That evening, as the sun set, we opened the wine and celebrated our findings and our trip while enjoying the view from our balcony. I was quite satisfied, and we decided we were ready to return to the airport the next day. However, not wanting to entirely give up on this venture, we would travel along the rest of the shore around the island and maybe sample a few of the black sand beaches along the way, something to add to our memory of Tenerife.

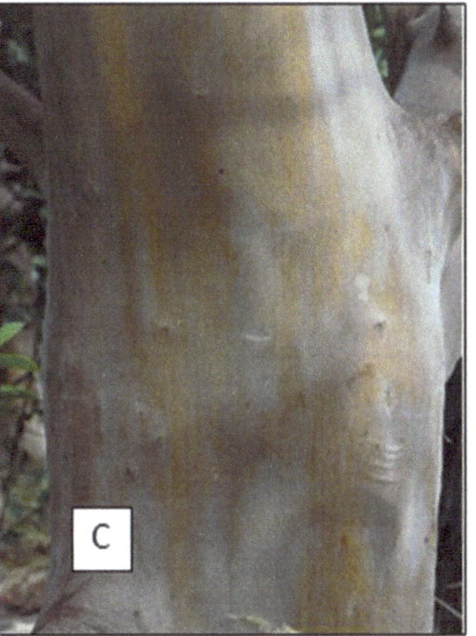

Figure 4.1 An *Arbutus canariensis* tree at elevation of 3891 ft (1.19 km) on the rainy side of the mountain on Tenerife. (28.34423°, -16.58424°) A, B, C progressively expanded views of the tree. C. Note the coloring is different from the exfoliated *Arbutus menziesii.*

Figure 4.2 Three views of the *canariensis* trees growing in the same location as Fig. 4.2. A. Shows the twisted growth of some of the trees, B. Illustrates the large leaves of the trees at this elevation and position on the mountian, C. Cluster of the berries present on many of the trees.

Figure 4.3 A. Lichen growing on volcanic rocks on rainy side of Tenerife Island., B. Expanded view of A., C. *Arbutus canariensis* berries waving at us on Tenerife Island.

Figure 4.4 View of an Arbutus canariensis growing at elevation of 200 ft(61m) near the ocean. A. The tree, B. Expanded view of the trunk, C. View of the upper branch illustrating peeling bark, D. Close up of leaves and blossoms, (note color of the flower and size of the leaves), E. Ancient wine bottle at the wine museum.

Chapter Five:

An Entanglement - The Greek Love Triangle

What is this Greek entanglement? This expression has been used to describe the triangle of complex relations of Italy, Germany, and Bulgaria (members of the Axis Powers) during their occupation of Greece during the latter part of World War II. Truly a snarl of competitive force, but no, it is not this military tragedy I am referring to. Looking back even further, into ancient times, the mythology of Greece might be invoked. For example, the convoluted amorous relationships between Aphrodite, the Greek goddess of beauty, love, and eternal youth; Anchises, her mortal, human, lover; and Ares, god of war, who was both Aphrodite's half-brother (Zeus being their common father) and, despite her marriage to another deity (Hephaestus), her frequent paramour – thus making her relationship with him not merely adulterous, but incestuous as well. But again, no, nothing of such fantasies or devious nature; I am referring to a rather a very down to earth triangle but nevertheless a strange one.

Specifically, the interaction of the two species the *Arbutus andrachne* (Greek Strawberry tree) and *Arbutus unedo* (the western Mediterranean Strawberry tree) both of the same genus form two tips of the triangle. The result of this interaction is a naturally occurring hybrid called *Arbutu*s *xandrachnoides*. Indeed, there are many conflicts and mysteries associated with the mating. First, one may ask how such an unlikely pairing might occur in the first place? The *unedo* is a fall bloomer, while the *andrachne* blossoms in the spring. How could one naturally pollenate the other? Generally, such a phenomenon requires that both plants bloom at roughly the same time in roughly the same location. Further, some insect or, as in rarer cases, a humming-bird, must retrieve the pollen from one plant and then deposit it into the pistil (female organ) of the other. Natural cross pollination has also occurred between *A. unedo* and the *A. canariensis* on Tenerife Island in the Canary Islands, resulting in the natural hybrid *A. xandrosterilis* (Pascual (1993).[53] However, this mating is much less surprising, as both the *unedo* and *canariensis* are fall bloomers.

Nevertheless, one must contemplate and even scrutinize this *unedo* or maybe just call it a *bad boy*. In Chapter Two I described how it had jumped across the Atlantic and propagated itself along in the Pacific Coast but now we see it even somehow has mated with two other Eastern Hemisphere *Arbutus* species as well. It makes one wonder if the *unedo* is the Don Juan of *Arbutus* trees?

Returning to the birth of the *xandrachnoides,* is it possible under abnormal circumstances, that the normal fall and spring blooming times might align, at least partially? The predominant factors known to affect blooming in plants are the photoperiod of the season; the temperature and particular variation of plant involved; the amount of rainfall in the region to which the plant is native; and the season in which the majority of that rainfall occurs. Because temperatures can swing so dramatically in a short span of time, sometimes as little as four to six hours, especially during the autumn and spring, plants which depend on a steady temperature within a particular, narrow range often struggle during these seasons. This is particularly true at latitudes where freezing can occur (e.g., late or early frost). Furthermore, while the photoperiod of a given season is more reliable overall because of the consistency of celestial patterns, the occurrence of volcanic eruptions, for example, can blacken the sky for an extended time, particularly downwind. Could such a natural phenomenon, or perhaps several such over the course of many eons, have assisted in giving rise to what otherwise seems the rather inexplicable mating of the two plants in question?

There is at least one study of evidence of the time-shifting of the blooming period of the *unedo.* Rainfall was artificially reduced in a control group of *unedo* trees over a two-year period. [54] The authors found that the peak blooming period was delayed by about twenty days the first year and fifty days the second. This result invites the question: might an extended drought, as surely would have occurred naturally at various points in the species' past, have once delayed the fall flowering of the *unedo* in such a way that it coincided with the spring blooming of the *andrachne*? Moreover, how might such a drought have affected the *andrachne*? Unfortunately, my research indicates that this latter question has yet to be studied.

The changing climate has rightly raised grave concerns, not only about its likely impact upon the animal world, including our own human habitat, but its probable effects upon plant life as well. Bertin, in a comprehensive review of the literature in 2008, [55] found a more consistent advancement of the phenophases of plants in recent years due to the warming effect caused by ever-increasing emissions of CO_2. One study of three deciduous trees, found that one tree's blooming period was delayed by temperature increases in the fall but occurred earlier when spring temperatures rose earlier than usual (Tao, et al., 2018). [56] The other two species were more influenced by the photoperiod. Of course, humanity's growing awareness of climate warming is only a recent event compared to the climate changes that have occurred in the past tens of millennia (e.g., several glacial periods) to which the *Arbutus* trees have gradually adapted via natural selection.

The *Arbutus xandrachnoides* grow more rigorously than its parents. It has taken on more of the characteristics of the *andrachne,* such as with respect to the color and texture of its bark, cinnamon-red and generally smooth, with a tendency to peel more easily than the *unedo* for example. Its blossoms are similarly shaped and interestingly, have been reported to occur both sometimes in the spring, like the *andrachne*, and sometimes in the fall, like the *unedo.* Further, the berries are of intermediate size compared to those produced by its *parents*, while its surface is smoother and less granular than that of either, the rough pyramid papilla of the *unedo.* On the other hand, they fruit in the fall just like the *unedo.* The leaves of the *child* are also of an intermediate size as compared with those of its parents, the *andrachne*'s being substantially the largest of the three (Bertsouklis KF and Papafotiou M, 2016).[40]

As I studied the relevant literature, I considered the role that male sterility, fairly common among hybrid plants, might have played in these various properties of the trees. In his 1993 paper, Pascual reports that *A. xandrosterilis*, the Canary Island natural hybrid, is sterile.[53] He provides a picture of each of the male stamens of the *unedo*: the *cannariensis* and the cross, *xandrosterilis.* The *xandrosterilis* stamen is quite distorted, unlike either of the others. I mused awhile about sterility of the Greek cross, x*andrachnoides*, before eventually I contacted Professors Bertsouklis and Papafotiou of the University of Athens. Dr. Bertsouklis was kind enough to check out a grove in Varympompi, about 24 kilometers northwest of Athens, in the spring, where he found examples of *andrachne*'s and *xandrachnoides*'s blooming concurrently. He examined under a microscope the blossoms of x*andrachnoides* and found pollen present in the dual sacs of the anthers, which seems to have settled the question regarding their fertility, at least in connection with pollen production.

Our arboreal "love triangle" takes on yet another interesting twist vis-à-vis human intervention, with reports of crossing and even double-crossing recurring in the literature. This is beginning to sound a bit like the plot of a John LeCarré spy novel.

A 2004 paper by the French botanist Jean-Pierre Demoly in particular yields several fascinating insights. [57] The main feature of this paper is the origin and naming of two *Arbutus* hybrids: *Arbutus* x *Thuretiana* Dem and *Arbutus* x*Reyorum* Dem, the Dem is added here to show the naming of these by Demoly. The first, *Arbutus* x*Thuretiana* is a cross between Arbutus *canariensis* and the *Arbutus andrachne.* The second, *Arbutus* x*Reyorum* is a cross between the *Arbutus* x*andrachnoides,* the Greek hybrid, and the *Arbutus canariensis (i.e. the double cross).* Both of these were cultivated in southern France. The names of the first was chosen to honor Gustave Thuret who founded the starting of many exotic plants at Cote d'Azur (French Riveria). The second was to honor Jean Rey and his son Jean-Marie Rey who tested and propagated the *A.* x*Reyorum.*

However, the initial date of when the first hybrid occurred is not given. Demoly then implies that this latter hybrid was displayed in the 1915 Panama American Exposition in San Francisco [58] but doesn't indicate how it could have got there. He also writes that a plant very comparable called *Arbutus* 'Marina' was introduced into France in 1993 from an English nursery, Madrona Nursery.

Now turning to the present in North America, a popular cultivar called the *Arbutus* 'Marina' is prevalent in the Mediterranean like regions of California. I pondered: "Could this be the same tree?"

In follow up communication with Demoly my impression is that he does have ready access to *A.* 'Marina', the now mature trees that were introduced into France. Comparing their morphology of blossoms and bark he wrote me that he feels justified in giving the name of the cultivar as: *Arbutus xReyorum* 'Marina'.[59]

I visualize Demoly as the detective of trees. Our communication was a bit clumsy in my Google translated English – French. Notwithstanding, Demoly is an authority and gained considerable botanical experience in southern France having written a 304 page book with 388 photographs of the extraordinary and famous botanical garden *Les Cèdres* which is located on a small but renowned peninsula just east of Nice, France, called Saint-Jean-Cap-Feratt.[4] [60]

I don't picture myself as a plant detective, nevertheless, I feel it necessary to try to unravel the rest of the story. Just how did this tree, if it was the same tree as in California, appear in France? I managed to get ahold of Liam Mackenzie, the founder in 1986 of the Madrona Nursery, located in Berthersden, Kent, UK mentioned by Demoly. Evidently, Lian selected this name for his nursery because of his passion for the *Arbutus* genus. Mr. Mackenzie informed me that, back in the early 1990s, he had traveled with some regularity to the Courson Flower Show, held south of Paris, where he had sold a wide variety of plants. He suspects that *Monsieur* Demoly or others that he had close interaction with might have bought some *Arbutus* 'Marina' from him. However, Mr. Mackenzie relayed that he had not grown them himself but had acquired *A.* 'Marina' plants from Peter Catt of Liss Forest Nursery in Hampshire, England. [61] As it turns out, Liss Nursery is essentially closed, but in a brief exchange by e-mail, the since-retired Mr. Catt, told me that, while he was unsure of when, exactly, he had purchased these botanical treasures, he recalled quite clearly the name of the outfit from *which* he'd procured them: a little place called Briggs Nursery, located in Elma, Washington. He added with nostalgia: "I was buying lots of micro-propagated liners from Bruce Briggs in those very happy days."[62]

Now, what does Briggs Nursery [63] have to do with any of this? To answer that and related questions, we must look more closely at the 1915 Exposition I mentioned earlier. This exposition was held in part to celebrate the completion of the Panama Canal on August 15 of the previous year.[5] The canal had opened to much fanfare, and the scale of its impact - enormous, by any measure – upon maritime transport between the world's two major oceans, the Atlantic and Pacific, was already apparent. This Expo took place in the long shadow of World War I, then at its height in the European theater. The United States would not enter the war for another two years; however, its effects upon the World's Fair were no doubt less dramatic than they would have been had we intervened sooner.

The Expo ran from February to December of 1915. In its wake we find a mysterious trail leading to the propagation of a beautiful *Arbutus* hybrid, one with pink or ruby blossoms and its trademark cinnamon-red, peeling-prone bark, later called the *Arbutus* 'Marina'. The following sequence of events involving this genetically curious botanical species has been published on the website of San Marcos Growers [64]. In the beginning, a nursery, the Western Nursery, in 1915 was owned and operated by Charles Abrahams and until it closed was

4 This cape has property owned by many famous people, both historically and presently, including the now deceased Paul Allen, the co-founder of Microsoft Corp.

5 Some commentators have speculated that the *real* impetus for the event was to showcase the city's recovery from the devastating (7.9 Richter scale) earthquake of 1906, which had decimated vast swaths of the northern California coast, including about 80% of San Francisco itself.

located on San Francisco's famously serpentine Lombard Street in the Marina District. Mr. Abrahams had reportedly obtained cuttings from an assortment of trees sent from Europe featured in a horticultural exhibit at the 1915 Expo, including the specimen of *Arbutus* 'Marina'. He then later successfully propagated this tree. At his nursery's closing sale, Eric Walther, then the director of the Strybing Arboretum, purchased a boxed tree from him which has been later identified as the *Arbutus* in question.

Comprising fifty-five acres of land, the beautiful sanctuary now known as the San Francisco Botanical Garden (formerly the Strybing Arboretum) lies entirely within the Golden Gate Park, itself located just southwest of the now defunct nursery. *I describe later a visit to this Botanical Garden.* Continuing with the trail of this tree, Victor Reiter, a well-known plantsman in the area, acquired cuttings from the tree, still flourishing in the Garden even today, and began propagating it in 1933.[65] [66] He and his wife developed a gorgeous garden of their own, in which one of the resulting specimens grew to considerable proportions. However, at least as regards the production and sale of native trees, the nursery trade in California at the time was far from vigorous.

The Saratoga Horticulture Foundation, Inc. was founded 1952, in part to correct this shortcoming and to research interesting flora compatible with California's mostly warm, dry climate. [67] The Foundation opened a nursery in San Martin, California. Mr. Reiter apparently played a pivotal role both within the Foundation itself and, later, in the day-to-day operations of the San Martin nursery. A specimen of one of his *Arbutus* trees, and/or cuttings from it, led to the planting of one outside the Foundation's home office, a tree which by all accounts flourished from the outset. During the 1970s and 1980s, offspring of this *Arbutus* were raised and distributed on a limited basis. It was also during this period that the cultured hybrid was given the name *Arbutus* 'Marina,' to reflect its geographical provenance and distinguish it from its genetic forebears[6].

Awkwardly, it appears that the Saratoga Horticulture Foundation could not reproduce the *Arbutus* 'Marina' fast enough for wide distribution. Therefore, Lowell Cordas, the Foundation's director, contacted Briggs Nursery, Inc. in search of assistance. Cordas was aware that the founder of Briggs had developed mass-production methods of cultivating large numbers of plants simultaneously through the use of micro-propagation techniques. This is a recent human innovation that would probably impress even those Greek gods of yore. Put simply, it involves taking meristematic tissue (undifferentiated tissue in the region of a plant where cells grow) and placing it in a solution containing hormones and nutrients designed to rapidly stimulate growth. If successful, this tissue will sprout roots which are divided into perhaps a dozen sections, each of which is then deposited into a separate container with a new solution which promotes further growth.

A large quantity of plantlets can thus be produced in a small physical space and within relatively short growing time. The plantlets are usually assembled in multi-row liners which are easily distributed. The only apparent drawback to this otherwise extraordinary technique – is that each plantlet is, necessarily, a genetic clone of the original *parent* plant. Therefore, the resulting specimens do not profit from the reproductive mechanism, enjoyed by purely naturally growing plants, that yields adaptive environmental advantages for each new generation, for example, cross-pollination between trees.

It is rumored that the Saratoga contracted Briggs to grow five thousand plantlets for the Foundation. They received these piecemeal throughout 1993 and later grew them to be distributed to nurseries. The Saratoga Foundation has since been decommissioned. Now it becomes clear how the *A.* 'Marina' passed from Briggs Nursery to Liss Forest Nursery in Hampshire, England, to Madrona Nursery in Berthersden, Kent, England, and finally to the Courson Flower show south of Paris, France. As further support to this trail, Liam Mackenzie of Madrona Nursery sent me the brochure that he used to advertise the *A.* 'Marina' when he was selling it and

6 In 1989 the San Marcos Growers in Santa Barbara acquired a plant which has since blossomed into a large tree in its own right. Measured in 2013, it was found it to have a circumference of 2.74 meters, a height of 13.7 meters, and crown width of 16.3 meters.

the wording and content reflect very closely the brochure that the Saratoga Foundation had produced when advertising the tree in California.

As I understand the situation, growers such as San Marcos now obtain their plantlets directly from Briggs in wholesale quantities. My contact at San Marcos Growers, Randy Baldwin, told me they have sold 11,184 *Arbutus* 'Marina' trees in the quarter-century since they acquired their first specimen from Briggs. In San Francisco alone, there are now any number of sites at which one can inspect these trees for oneself. There are two good books offering descriptions and locations of them. One, provided by Matt Ritter (2011), is near the city's marina area.[68] Seven additional sites are listed by Mike Sullivan (2015).[69]

Notwithstanding this illuminating account of the tree's colorful if somewhat convoluted history, several mysteries remain unsolved. First, what are the actual parents of this hybrid? Are they *Arbutus* x*Reyorum*, as Demoly speculates (i.e., a double-cross between *Arbutus* x*andrachnoides*, the Greek hybrid, and *Arbutus canariensis*), or some other species altogether? According to Baldwin, Cordas had always insisted that the tree's true genesis lay in cultivars of the *Arbutus* **x***andrachnoides. [70]*

Compounding this riddle are two other thorny questions: first, what time of year is the tree's blooming season, and second, is the *A.* 'Marina' sterile? With regard to the former, the *A.* x*andrachnoides* was reported by Professors Bertsouklis and Papafotiou to bloom in Greece either in the spring, like the *andrachne*, or in the fall like the *unedo*. Mr. Baldwin relayed to me that the *A.* 'Marina' blooms in the spring in Santa Barbara, as well as in October and December! He further mentioned that flowers often bloom in the San Barbara area at unexpected times. For example, he sent me a picture of an *Arbutus canariensis* specimen he and others at San Marcos had grown from seed given him a few years ago. This tree was found to bloom there in late May, while in the Canary Islands it typically blooms in autumn. He was also kind enough to supply me with some photos of *A.* 'Marina' trees blooming in October in Filmore, California, located about thirty miles to the southeast of their nursery. On their website [71], San Marcos Growers state that the tree flowers all year round, with cresting taking place in the spring and fall. They also note that it has been observed to produce yellow berries at the same time as a more mature ilk bearing the dark red hue most commonly associated with the fruit.

Lurking behind these facts, once again, is the specter of the sterility question. Mr. Baldwin says that neither he nor his colleagues at San Marcos Growers have ever observed the growth of any young seedlings within the immediate vicinity of their big *A.* 'Marina' Now, of course, even a flower with a female pistil and even sterile male stamens can be pollinated by one of its fertile parents if located nearby. However, whether such a pollination can produce seeds that are fertile I don't know.

I recently had occasion to examine under a microscope some flowers from a specimen of a closely related tree, the so-called *Arbutus* 'Spring Frost', which I'd discovered at a nursery in Portland, Oregon. The flowers had bloomed in early May of 2018. My goal was to establish either the presence or absence within the flowers of normal stamen. The species of tree in question is a patented cultivar of an *A.* 'Marina' with variegated leaves. According to Randy Baldwin, these leaves were a "sport" of this particular class of tree. (In botany, a sport, or *lusus*, is a part of a plant that shows morphological differences – in plain English, has different visible attributes - from the rest of the plant.) Of great additional help were some blossoms, generously sent me by Mr. Baldwin, from one of San Marco's 'Marina' trees.

In examining these flowers, I spotted what appeared to be normal stamens with pollen clearly present in the dual sacs. But upon closer inspection, I also detected something slightly different from what I had consistently observed in the specimens of *A. menziesii*, *peninsularis*, and *unedo*: the appendages attached to the anthers of the stamen botanically called "spurs" (Figure A2 & A3) were noticeably shorter and less pronounced, curling inward only slightly at around the two-thirds mark. What evolutionary purpose these appendages serve, exactly, is unknown, just another mystery of the tree. For illustration, if the appendages growing out from the anthers of the *menziesii*, etc. resembled the horns of the Texas Longhorn breed of cattle, I decided, then these (i.e., those of the *A.* 'Marina' and *A.* "Spring Frost" specimens) horns were more akin to those of farm-variety bull. While reviewing the aforementioned photograph provided by Pascual of *A. canariensis*, I saw that the spurs on the anthers of its stamen were truncated in a fashion similar to those of the 'Marina' and "Frost." Furthermore, upon examining the stamens of some dried blossoms from a specimen of *A. canariensis* already in my possession, I was able to identify the same phenomenon again, namely, comparably truncated spurs. This finding I believe is new and suggests that *A. canariensis* most likely figures prominently in the ancestry of *A.* 'Marina'.

In order to explore this finding more thoroughly I flew to San Francisco in April 2019 and visited the San Francisco Botanical Garden. They had several *A.* 'Marina' trees blooming there (Figures 5.1 & 5.2) and two *A. canariensis* trees of which one still had some flowers (Figure A2B). The curator there, Ryan Guillou, gave me permission to acquire some flowers from them to study. At my hotel that night and next morning, I spent hours dissecting and examining them with a portable microscope. I found in flower after flower the spurs of the *A. canariensis* and *A.* 'Marina' were very similar, again shorter than those of the other *Arbutus* species I previously examined.

So, what do the appendages of the *A. andrachne* and *A.* x*andrachnoides* look like, you might ask, since according to Demoly these trees are involved in these crosses? Fortunately, those learned Greek professors I mentioned earlier once again came through with the answer. By studying blossoms from both types of trees, they were able to deduce that they were similar to those of *A. undeo*. Thus, it appeared that the shorter, less dramatic spurs of the *A. canariensis* and *A.* 'Marina' are probably unique to these species, supporting in part the premises of the Demoly as to the heritage of the *A.* 'Marina' as being the *Arbutus* x*Reyorum*. However, based on my observations it doesn't rule out the alternate *Arbutus* x*Thuretiana* a cross between *Arbutus canariensis* and the *Arbutus andrachne*. Well, even Hercule Poirot didn't solve all of his mysteries to 100% satisfaction.

Nevertheless, of all the foregoing mysteries, perhaps the one that I'd most like to see unraveled one day is that of how the *A.* 'Marina' arrived in America in the first place. In the course of my correspondence with Randy Baldwin, he mentioned that records of the Expo are stored in the archives of the University of California Berkeley's Bancroft Library. Acting on this tip, I had a library researcher perform a search of any and all records kept there, looking for any relevant mention of agriculture or horticulture sent from Italy, Sweden, or France. Unfortunately, the effort produced nothing pertinent, and I am afraid that any other leads which might surface in this matter will similarly prove to be dead ends – leaving *this* mystery, at least, permanently unsolved.

Then again, perhaps some future DNA analysis, will eventually shed some light on the question. In the meantime, one almost can't help but picture the knowing smiles doubtless etched upon the faces of those old Greek gods – smiles, we may suppose, unlikely to fade anytime soon.

Figure 5.1 *Arbutus* 'Marina' growing at the San Francisco Botanical Garden April 2019.

Figure 5.2 *Arbutus* 'Marina' A. A different tree than Figure 5.1 but at the Garden, B. Cluster of blossoms on the tree, C. Two berries still present on April 2019.

Chapter Six:

My Love Goes South -The Lady's Legs of Texas (*Arbutus xalapensis*)

The Chihuahuan Desert, dotted with prickly pear, dog cholla, blooming claret cup cactus, yucca plants, and an occasional agave plant, flashed by as Darlene and I pushed slightly over the 70 MPH speed limit. For a while, the scenery repeated itself: more peppering of shrubs, bleached hills, dry coulees, and wavering heat. Then, all of a sudden, a Welcome to Texas sign, shaped like the state itself, appeared. This was followed by a 75 MPH speed limit sign; my finger responded by clicking the cruise control up a few notches. We were well on our way to the Guadalupe Mountain National Park, following Highway 62/180 on this June 2017 morning.

Several days previously, as our plane lowered its wheels to land in Albuquerque, New Mexico, I thought to myself, I know nothing about Albuquerque. Even so, Glen Campbell's popular song words, "By the time I make Albuquerque she will be working . . ." kept replaying in my mind. Siri on my phone, quickly provided me with many facts about Albuquerque. Among them was that famous Carlsbad Caverns National Park was nearby. I made a mental note that we should see them after we accomplished my primary mission.

"Where is the best place to see the Texas Madrones[7]?" I had asked the ranger over the phone the previous afternoon. The McKittrick Canyon, he'd answered. He had recommended hiking up the side of the canyon, perhaps to the Pratt cabin and back, a roundtrip distance of about 4.8 miles. He'd added, "The trail is easy, and they're about fifteen big Madrone trees growing along the way." How young was this ranger, I wondered, trying to gauge what he meant by *easy*? The map showed the turn-off to be not too far ahead.

Shortly after passing a rest area with tall, blooming agave plants stippling the surrounding area, we came to the well-marked side road. Turning on to it, we were welcomed by a National Park sign and informed that we were now officially in the park. The road wound through gullies and over small rises, weaving its way along a dry creek bed as we searched for the parking lot where the hiking would begin. My heart rate began to increase; I sat up straight, now fully awake. I had been looking forward to seeing the Texas Madrone for some time. From what I had read, it should have been a lot like the Pacific Madrone, perhaps the most closely related species.

Suddenly, I brought the car to a stop. Right there on the side of the road stood a Texas Madrone. At least I thought it was; it appeared to have all the characteristics I'd read about. I jumped out of the car with my camera and approached the tree like I was stalking it. The leaves had the *Arbutus* look, and the canopy spread wide above. Some dead tree branches lay in front, and upright dead trunks partially obscured the lower view. However, a bare upper trunk and upper branches were visible, and the trunk was distinctly contorted. But, far from bearing the typical colors of the Pacific Madrone (green, tan, cinnamon), this tree's bark was stark white. Maybe that is why the local name, Lady's Legs for the Texas Madrone, arose.

First circling the tree at a distance and then moving inward, I noticed green berries, about four millimeters in diameter, distributed among the green leaves. This was to be anticipated, considering the time of year. Mixed with the tortuous white branches were also some black dead ones. I wasn't sure if they were diseased or had died for other reasons. Brown, scalloped bark covered much of that portion of the lower trunk, which was still viable, with some dead regions interspersed throughout.

---

7 Scientific name: *Arbutus xalapensis* colloquial name: Lady's Legs

Returning to the car, we headed up the road while watching for more Madrone trees. The parking lot emerged around a corner, and abruptly we were at the head of the trail. A small visitor center was located there, a sign on the wall announcing the elevation as 5,013 feet (1,528 m). An array of display boards described the local flora and fauna. One even warned about diamondback rattlesnakes. I shivered even though, having grown up in Montana, I had the privilege of meeting them many times. I quickly steered Darlene away from that display as I didn't want to abort our hike before it started.

A seven-minute video by Wallace Pratt told how, in 1921, he had discovered for himself the beauty of the McKittrick Canyon. [72] He was working at that time as a geologist for Humble Oil in Pecos, Texas. One of his associates invited him on a trip to see a very beautiful place in the nearby mountains. Out of curiosity, he agreed to tag along. The two men set out across the desert despite the lack of available roads. After a few hours of monotonous travel in the hot and dusty climate, he began to doubt whether there was such a place as his friend had described, or if perhaps he was being led on a wild goose chase. Once he saw the canyon with his own eyes, he immediately fell in love with it. He later had the opportunity to buy a portion of the canyon, which was owned by the McKittricks, the same family that owned the accompanying ranch. Pratt purchased it and, after the stock market crash of 1929, was able to extend his holding to a larger area.

In 1931, he commissioned the construction of the cabin, later known as the Pratt Cabin. This building, completed the following year, was assembled primarily with rock and wood and ultimately would function more as a lodge than a cabin. Among other features, it boasted four beds, hammocks, and a table big enough to accommodate a dozen people. It soon evolved into a summer home for the Pratt family and their guests that would remain the Pratts' private property for the next several decades. Then, in the early 1960s, they donated both the cabin and over five thousand acres of the canyon to the National Park Service.

Heading up the trail, we were soon surrounded by juniper bushes and other shrubs. Among these were some Sotol plants, with their tall, toothed leaves radiating out from a rosette. Some of these were in, or nearing, full bloom. Also quite prominent were the heavier and thicker blue-green stalks of the *agave*, many of them projecting several feet into the air from their rosettes. (Figure 6.1B)

Presumably, the recent rains caused the agaves to bloom in profusion. Our timing was fortuitous: the phenomenon occurs only once in the plant's lifetime, usually after about ten years, depending on the environment and the climate conditions of where it is located. Some people had called it the Century Plant because it bloomed so infrequently that, to the casual observer, the occurrence seemed considerably rarer still, closer to once per hundred years. However, this observation was made of agave plants growing in an environment very remote from their native conditions, which also helps explain the nickname's origins.

Delightful configurations of rock decorated the path we were following. When we came to the dry creek bed, layers of yellow-tinted rock cut by water guarded the channel. The creek bottom itself was composed of gravel, rocks of mixed sizes, and beds of sand. Here, Alligator Juniper trees with scaled bark jutted out from the higher rock banks, with branches twisting in bizarre shapes. Dead, sculptured trees stood along the hills like tombstones, reminding us of their past, beautiful growths.

Crossing the dry creek and proceeding along the rocky trail brought us to our second Texas Madrone. The tree's upper branches were beautifully formed in digressing curves but were reddish in color, not white. Quite magnificent! Again, a dead, dried trunk and large branch seemed to be married to the tree. Small trees were growing a meter or two away, clearly offshoots of berries or shoots originating from the parent tree. As we continued, we encountered more Madrones with a variety of appearances. (Figures 6.1-6.6) Some of the trees' upper branches were noticeably white, like those of the first Madrone we had encountered. This was in sharp contrast to the black branches, which by all appearances were dead. Was their death due to a fungus, similar to the one that plagued the Pacific Madrone. However, the dry conditions here were quite different from the Pacific Northwest conditions, so perhaps they had died during a drought.

Pausing to rest, I imagined how it might have been had Darlene and I been making this trek in the early 1800s. We may well have been walking very cautiously up the gulch and, upon hearing the snorting of a horse, dropped down behind a juniper tree. Quietly peering through the branches, we may have seen a band of Mescalero Apaches approaching single file along the creek bed. I could picture them with almost unnerving clarity, long hair down to their waists; weapons slung over their shoulders, buckskin apparel ragged and minimalist, all of it handmade. The leather saddlebags, draped over the backs of their horses, would likely have sagged with the weight of their provisions. With their variously colored manes, these ponies would have trotted briskly along as though carrying their riders on a warring mission. The sudden anxiety no doubt would have raised the hair on the napes of our necks, occasioning further retreat into the bushes.

Around 1869, the Guadalupe Mountains were known to be home to Mescalero Apaches, until the US Army raided their settlement and forced them out. This group of Apaches had the Mescalero prefix added to the name of their tribe because of their widespread use of the heart of the mescal (agave) plant for cooked and dried food. The leaves, once allowed to rot, were then beaten, permitting extraction of the fiber. This, in turn, was used for baskets, twine, rope, and even bowstrings. Other uses of the Mescal involved making liquor, perhaps similar to the way tequila is made today.

Resuming our hike, we found the trail easy, as the ranger had predicted. More Madrones appeared, impeding our progress since I stopped to snap picture after picture. As usual, my longsuffering wife endured these interruptions without complaint. Arriving at the next creek bed crossing, we finally came upon some flowing water. We easily crossed it by hopping from one rock to the next. The water seemed to appear out of the ground, then disappeared again, a phenomenon known to occur along the creek. Tall stalks of agave caught my eye. Their blooming branch protruded at roughly ninety degrees from the stalk in intervals of approximately eight inches before bursting into blossoms, a quite remarkable sight. (Figure 6.1B)

Each new Madrone we encountered had a different look. The younger ones appeared similar to each other, with red, green, or cinnamon bark. The majority of older ones were scarred with dead or black branches. The largest older tree had a diameter of eighteen inches at the height of four and a half feet. (Figure 6.5) Based on Mike Prochoroff who grows and raises Texas Madrone from seeds then markets them and Professor Rebecca Kidd's (Stephen F. Austin State University, TX) study of the rings of two Texas Madrone trees, this eighteen-inch tree must be somewhere between 288 and 371 years old. Certainly, it would have started growing when the Mescalero Apaches ruled the Guadalupe Mountains. The main trunks of these trees rose over ten feet without causing branching to occur. The heights of some of trees were over twenty-five feet. The Madrones growing near other trees or shrubs had the characteristic twisted structure, a growth adaption allowing them to capture sunlight. Some had emerged among ledges of rock, which afforded a striking contrast with the bark and leaves of the trees themselves. (Figure 6.1A)

Our legs felt as though we had traveled more than two miles when the gulch began splitting, with a new branch deviating to the right. A little farther on, a portion of a rock fence became visible through the undergrowth. It became more definite as we continued, and then a clear break materialized in the form of a pathway at the foot of an open gate. Passing through the gate and proceeding up the path, we came across a small rock building on our left. Then out of nowhere emerged the famed and rather extraordinary Pratt cabin.

It was a significant statement of Pratt's ingenuity: a home that blended into the surrounding rock, adding rather than subtracting from its natural beauty. Its straight walls and window indentations looked as firm now as they must have eighty-six years ago. Several weathered Madrones, lacking the heavily scaled bark at their bases, grew behind the house. Scattered in the adjacent woods were more Madrones. They, too, appeared rather anemic, perhaps because the sun didn't penetrate the understory well. At the front of the cabin, a number of chairs, including some rockers, sat on a porch that looked out over an opening in the woods. They looked like they were there waiting for us to sit in them. Stark cliffs at the edges of the gulch provided the background. Some foliage obscured the view but probably hadn't been present in Pratt's day. Darlene and I walked around the cabin, noting signs of infrequent use; the large, flat rock table outside had developed a crack across it, due to uneven settling of its supports.

Looking at my watch, I saw it was time to go. I later learned that if we had continued further up the trail, we would have come across a more aggressive water flow in the creek, which purportedly contained pools of rainbow trout. Heading back, we picked up our pace, snapping only a few more photos. Once back on the road, we turned west toward the visitor center. Several Texas Madrones were growing outside the center. One was labeled *Arbutus xalapensis* var. texana. This brings up the interesting botanical question of whether the *Arbutus texana* is a species wholly separate from the *Arbutus xalapensis*, or merely a variant. The sign cast it as a variant, but other sources leave room for doubt. A broad range of writings on the internet and elsewhere treat it as a separate species, others as a mere variant, and still others simply as *xalapensis*. At a glance, the scientific publication history appears as tortuous as the tree itself.

The scientific name and first botanical description of *Arbutus xalapensis* are credited to Karl Sigismund Kunth, who reported it in 1818.[73] Kunth was born in 1788 in Germany and became interested in botany while studying at the University of Berlin.[74] He later worked in Paris as an assistant for Alexander von Humboldt [75] where he classified plants that Humboldt and Aim Bonpland [76] had brought back from their five-year expedition to America between 1799-1804. Incidentally, the ship in which Humboldt and Bonpland had embarked on their excursion, the *Pizarro*, had docked for a few days in the Canary Islands, on the island of Tenerife. The two men explored the Teide volcano, which had been previously active (see Chapter Four on *Arbutus canariensis*). They made no reports about having seen any *Arbutus* trees there, however.

Kunth eventually became a famous botanist and died in 1850. His description in Latin of the *Arbutus xalapensis* includes the location in the mountains of Mexico, where it was found near Xalapa. The city of Xalapa lies along the coast, about a thousand miles (by road) south of Austin, Texas.

A second report by Samuel Botsford Buckley has a bearing on the tree's name. Buckley was born in 1809 and died in 1884. [77] He had a diverse background, having trained in botany and mineralogy. He received a Master of Arts from Wesley University in 1836. In 1859, he traveled to Texas and was part of a geological survey. During the survey, he collected specimens, which he attempted to bring back to Philadelphia at the start of the American Civil War. Unfortunately, many of them were lost or weren't successfully transported, given the conditions at the time. He then wrote and presented his findings to the Philadelphia Academy. [78] In 1862, he reported to the Academy what he thought was a new species, *Arbutus texana*, that he'd found in Hills, Texas, in Lee County near Austin. He also identified trees in West Texas which were fifteen to twenty feet in height. However, there seems to be no specimen of this tree at the Philadelphia herbarium, although one was reported to have been deposited there.

This was confirmed by Dr. Paul Sørensen, professor emeritus and curator of the herbarium at Northern Illinois University, [79] who in 1999 published a seminal paper on the *Arbutus* with significant emphasis on the species growing in Mexico and northward into Texas [1]. He searched the herbarium in Philadelphia and found only a non-*Arbutus* specimen labeled *texana* in Buckley's handwriting. A herbarium founded in Philadelphia by Elias Durand (1794-1873) [80] hosted an extensive collection of North American species during the time Buckley compiled the findings in his report. This herbarium was subsequently transferred to Paris, and an *A. texana* specimen was discovered there by Dr. Lourteig; it was labeled by Buckley, according to Sørensen. It is widely considered a lectotype, a specimen selected to serve as the single type specimen for species originally described from a set of syntypes (in simpler terms, a specimen selected to represent an original.) However, he goes on to describe from his own experience some of the difficulties presented by single herbarium specimens.

The *A. xalapensis* tree is widely distributed from Texas southward into the Neotropical region of Mexico. There is a natural variation in the trees due to their location and environmental conditions: larger, more puberulous (hairier) leaves in the southern part of the region and smaller, more glabrous (smoother) ones in the northern regions. Sørensen further suggests that studies of sample specimens alone, which fail to account for the whole tree in a variety of ecological environments, can be misleading. It seems that Buckley thought he had found a new species but reported on perhaps only the northern morphological form of the *A. xalapensis*. Kunth's specimen also probably represented the morphed state of the tree in the mountains near Xalapa. However, historical records show that Kunth reported it first and thus is credited as the botanist who discovered the species. Consequently, it is his name that is used rather than Buckley's, which is now the most commonly cited in reference to the tree, notwithstanding that he never saw a living specimen. *Texana*, on the other hand, is generally regarded as the taxonomical designation assigned by Buckley to actual, live *xalapensis* specimens found in the northern region. Should the northern species, therefore, be classified as a variant of *xalapensis*? I leave that to the experts to debate.

However, there is another twist in the plot. A 2001 paper by Hileman, Vasey, and Parker brings genetic analysis into focus. [81] While the paper's objective was to test a certain hypothesis regarding the evolution of trees spreading to the eastern and western hemispheres, Figures 1 and 3 in the report indicate from their genetic analysis that *A. xalapensis* and *A. texana* may be separate species. The analysis used single samples of each. The *texana* came from Coahuila State, Mexico, which borders Big Bend National Park in west Texas, and *the xalapensis* specimen came from Nuevo Leon State, Mexico, which is more to the east and south. In my correspondence with Dr. Parker, professor at San Francisco State University, [82] one of the paper's authors, he was uncertain whether the slight differences in ribosomal genes they found would or would not indicate a division of species. He felt that a more comprehensive genetic study would be required for such a determination to be made.

As we move forward in time, we can anticipate that genetic analysis will become more and more sophisticated in the classification of species. In the meantime, other, more common colloquial terms such as Texas Madrone and Lady's Legs should well suffice in everyday conversation.

As we departed Guadalupe Mountain National Park, the sitting sun reflected off a sign outside the visitor center, informing us that we had been driving on the Madrone Circle.

Figure 6.1 A. Texas Madrone (*Arbutus xalapensis*) in McKittrick Canyon, Guadalupe Mountain National Park, Texas (Note the picturesque setting and that portions of the tree are dead.) B. A blooming *Agave ameicana* sometimes called the Century Plant because it blooms so rarely.

Figure 6.2 An *Arbutus xalapensis* that has peeled but its coloring is non-white in contrast to Figure 6.6 D&E.

Figure 6.3 A. Close up view of the upper branches of tree in Figure 6.2. B. An even closer view of a branch with green berries and leaves. Compare the leaf sizes to the hand in the picture.

Figure 6.4 An *Arbutus xalapensis* that looks like a sculpture. This was my favorite tree that we observed in the Park. The combination of dead regions, white bark, and green leaves mixed into the beautiful form was striking to the eye.

Figure 6.5 Another beautiful and large tree which offers heavy bark near its base, white upper branches, some dead blackened dead regions and it is partially hidden in the leaves of an adjacent deciduous tree.

Figure 6.6 Several *xalapensis* trees. A. and B. Offering a mix of dead branches, various colored branches and interesting form. C. White upper bark in twisting branches and heavy bark towards the base of the tree. D. A close up of some of the branches of C. demonstrating their texture and color.

Chapter Seven:

A Mexican Fling - The Baja Connection (*Arbutus peninsularis*)

In the dark, at 5:10 a.m. on February 26, 2018, I entered the divided highway, heading west. Still sleepy, I turned on the radio and was greeted by a lively Banda band on the Mexican station. Few cars were on the road (Highway 1) as I headed toward Cabo San Lucas, the resort town at the southwest end of the Baja Peninsula. Cruising at 90 km/hr, I was soon turning north onto Highway 19, away from Cabo San Lucas and toward Todos Santos, my first destination of the morning. This latter town lay about seventy-seven kilometers to the north. My appointment was at 6:45 a.m.

I yawned when I thought about Darlene still sleeping back at the condominium. When she had heard what I was planning to do today she had declined to accompany me. For some reason, I did not understand, she didn't think it sounded like fun.

My thoughts were interrupted by a flashing blue light ahead of me. It sent warning signals to my brain, reminding me of police we had regularly seen parked with similar lights between Cabo San Lucas and San Jose Del Cabo. The last thing I wanted was to be stopped, so I slowed down and gradually crept closer to the lights. They seemed to be moving. I let a car pass me and, as it approached the vehicle in question, I could see from its illumination that it was a truck with flashing lights, not the *Policia Federal*. Unlike amber or red warning lights on slow-moving trucks in the USA, in Mexico such vehicles seem to use blue lights. Accelerating around the truck, I was on my way, traveling faster now, and arrived a full fifteen minutes early. I parked outside of the hotel where I was to meet the nephew of Carlos, the owner of several mules, and as it was prearranged my guide for the day,

As I waited, the first hints of dawn appeared in the sky, and, in anticipation, several roosters began crowing in the distance. Todas Santos is a small town with a history originating with the mission founded there, and along with it the beginnings of local agriculture, circa 1723. It has a picturesque downtown area with many art galleries and restaurants. Darlene and I had visited a number of these previously and had sampled some of their memorable delights. It isn't just tourists who find the town intriguing; many expatriates have moved there as well, many of whom are artists displaying their work in the galleries.

The occasional car went by as I stood there waiting in the parking lot, but otherwise everything was quiet. Finally, a white, dusty, and recent vintage pickup pulled up and a young, hardy-looking fellow hopped out of the driver's seat. "Roy?" he asked me, smiling as he extended his hand.

I replied: "Yes.".

He articulated: "I am Antonio, Carlos's nephew, and I will lead you to meet Carlos. It will take about one hour."

Out of Todas Santos, we turned north onto Highway 19, but stayed on it for only a moment (not even half a kilometer, I would estimate), after which we exited onto a dirt road and headed east toward the *Sierra de la Laguna* (the mountains of the lagoon). Its naming is evidently influenced by the numerous pools, or lagoons, present there, particularly during and after the wet season. The *Sierra* is composed of a series of ascending foothills and rising central projections composed of granite and other rocks reaching between 1,000 to 2,200 meters (approximately 0.6 to 1.4 miles) in elevation. They form the backbone of the southern Cape region of the Baja peninsula, a range separate from the other mountains that stretch the length of the peninsula.

According to Drs. Ortega and Arriaga [83], the temperatures throughout the range vary from an average of 13°C in the higher altitudes to 25°C in the lower, with rainfall totaling each season around seventy cm (27.6") in the former and thirty cm (11.8") in the latter. This creates an opportunity for wide plant diversity at various heights. Furthermore, from a biological viewpoint the range functions rather like an island, in that the peninsula is separated first by ocean from the mainland, and secondly by desert from the sea and the other mountains. Geologists surmise that the peninsula detached from the mainland about 140-100 million years ago [84], affording the flora ample opportunity to develop their own unique characteristics, thus resulting in the many plants today considered endemic to the region. For this reason, among others, the area has been declared a UNESCO (United Nations Educational, Scientific, and Cultural Organization) Bioreserve. [85, 86]

As we proceeded along the road, it turned almost immediately into a washboard restricting driving speed to about 20 km/hr or less. As I bounced along the sun began peeking over a ridge in the mountains. Its light brought into view the cactus and shrubs that grew on each side of the sand-swept road. A tall elephant cactus (Pachycereus *pringlei*) with multiple branches was highlighted against the haze of the valley west of the mountains, the first deep, orange-red tendrils of dawn's light now creeping fully into the sky. The term "elephant cactus," incidentally, derives from the way the base trunk of the cactus mimics an elephant's leg. It is also called the Cardon cactus.

The road was quite interesting, sometimes several feet below the surrounding desert while at other points well above it, weaving up, for example, over a small rise with rocky surfaces protruding out of the road. In still other spots it was heavily infiltrated with sand, indeed, not a good spot to stop and try to restart. We passed a few junctions and some flimsy signs erected, presumably, by rancheros, one pointed to a mule ranch. My guide kept raising dust ahead of me, which of course I had to "eat"; luckily, it wasn't as powdery and therefore much less of a nuisance than what I'd encountered on certain other roads in the past.

After negotiating a sharp curve in the road, he stopped rather abruptly beside a pickup pulling a trailer that looked like it had been built from a number of mismatched pieces of metal held together with wire. Two mules were standing in it. The trailer was open-ended, with a small rope tied across the back perhaps to hold ends it together rather than keeping the mules in. The mules themselves were each secured each with a halter and ropes to the front of the trailer, their black tails swishing restlessly, perhaps at flies.

Antonio introduced me to Carlos. I asked him to relay to him what my purpose was and where I wanted to go, as Carlos didn't speak any English and I didn't speak any Spanish. As it turned out, he already knew, as the adventure group that had set up the excursion had passed this information along to him. This trip was the consummation of a month and a half of correspondence between several people, finally establishing the right contacts and arranging all the details. A key person I'd like to thank for it, is Dr. Jon Rebman, the Curator of Botany at the San Diego Natural History Museum, in San Diego, California. Among many other distinctions, he is a co-author of *The Baja California Plant Field Guide* [87], and as such has remarkable experience traveling in Baja. He was kind enough to tell me where I could find the *Arbutus peninsularis*, locally called the*madroña*, of course this was precisely the Baja connection I was after!

Carlos and Antonio exchanged a few brief words before Antonio relayed that I could leave my car there or, since Carlos was a local ranchero, we could pass through a gate and then park on the inside for two hundred pesos. That seemed like more secure parking to me, and well worth the peace of mind for just ten dollars (USD), so I opted for the latter. However, I didn't think to inquire about the conditions of the road, something I'd soon discover was a big mistake. Antonio held the gate open and I followed Carlos through. In a few hundred meters I was faced with an extremely rough, sandy road going down a sharp decline, with huge holes that had been gouged out in the past by spinning wheels. Carlos was already well along, his pickup bouncing on the uneven terrain, the mules making a heroic effort to stay upright in the trailer.

I thought to myself, *Am I going to get back out of here?* Despite my nagging doubts, I was anxious to get on with the trek. I told myself I'd worry about it when the time came.

Negotiating the dips and bumps as slowly and carefully as I could, jockeying my car to minimize the number of potholes I'd no choice but to drive over, I worked my way over this mistreated stretch of road. Soon the road conditions improved and I followed Carlos to an encampment with several empty pickups sitting there. Carlos stopped, and I parked a short distance away.

He started backing the mules out of the trailer one by one. This involved a lot of yelling on his part and fussing on theirs. They weren't particularly happy to exit, but with Carlos' friendly persuasion they eventually cooperated. He then saddled them. My mule was the smaller of the two. Since I can't easily spell or pronounce her Mexican name, I will call her Rosie. As I got into the saddle with a little help from Carlos, I had difficulty getting my wide-toed hiking boots into the stirrups. This was compounded by the fact that the stirrups had hooded covers *tapaderos*, making it extra difficult to slip my feet in completely. This configuration was new to me. All the stirrups I'd ridden with in the past had been of the open variety. I was to learn later it had this hood to protect the foot when brushing against shrubs and boulders which occurred often on this ride.

Carlos indicated by holding up four fingers that it would be about four hours to the site with the *madroñas*. We headed out along the dry creek bottom, soon passing a sign that said *La Barrera*; the starting location Dr. Rebman had told me about. The trail began to climb almost immediately. It had been well traveled but it was definitely a mountain trail: rocky, sandy, cutting between brush, boulders, zig- zagging as it climbed. Rosie began to grunt, her ears bending back against her head at times. I am unfamiliar with mule psychology, but I knew well that when a *horse* manifested such behavior, its rider had best heed. While Rosie seemed to be tame enough, she quite clearly did *not* want to climb the mountain at the same pace as Carlos' mule, so she and I tended to lag behind. Periodically, Carlos would have to stop and wait for us. I kept encouraging Rosie with little taps of my heels and flicks of the reins, which had a whip at the end. I was hesitant to provide excessive encouragement, since had no experience with mules at all, much less this one. I guess I felt a little sorry for her, having to haul me up the mountain like this. As we climbed up through narrow, rocky regions, and across hard rock platforms, I began to better understand why one wanted a mule for this journey. I don't believe a horse would have fared very well. (Figure 7.1 E&F)

My legs began to ache, and I kept fidgeting, trying to get my feet into the stirrups more cleanly. After about an hour and half we came to a flattened place along a creek. Carlos dismounted, and when I caught up, I gratefully swung down to join him. He indicated to me that I could ride the mule he had been using, I guess hoping I would keep up. I managed to communicate that I was okay with Rosie but that the stirrups were set too short for my leg lengths. He therefore undertook the process of unlacing the straps which held the stirrups and adjusting the length by several inches. Meanwhile, I seized the opportunity to stroll around a bit and loosen up my legs. They weren't used to this kind of riding since my *riding*, over the last 50 years or so, was in motorized vehicles.

Soon Rosie and I were following Carlos up the trail. My legs felt better as I could now stretch them more easily. The trail twisted up through the rocky foothill. In several spots along the way, smooth boulders jutted prominently. Some even encroached upon the trail, requiring Rosie to squeeze by them. I had to lift my backpack, which was hanging on the saddle horn, to keep it from dragging on these boulders, yes, they were that intimate. At other times the trail went up through slender washes. One of them was about six feet below the surrounding hillside.

In the more open areas, the *Cardon* cactus mentioned earlier appeared frequently, growing along the trail with varying numbers of green arms protruding into the sky and thorns sticking out. Other shrubs seemed ever-present. Sporadically, Rosie would try to reach out and grab a bite off a bush. She continued to grunt and flick her ears back and forth and fall farther behind Carlos, until eventually he stopped and waited for us once more.

Every now and then there was a shrub, several meters in height, with bright yellow flowers which caught my eye, yellow being my favorite color. The flowers looked like daisies or black-eyed Susans, but with a duller center surrounded by perky yellow pedals emerging at regular angles, Brittlebush (*Encelia farinose*) I believe. [87] These brightened the otherwise bleak and dry landscape. The terrain changed continually as we climbed higher. An oak, I believe an Encino roble (Quercus *albocincta*), to be exact – soon appeared. It didn't seem to mind growing on the edge of coulees, perhaps monitoring the lack of activity below.

Finally, after about two hours, we climbed up over a hump and the trail opened onto a flat knoll at the edge of a deep canyon. Carlos stopped there and dismounted, and with relief I slid off my own saddle. He got his lunch out and suggested we take a break to eat. I thought it was a little early, but my stomach didn't argue. He was having some large, clearly homemade, tortillas on which he spooned some form of blend. He offered me some, but I declined. Although the dish looked intriguing, I didn't want to disturb my gastrointestinal tract with something unfamiliar, especially so early in our stay in the Cabo area. So instead, I munched on some sandwiches I had brought along. Rosie and the other mule stood with their heads slightly drooping and the sweat drying on their shoulders and flanks. They, too, no doubt appreciated the rest.

While I was eating, I had time to recall that the full scientific name for the tree I was looking for was *Arbutus peninsularis* Rose & Goldman. These last two names were added to assign honor to first Rose for his 1911 description of it [88] and second to Goldman because a specimen was initially acquired in 1906 by him and Nelson when trekking in the *Sierra de la Laguna*. This specimen was then stored in the U.S. National Herbarium as no. 565524. However, one might ponder what happened to Nelson's name on the scientific description since he helped find it? I don't know. Adding to this mystery is the actual description of the tree in the herbarium was written by E. W Nelson. Early on there was also some concern about whether this tree was a new species as it was thought to might just be an *Arbutus menziesii*. However, when studying more carefully the published description, the *peninsularis*' leaves are more tomentose, having wooly hairs, and the calyx lobes of the blossom are larger.

Looking around, we must have been about a kilometer above sea level by now. The view at this elevation was quite magnificent. As I looked back along the trail we had traveled, I gazed upon a dry riverbed that meandered off into the distance far below. The horizon included hills covered with small, pale green patches of foliage disappearing toward the sea in the west. With some imagination, I could see where the sea met the land, but it may have just been the distant haze. Looking on the other side of the knoll, the view plunged into a drier-looking gully that quickly dropped into a series of broken hills. (Figure 7.2D) The distant hills blurring under a stretch of clouds. To our right the upper slope was dotted with dark olive-colored bushes. Crossing back to the other side of the knoll and looking up, I could see what looked like a collection of foliage I took for a grove of trees. *Perhaps*, I mused, *we are approaching the bosque with the madroña trees that Dr. Redman had told me about.*

After half an hour or so, Carlos remounted his mule and I reintroduced myself to Rosie. The trail climbed along the backbone of the ridge. It wasn't long before Carlos stopped and started pointing and motioning for me to look. I stopped and began scrutinizing the hill across the draw but couldn't see what he was motioning about. He kept pointing and saying something, but I couldn't understand. Then it hit me: there was a *madroña* tree, an *Arbutus peninsularis*, right beside Rosie! I would have ridden right past it had Carlos not pointed it out.

It was a good-sized tree, but much of it was dead on the side nearest me. Looking higher upon it, I saw the telltale red peeling bark, as well as the distinctive leaves of the *Arbutus*. (Figure 7.2 A-C) Some inflorescence was present, but most of the blossoms seemed to have fallen off. There were dead branches, and my first reaction was to note that it looked a lot like the Texas Madrone that my wife and I had seen in the Guadalupe Mountain National Park in the previous June. However, upon closer inspection, I observed that the regions under the peeled bark were not white, but in fact a lighter shade of red. Perhaps this color denoted areas where peeling had occurred the year prior, but in which the outer red bark remained more or less intact. (Figure 7.2A, & 7.1)

I began photographing the trees, which were intermittently distributed up the draw among various other trees and bushes. The distance between the *madroñas* varied, from a few meters to seventy or more. I never did see a *madroña* isolated from other trees or shrubs. Many of the trees had dead branches or defunct regions of trunk. There was no evidence of blackened branches such as would have been indicative of a fungal attack, as we often see in the Pacific Madrone. I don't know exactly why large segments of these trees had died, but I speculate it may have been during times of drought or perhaps in sudden freezes where the trees had no time to adapt.

Studying the leaves, I noted that on average they were ten centimeters in length, with a width of four centimeters, and had serrated margins about one millimeter apart. (Figure 7.3 A) Were the leaves more tomentose than the *A. menziesii*? I couldn't tell. The stalks of the leaves were a little over 1 cm in length. The underside of the leaves was paler than the glossier, greener upward-facing side. Most of the trees had dense, heavy bark at their bases, and in some cases, it reached quite high. It had vertical fissures with a "tiling" pattern in between. The recesses were darker gray, while the tile was lighter in color and had a smoother surface. Each tile, or separated region, was approximately one centimeter in vertical length and a half- centimeter in width, running in nearly vertical rows (Figure 7.6 C). Depending on how smooth the tile's surface was, it reflected light, appearing almost white in contrast to the rough regions, which diffused the light and produced a darker appearance. Regarding the rest of the tree, it generally was quite red, and in regions where the red bark had peeled, a lighter red was present underneath. (Figure 7.1 & 7.5) This contrasts with the Pacific Madrone, in which green typically can be observed under the thin, peeled red bark. However, this finding on the *peninsularis* may have been due simply to the time of year, early in the season for peeling. Thus, this dark red/light red juxtaposition was probably due to a full year's passing without the thin red bark's completely peeling off, and the under-bark's having turned red again. In one tree it was a quite different case: the peeled bark region was bone-colored, more akin to what I had seen on the Texas Madrone. (Figure 7.4)

The inflorescence of the trees was very noticeable; the blossoms themselves were white clusters which stood out against the green leaves. Some were composed of buds yet to open alongside many fully opened blossoms. Closer inspection revealed that some of the blossoms had been torn or cut toward their bases, perhaps by ants or other insects.[8] The blossoms had a shape more convoluted than that of the Pacific Madrone's or the *Arbutus unedo*, with the "mouth" of the blossom appearing smaller. (Figure 7.3C) There were wooly hairs along the stems of the blossoms. I was watching carefully to see if hummingbirds were working the blossoms as had been reported by Arriaga [89], but all I saw was one large bumblebee several times larger than the flower, attacking it rather aggressively. (Figure 7.3 B & D)

After advancing through the grove, we reached a flatter region along the trail. A large sign was posted there. Its message was written in Spanish, but I was able to translate its meaning later: here was the start of a more restricted region of the Biosphere. As I checked one last *madroña,* Carlos ambled farther along the trail. When he returned, he seemed to indicate there were no more *madroñas* in the immediate area. We had seen about fifteen by that time. I sensed he was ready to turn back; looking at my watch, I realized we had already spent at least an hour looking at the trees. Later, when I looked at the Google map and punched in the latitude and longitude of this last position, I saw that we'd been only a mile or so from the La Cienequita, and just two and a half miles from the Segundo Valle (second valley) of the Sierra de la Laguna, areas in which others had recorded the presence of *madroñas.*

Reluctantly, I agreed to head back before the day grew any later. We returned down the trail much faster than we had come up, aided by gravity on the downslope. We arrived at our vehicles around 2:30 p.m. Though I'd grown quite fond of her over day, as sore and stiff as I was, I couldn't dismount Rosie fast enough. (Figure 6A) I began stretching my legs while Carlos unsaddled her, then helped him load her into the trailer. After some more friendly coaxing by Carlos, she finally jumped in, the other mule following her lead without much fuss.

The final step was to get my vehicle back to the road outside of the gate. I followed Carlos, onto the dirt road leaving him ample space just in case he had to back up in the soon to come difficult region. When he arrived, he bounced up and through this war-torn area (from spinning tires, soft sand, and the steep incline) with hardly a hesitation. His trailer jumped violently over the bumps and holes. The mules were trying to stay on their feet. Poor Rosie fell once, but thankfully got right back up again a testament, I suppose, to the resilience of mules. My turn now came to transit this terrain. I approached with moderate speed, trying again to select the sections of the road of with the fewest mounds and excavations. Zig zagging from one side to the other, I almost made it, but then the car slowed to a halt, spinning out in the sand. Now what?

---

8 (Laura Arriaga and her coauthors reported in 1990 that ants often cut the blossoms, destroying their natural pollination mechanism, and they studied hummingbirds feeding on the nectar or pollen in the blossoms.) [90]

The only choice was to back down as best I could, ensuring I stayed on the road until I could extricate the car from steep sandy portion. So, I put it in reverse and proceeded very slowly, with utmost caution, my eyes alternating between the rearview and wing mirrors. At last I reached a flat area. There, I hoped, I could make a good run at the eroded section. This time I threw caution to the wind, arriving at the first soft region at a risky speed, each sand fissure slowing me. I had almost reached the end of the battered sand mounds when my tires started spinning out again. *I dare not stop now.* I kept my foot pressed firmly against the pedal. Fortunately, I had just enough momentum to catapult the car over the last crest.

Whew! I made it!

After a short dialogue consisting mostly of more hand gestures, Carlos and I bade each other *adios.* I sank wearily into the driver's seat, groaning from the stiffness in my limbs, and a moment later was back on the road, bound for the highway. The trip along the dirt road was uninspiring, save for the intriguing Baja foliage that kept distracting me. After a good hour of continuous driving, the washboard road finally came to an end. With considerable relief, I merged onto the welcomingly smooth, oiled asphalt of Highway 19.

I dialed Darlene, who sounded grateful and happy that I had survived. I opened a drink and settled into the drive back to our condominium.

My mind kept flashing back to certain scenes from my adventure: Rosie standing at the end of the trek, looking at me with her big brown eyes, her head slightly drooped, one ear forward the other back. I reflected, too, a little somberly, that I'd spent only an actual hour or so marveling at the beauty that had been guided by millions of years of development and I had visited during only a very small portion of the yearly botanical manifestations. If only I had more time and energy I mused. However, I was sore and exhausted but still exuberant.

I had seen it at last, the *Arbutus peninsularis* in its high mountain abode, its island in the sky!

Figure 7. *A. peninsularsis* shedding bark with its surrounding *Arbutus* leaves.

Figure 7.2 Collage of pictures on the trip to see the *Arbutus peninsularsis*. A. Colorful *peninsularsis* trunk shedding bark, B. An older tree with dead sections, C. The upper trunk of tree in B, D. The view west towards the ocean from our lunch stop. E. My guide heading up the trail. F. The author on *Rosie* ready to start the trek. Coordinates: 23.5454° N, 110.046653° W, Elevation 484 ft (148 m).

Figure 7.3 A. A leaf with a scale. The upper minor divisions are in mm. B. An expanded view of a section of D showing a bumble bee seeking nectar from a blossom. D. C. Blossoms with a scale (minor division in mm). D. A branch with leaves and some blossoms.

Figure 7.4 *Arbutus peninsularsis* trees in the woods. Note the white trunks and adjacent palm tree.

Figure 7.5 A view looking up along the main trunk peeling and a large branch, on the right, still retaining heavy bark.

Figure 7.6 A. *Rosie* is exhausted at the end of the trip., B. Sunset at our condo that evening., C. A study of the heavy bark on one of the *A peninsularsis* trees with cm scale. Note the almost checkered pattern of the bark.

Chapter Eight:

I Broaden My Craving During the Pandemic-Arizona Madrone (*Arbutus arizonica*)

One cold December morning in 2019, I found myself shivering, thinking of palm trees and warm sand, when I realized Darlene and I needed a decision. Our time-share contract required that reservations be made thirteen months in advance to secure lodging at a desirable location during the winter. Somewhere warm was foremost on our minds. Arizona was a destination we had not previously considered, and, as it happened, there was a vacancy north of Tucson in the Oro Valley in late January 2021. In the back of my mind, I was thinking while we were there, we might also search for the Arizona Madrone I had yet to see! Although I did not initially voice this thought to my wife. Instead, I kept my focus on the "warm and sunny" part. She happily agreed, we booked the condominium, and for a time all looked well.

As time went on, I decided that I would gradually slip into our conversation that there was still one Madrona in the United States that I had not seen. Later I would mention that there was probably some growing near Tucson. When I did voice these thoughts, she looked at me, with that look that said: "So you have an alternative motive for this trip, I should have known." It is hard to fool my wife. However, she is a good sport and generally is game for going on another Madrona adventure, especially if it is a new and interesting place.

Then the pandemic struck, COVID-19. Though initially optimistic that it might wane sufficiently to permit normal travel in time for our trip (especially if a vaccine became available as quickly as we all hoped), by December 2020, with just a month before we were scheduled to leave, we were forced to acknowledge the reality of the situation - the pandemic would be around for a good while longer. We debated whether to simply cancel our reservation and perhaps rebook for a date later in the season. However, before we could make up our minds, we discovered that cancellation was no longer an option, at least, not without losing our valuable credits. We ultimately decided that we'd drive but would try to minimize the number of nights we spent in hotels along the way, thereby both saving money and reducing any risk of contracting the virus. Once we were there, we figured, we'd be staying in our own private condo for two weeks, and therefore ought to be safe. Our prediction proved accurate, albeit with a deeply ironic twist.

The condo was located in the Oro valley north of Tucson, which features broad, quiet streets and sidewalks dressed in desert flora with the background of the Santa Catalina Mountains. During construction, natural *washes* were left between groups of homes to provide drainage during downpours and to preserve some of the habitat. These washes are home to birds, rabbits, and even the Javelina (*Tayassu tajacu*), a breed of Arizona wild pig.

One evening during our stay, I was elated to observe a group of these pigs come scurrying out of the wash adjacent to our condo complex, searching for food. They are small compared to domestic pigs, about eighteen inches in height and two feet in length, with bristles on the backs of their heads, resembling in many ways miniature versions of the ferocious wild pig one can read about in the literature. Even more fascinating, was a baby Javelina scuttling behind its mother, its little legs scampering to keep up. It would squeal whenever it fell too far behind and its mother would pause, giving her young a chance to catch up.

Darlene and I enjoyed frequent leisurely strolls, when the temperatures were most agreeable. Of particular interest on these walks were the different cacti abundant in the area. We were especially intrigued by the number of forms of Cholla that we encountered. These were often interspersed with diversely sized barrel cacti and some prickly-pear, and the awe-inspiring giant saguaro, with arms branching at a variety of angles and stages of maturity. Much to our disappointment, there was far less sunshine than we had hoped for, the daytime temperatures often similar to home.

As we settled into our stay, the pertinent question for me of course became the familiar one now - where could we see the Arizona Madrone (*Arbutus arizonica)*? I quickly learned that this species name does not appear very often in the literature. In fact, it is hard to find anything about it at all, even in the vast depositories of research available online. I found this very puzzling.

One Google search did produce a website offering a "Chiri" Arizona Madrone for sale. This nickname, "Chiri," apparently derived from the tree's origins in the Chiricahua Mountains. These were located east of Tucson. In fact, the Chiricahua National Monument there is, roughly 133 miles east of our condo, a mere two-and-a-half-hour drive. I telephoned the visitor center at the Monument and was told that in light of COVID, they were open but with restrictions. And, yes, there were indeed *A. arizonica* trees to be found in the vicinity, some on a trail near the center of the park and others just a short distance away, at a campground along the Bonita Canyon.

The following day, Darlene and I packed a lunch and took off for Chiricahua Monument National Park. I wondered during the drive what was monumental there? Why was the park called that? I knew it wasn't because of the trees I sought particularly since I could find very little about them. Nevertheless, as we drove through the semidesert, I mused on what I *had* thus so far learned about the species.

The earliest and most definitive description of the tree was given by Charles Spraque Sargent in 1891. [90] Sargent, a famous botanist born in 1841, was appointed at Harvard University as the school's Professor of Arboriculture in 1879. He died in 1927. His life and work overlapped with those of another famous botanist at Harvard, Asa Gray, who lived from 1810 to 1888. While Gray was given first credit in 1891 for describing the *A. arizonica*, Sargent describes Gray's preliminary assessment as rather confused and inaccurate. For example, Gray initially believed the Texas Madrones to be an ilk indigenous to the Pacific coast, specifically, A. *menziensii* rather than a separate species itself. He drew no distinction between this family and that native to Arizona, though later changed his mind, categorizing the Texas *texana* as well as the *arizonica* as variants of the *A. xalapensis.* Eventually, in defense of Gray (and, indeed, younger botanists in general), Sargent conceded the difficulty of drawing reliable conclusions merely from specimens in the herbarium. He acknowledged there was no substitute for examination of the actual trees themselves.[9]

My reflection was interrupted by our arriving at the first and only rest stop along the section of highway we were traveling. I must say that, after the long semidesert drive, being able to get off the interstate, if only for a few minutes, was quite a relief. Of greater note, however, was that this particular rest area was situated on a very distinct knoll composed of huge boulders of diverse shape and size, many of them stacked on top of one another. These boulders lay in stark contrast to the vast, flat stretches of semidesert that extended as far as the eye could see. How did this bizarre knoll form in this spot, I wondered? To me, at least, it constituted a geological mystery.

About an hour later, we finally arrived at the entrance to the Chiricahua National Monument. Now emerging from the semidesert and into a forest, I began looking carefully at the trees. Could I pick out an *A. arizonica*? Quite frankly, I didn't know what I was looking for. I had in mind only images of other *Arbutus* trees. In any event, I saw nothing familiar, and within a minute or two we arrived at the visitors center. There we decided to have our lunch and study the map they provided.

---

9 I should note in passing that, if possible, one must live very near the trees in question allowing repeated observations throughout the season. A single observation at a single seasonal point of a single tree will yield at best an incomplete understanding of the trees. Due to various practical constraints, however, sometimes that is all that is available to an observer.

There was a trail leaving the parking lot and heading up a valley, where presumably we could find some of the trees. However, the map showed the campground as only a short drive-up Bonita Canyon Road, which seemed a more promising course. We were told by the visitor center's attendant that the trees could be distinguished by the presence of their reddish bark near the tips of large branches. There were no trees like that around the parking area, so we started down the road that wound its way up the canyon.

Darlene suddenly spotted a small tree, more closely resembling a bush, on the side of the road, one with distinctly red bark. "Look!" she exclaimed. "There's one right there!" My wife has always been much quicker than I in spotting such details at a glance, as she has perfect color vision. Unfortunately, I have difficulty discerning red and green as discreet colors unto themselves, particularly within objects closely grouped together and where the brightness is muted. But this redness was bright, and the branches smooth – no clumps of older bark on them whatsoever. Wow!

There was no convenient place to stop and take photos, so I kept driving. More of these little trees kept cropping up along the way. Suddenly, the road to the campground appeared and I swerved on to it. Stopping I was about to hop out of the car when Darlene, rather calmly said: "Don't you think you should park the car off the road first?"

"Oh," I said and slid back into the car and drove further to the parking area. Nothing to stop me now. In mere seconds I was out of the car with my camera. The trees were much bigger here twenty to thirty feet high. Darlene soon joined me, and we began looking in earnest. Unsurprisingly, Darlene was the first to spot a tall tree with red bark on smaller branches, these sprouting from a main trunk (Figure 8.2C). Smooth red bark was featured prominently at the tips of these branches, but where the tips joined with the main branches, the tree's bark became increasingly bespeckled with splotches of gray. This was followed, in turn, by denser bark in which both colors were largely melded together, in visibly longitudinal strips. The main or *mother* branch was covered with a dense bark which was gray on the surface but discontinuously colored in deeper layers, with dark horizontal fissures irregularly punctuated by cross-fissure. As it descended toward the base of the tree, this heavy, checkered like bark became even more prominent. (Figure 8.2A) Interestingly, but only occasionally, on the upper side of the large branches there appeared regions where this heavy bark was diminished or missing, revealing instead a red *under bark*. This characteristic was more in keeping with the trait of the Pacific Madrone but still barely present. (Observable in the photograph of Figure 8.2A.)

The leaves were very much *Arbutus* in appearance: their color, lanceolate shape, and the way they fanned out from the supporting branch all a feature of a standard Madrone (Figure 8.2B). From a distance, the bark, structural form, and leaf formation could have been easily confused with those of the Emory Oak (*Quercus emori*), which often grew alongside the *Arbutus*. Upon closer inspection, however, one can distinguish the two by comparing the Oak's scalloped leaf against the *arizonica*'s smooth lanceolate form.

Having studied the trees at the campground, I returned to the road to inspect more closely the shrubs Darlene had pointed out on the drive in. Even I had noticed the unusual smoothness and deep, almost brick-like redness of their bark. Studying the trees closely, I was delighted by the way in which the branches extended from the main trunk with striking contortions. (Figure 8.7) Hanging on to several of these branches were bright red berries about one centimeter in diameter, with more sprinkled across the ground. The leaves, though, were much different from what I would have expected given my prior knowledge of Madrones. Later I understood when I learned that these trees were not *Arbutus* at all, but rather, Pointleaf Manzanita (*Arctostaphylos pungens*). I had seen a Manzanita before, but it was a larger tree, with shedding bark, and although I liked them, I did not feel they were as attractive as the Pacific Madrone. However, I must admit these shrubs were undeniably eye-catching and well worth remembering.

Upon my return to the campground, Darlene and I drove farther up Bonita Canyon Road and finally discovered the monuments that served as the park's namesake: gray pillars of rock marching along either side of the road, stretching tens of feet into the sky. New and interesting shapes of these rocks appeared along the way:

curious mixtures of cracked spires, piles of rocks carefully balanced, erosion-rounded profiles, grouped columns, individual edifices remarkable in their own right, and trees protruding between these structures. (Figure 8.1) We were awed at each turn. Upon reaching the end of the road, now high up in the mountains, we started back down, and were soon startled by an odd-looking animal, to which I courteously ceded the right of way. As it ambled across the road, Darlene commented that it looked like a raccoon, but its body was too slim and both its tail and snout too long. I would later learn that it was a coatimundis, a diurnal mammal native to South America but also fairly prevalent throughout the southwestern United States. The creature hesitated for a moment, but unfortunately not quite long enough for a picture, before scurrying into the bushes on the other side of the road.

During the following week, I inquired further of local knowledgeable sources about the A. *arizonica*. A worker at a garden/restaurant in Tucson informed me that they did not have any *A. arizonica* trees because the species is unable to survive the sweltering summer temperatures in the valley. Fortunately, however, he went on to say, such trees could be found easily in the Madera Canyon, located just fifty-three miles south of the city. Darlene and I set aside a day later in the week to make the trip, only to be met by all kinds of interesting surprises.

First, we were pummeled by torrential rains and heard warnings of a coming snowstorm. Whoopee, I thought! Here we were in Arizona, and we were being advised of impending weather far more common in our hometown in Washington (though, even there, snowstorms are a rarity), the very sort of weather we had come to this part of the country to escape. Rain? Sure, that wasn't terribly surprising, even in the desert. But snow? Surely not here in Arizona. Either we'd misheard the forecast, or the meteorologists were somehow woefully mistaken.

But we had *not* misheard, and the weathermen had made no mistake. The next morning, Darlene and I awoke to snow on the mountains and even to skiffs of it in the parking lot. Fortunately, we were not scheduled to drive to the Madera Canyon until a few days later, by which point I imagined the snow would be long gone. When the day arrived, there was still some snow at high altitudes but the canyon itself, I felt sure, would be free of inclement conditions.

I was wrong. When we arrived at the canyon a few hours later, we encountered dozens of people running about, throwing snowballs at each other and having a grand time with the white personification, something they saw only a few times in a generation. A forest ranger truck was parked beside an orange and black striped barricade, to which was affixed a sign announcing, ROAD CLOSED. I spoke with the ranger and learned that the road was a total mess farther along, so they were keeping people out for the time being. Having grown up in Montana, I wondered if the road conditions were genuinely hazardous or just posed a hazard to Arizona drivers unaccustomed to wintry conditions.

In any event, we scoured the picnic area, along with an alternate road leading into the campground, but found no sign of *A. arizonica* trees. While this was a big disappointment, on the ride back to the condo I contented myself that, if nothing else, I had at least acquired a detailed map of the Madera Canyon.

As the week progressed, I studied the map and learned there were several resorts situated along the route, along with at least one bed and breakfast. I made a few phone calls, and, luckily, got at least one answer, from Loren Moore at the Santa Rita Lodge. She knew the tree I was looking for and told me it could be found farther up the canyon than we'd previously explored. In fact, she said, at the end of the road there was a parking area. Toward the left was a trailhead leading to several trees of the kind I was after. I looked on Google Maps and discovered that this trailhead sat just a mile or so from where we had stopped at the parking area the afternoon of the snowstorm. I wacked my head with my hand, had I known this, I could have easily walked up there that very day. After that I periodically checked the local road conditions and kept seeing the same unwelcome news. For the time being, at least, the road to the Madrones remained closed.

On our last day in Arizona, we planned a trip to Tubac, a small, picturesque town about fifty-seven miles south of us. Darlene's friend told her about the many art shops and galleries there, as well as the Tumacácori National Historical Park, none of which we should miss. We left in the morning, arriving around lunchtime.

I had noticed that the destination was only about twenty miles farther than the turn-off to the road leading to the Madera Canyon. Such proximity presented a third opportunity to lay eyes on those elusive Madrones. However, I had perhaps already tried my wife's patience a bit more than was prudent. I had after all led her, on two separate Madrona-hunting excursions, one of them ending up what was essentially a wild goose chase. I thought it is probably better not to broach the subject.

Nevertheless, while in Tubac, I checked the local road reports, only to find that the pass into the canyon was still closed. Darlene and I enjoyed the day, nevertheless, visiting several interesting and informative sites. At one, a tour guide explained how, in the distant past, the local natives were quite frightened of the Chiricahua Apaches, who often emerged from the Chiricahua Mountains on raids, seizing food, livestock, and even female hostages. The locals apparently made little if any effort to repel these onslaughts, instead simply hiding once prospective raiders had been detected.

As we left Tubac, the Madrona hunting juices were still flowing in me. I began telling Darlene about the reported road conditions vis-à-vis Madera Canyon, expressing skepticism that they could still be dangerous given that there had been no further rain or snowfall over the past few days. It was downright hot in Tubac, How could there be much if any snow left in the mountains? She knew what it meant to me to see more of the trees and so, to her credit, finally voiced the thought I had been hoping, but not really expecting to hear: "Why don't we just chance it, Roy, and go?"

Shortly, we exited the freeway and drove towards the mountains, passing cars coming out of the foothills, and plenty more behind and ahead of us. Could the reported road conditions, simply be wrong? When we arrived at the picnic area, we saw once again that sign I had come to loathe so intensely: ROAD CLOSED. This time I did not hesitate. I parked the car. I asked Darlene if she wanted to go with me. She tentatively looked out the window and said: "I will stay and guard the car." I understood that to mean she didn't want to go out in the cold. I grabbed my camera and started up the road.

As I made my way, I encountered a few others along the same trek, and saw several cars which, having ignored the ROAD CLOSED sign, now whizzed by us. Growing short of breath, I had to stop several times as the elevation increased. I grew thirsty, my mouth very dry, and realized I had forgotten to bring water with me. There were still remnants of snow along the road, in the ditch and places shadowed by trees and bushes. Remembering my childhood in Montana, I reached down and grabbed a hand full of snow and began sucking on it. My thirst being quenched, I forged farther up the mountain, determined to find the Madrones.

Arriving at the end of the road, I found the trailhead that had been described to me. Large drifts of snow remained, but the trail itself looked clear. I scanned the trees. Some of them seemed to have *Arbutus*-like leaves, but I saw no red branches on their trunks. Dusk was approaching, exacerbating my red and green color-blindness. I advanced along the trail, mindful of the icy spots. Finally, I spotted it - a distinctly red branch growing on a small tree, speckled with patches of gray bark! And the leaves, yes, they definitely belonged to an *Arbutus*! I extracted my camera and began photographing.

Quickly inspecting some adjacent trees, particularly the smaller trees, I spotted more branches of a similar red hue, with more of that gray tinge laced throughout. A woman was coming up the trail, her hiking partner lagging about twenty feet behind. With the light bleeding rapidly from the sky and my ability to distinguish colors dwindling, an idea suddenly occurred to me. I would ask her if she could make out any red in the bark of the trees she was about to pass.

"Yes," she said, stopping her stride and crouching to have a closer look at a few trees. "I believe so." She pointed to some she thought looked red. She asked her partner if he could see any trees with red branches. He mumbled that he might have noticed a few but seemed more interested in simply ascending the path and enjoying the sight of the rare snow. Fair enough, I thought.

I took more pictures and climbed the slope off the trail, being careful all the while to avoid slipping and sliding in the snow. (Figure 8.3 & 8.4) In no time, I found myself surrounded by what I thought were *Arbutus* trees of all sizes. However, in the waning light, it was difficult to be certain that some of the bigger trees were in fact *Arbutus*. Oak trees were intermingled amongst them like we'd encountered at the Chiricahua National Monument Park. This oak looked from a distance like *Arbutus* thus I had to rely on some telltale red coloring for certain identification. Nevertheless, compared to what I *might* have found, especially at such a late hour of the day, this collection of Madrones was a treasure, and I left feeling quite satisfied.

As I descended the mountain, I realized how much better it would have been had Darlene and I come here during the season when the Arizona Madrone was in full bloom, as then the trees would have been far easier to distinguish from the other trees. I also began to realize why there had been so little written about the Arizona Madrone: evidently it survives only in the mountains and canyons at higher elevations, and the main trunk does not exhibit telltale peeling like the Pacific, Texas, and Baja Madrones. It does, nevertheless, boast its own special character and beauty, such as in those small red branches mentioned previously, as well as in its heavy, checkered bark, this latter sometimes resembling rattlesnake skin (Figure 8.5). Several months later I also would learn from some wonderful photographs that Lorena Moore was kind enough to send me, that the Arizona Madrone's blossoms and berries were like those of other Madrones throughout the Western Hemisphere, and, in their own way, equally beautiful. (Figure 8.6)

I arrived at the car just as dusk was giving way to night. Darlene, having begun to worry a bit, was visibly relieved to see me - especially in one piece. We made haste for the condo very tired at this point. With no hint of light remaining in the sky, an exodus of cars descended the canyon.

The next day we vacated the condo at noon sharp, setting off on our journey back to Washington. We had planned a few short stops along the way, including one at my sister's home, near Mesquite, Nevada. Heading northwest, we traced the outer edges of Phoenix before deciding to lodge in Kingman, Arizona, situated about two thirds of the way between Tucson and Las Vegas.

After breakfast the next morning, it was off to the Hoover Dam, just forty minutes from the gambling capital of the world. Darlene and I marveled at the structure of the dam. Constructed during the Great Depression, it is truly one of the most remarkable feats of engineering in the history of humankind. Exploiting the ingenuity, sweat, and toil of thousands of workers, many of whom lost their lives in the effort, those behind the project had managed, incredibly, to harness the Colorado River. It formed the extensive Lake Mead system that supplies both electricity and water to a huge swath of the nearby population. The lake itself is a recreational playground for residents of the Las Vegas area, standing in sharp contrast to the other, less innocent if undeniably more popular recreations the city has to offer. Originally called Boulder Dam, the site was later renamed in honor of President Hoover, whose administration oversaw the bulk of its construction.

Wanting to avoid Las Vegas and to explore more interesting sites, we traveled on the Nevada Highways 167 and 169, around the north side of Lake Mead and into the Moopa Valley, eventually meeting up with US Interstate 15 near Glendale, Arizona. Of particular interest to us were the red-colored hills, their tint apparently caused by an abundance of iron oxide in the soil. These hills were woven into badlands and some interesting pock-marked outgroups. We felt compelled several times to stop and get our cameras out. Once back on the freeway, we reached Mesquite in no time.

We enjoyed two full days with my sister, admiring the most recent of her artistic output. A retired art teacher, she worked in multimedia art for decades and for a time owned a gallery in Miles City, Montana. After moving to Mesquite, seeking a warmer climate, she and her husband had converted part of their home into a personal gallery. Blessed with a fertile imagination, and naturally inventive, my sister is forever creating the most interesting things out of the most seemingly mundane materials. Numerous of these creations are on full display all around her yard, for the aesthetic enjoyment of visitors and passersby. I must admit, amazing as her talents are, just thinking about what she does makes me tired!

Leaving her home, we drove for about nine hours straight, arriving in Twin Falls, Idaho utterly exhausted. The next day's drive was mercifully much shorter. After about six hours on the road we arrived in Kennewick,

Washington, leaving us just five hours from home. Alas, winter fate intervened. The mountain passes, we learned, were likely to be closed the next day due to heavy snows. So, reluctantly, we decided to head west and drive around Portland, then north to Anacortes, thus bypassing the mountains altogether.

Then came the cruel irony. For the entirety of the two-week trip, we had taken great care to avoid any significant risk of contracting COVID-19. We wore masks in public, diligently practiced social distancing, eschewed dining in restaurants in favor of getting takeout, and so on. Yet, by the time we finally arrived home nine hours after setting out from Kennewick, our relief was largely overshadowed by how poorly we felt.

We climbed into bed, grateful it was our own, and told ourselves we were just worn out from the trip, that we would feel better in the morning.

Unfortunately, this proved to be mere wishful thinking on our part. Over the next two days, Darlene and I both remained extremely fatigued, suffered severe headaches, and just felt miserable overall. At some point we agreed we should get tested for the virus. We did, and a day later were told over the phone that we had both tested positive, and so should remain quarantined for two full weeks. Wow! This, certainly, was *not* what we had expected. This highly unwelcome news, once we shared it, set off all kinds of alarm bells with our four adult children and their families.

Our eldest son, who happens to be a doctor of infectious disease, was called to front and center by his siblings. He arranged for us to participate in a trial study called "REGN 2067," in which antibodies, derived from people who had tested positive for the virus but had not become ill, were being evaluated. The doctors running the trial (a double-blind study) were testing two antibodies, REGEN10933 and REGEN10987, utilizing a random administration of them with a placebo. We agreed to participate and soon thereafter received our infusions, which could, of course, have been either the placebo or one of the two antibodies. At the time of this writing, we still do not know what we were given. We've been told that we'll find out one year from the date we received the infusions. We have since learned that two months after we'd received our doses, the placebos were discontinued because the initial results of the study having shown such remarkable promises, further administration of the placebo was deemed unethical. Thus, from that point onward, all participants in the study were given the antibodies, and apprised of this fact.

Thus, at least for another six months or so, it shall remain a mystery as to why we did not become terribly ill. Within a week we were feeling almost normal, and within two weeks our health had been fully restored. What, we still wonder, kept us from ever getting particularly sick? Did we receive the antibodies? Was it just our strong immune systems and overall good health, just the power of mind over matter, simple good luck, or perhaps even Divine intervention? We know our children and others were praying for us.

As a retired professor, I take certain academic liberties in forming a theory. It has been said that happiness keeps the immune system itself happy. Personally, I'm convinced that, at least in *our* case, it is our mutual love of Madrona trees, radiating all throughout us, that must be responsible!

Admittedly, sometimes even professors' theories don't hold water, but since no water is involved here, I daresay mine strikes me as perfectly credible.

Figure 8.1 *Monuments* at the Chiricahua National Monument.

Figure 8.2 Photographs of *Arbutus arizonica* (N 32° 00′ 43.009″, W 109° 21′ 16.38″) Altitude 1625′ (495 m) A. Main trunk with some heavy bark gone on the upper side, B. Leaves, C. Small red branches observable.

Figure 8.3 C. A tree with snow in the background, A. Closer view of the tree in C, B. A closeup of one of the branches of the tree in Figure 8.2 C.

Figure 8.4 Two views of the trunk and branches of *Arbutus arizonica* trees illustrating the red coloring and reduced bark on the small branches.

Figure 8.5 Photograph provided by Loren Babcock Moore taken 4/14/2019 *A. arizonica* illustrating the interesting heavy bark structure.

Figure 8.6 Photograph of the *A. arizonica* A. Ripened berries, C. Close up of the blossoms of C. (Provided by Lorena Babcock Moore).

Figure 8.7 Photographs of Pointleaf Manzanita (*Arctostaphylos pungens*) we had initially mistaken as *A. arizonica*. A. Leaves, B. Close up of a branch of D, C. Berries on the ground, and D. The interesting branch structure of the bush.

Part Two Introduction: My Romance Ripens: Giant Pacific Madrone Heritage Trees

The favorable climate of the Pacific Coast promotes trees growing to enormous size. Many of the Pacific Madrone have taken full advantage of this and are indeed regal. Some of these specimens are honored by calling them Heritage Trees.

What is it about these trees that calls to our inner selves? Is it how insignificant, how temporary and infirm, we feel standing next to them? Is the longevity of a living thing which has endured decades, even centuries of adversity at the hands of Mother Nature? Perhaps, it's simply the awe that these towering symbols tend to inspire? The lure of finding, observing, admiring, photographing, measuring, and even simply basking in the shades of these beautiful trees has proven irresistibly enticing to devoted tree-hunters over the ages and all over the world. In particular two authors Al Carder [91] and Audrey Grescoe have each written a book about Giant trees of which many reside in the Pacific Coast. Further, Grescoe devotes a special section to the *Arbutus* trees themselves. [92]

One might ask, when one arrives at such a tree what does one do? Of course, taking pictures with you or a friend standing by them seems mandatory. Trying to capture the whole tree is a challenge with often only pieces of it appearing in the resulting images. Actual tree-hugging is optional, of course but not much of the tree will be included in that hug. Another popular activity is to measure the dimensions of the tree: circumference with a cord or measuring tape, diameter by simply averaging the shortest and longest sides of the trunk and the height and breadth of the crown by surveying techniques, sometimes possible if the this structure is not hidden by the upper stratosphere of adjacent trees. The proper method to measure a tree has been given.[10] With a bit of luck, you might even stumble upon a candidate for inclusion in the Heritage Tree listing.

Measurements, however, hardly tell the *story* of the tree. Certainly, we would like to know how old it is? How did it live so long whereas other trees nearby died? How healthy is the tree? Are there daughter trees? What is the history associated with the tree? How, if at all, has it affected other people throughout its history? There are of course lots of botanical questions, as well, perhaps the most modern being: *What is the genetic heritage of the tree and its genetic relation to other big tree*s? Such questions will be more readily and thoroughly answerable in the future.

I find these questions and measuring of the trees all very interesting and fun, but it is the chase of the big Madrones that I find *most* exciting. Of course, everyone will have to pursue their own questions – and adventures; but in meantime you can explore the next seven chapters with me, as Darlene and I travel to see some of these magnificent expressions of nature.

10 "Measuring Guideline Handbook," an 84-page treatise on the topic. https://californiabigtrees.calpoly.edu/how-to-measure-a-tree.

Chapter Nine:

A Virtual Fantasy - The Council Madrone

The trails of the giant Madrones are often as twisted as the Madrone trees themselves. One of the most famous of the trees begins in Northern California, in Humboldt County, about eighty miles south of Eureka along Highway 101 near Garberville, then west to a site on the southern side of Fox Spring ridge near the Mattole River and Ettersburg. On this trek we will travel, out of necessity for which the reason will be revealed later, through the eyes and experience of others.

A unique event occurred about the time Columbus dropped his anchor in the Bahamas. A new Madrone life pushed itself through the soil, dropping bits of covering debris and tasting its first rays of the glorious California sunshine. No one was present to witness this momentous event except perhaps *The Indigenous People*, who lived in small distributed villages along the streams in this area[11]. The Hupas for example resided in houses of cedar planks, with their lives very occupied with the basics of survival, hunting, foraging, etc.[93]. Other tribes in the region were also of the Athapascan heritage, as indicated by their common languages.

The story continues approximately, three hundred fifty years later on a homestead in 1857 in Araquipa Hills near Vacaville, which is about forty-five miles northeast of present-day Berkeley on the road to Sacramento. [94] Here William and Martha Ann Jepson had traveled from Missouri by oxen-drawn covered wagon to establish a new home. On August 19, 1867, a boy they named Willis Linn was born. He had three sisters already and would soon have a younger brother. Willis grew up on the family farm and so likely helped in the cultivation of the land from a young age as was, and largely remains, the custom among children born into farming families. His father believed in hard work. He had little patience for reading or other scholarly activities, regarding them as a waste of valuable time better spent planting and harvesting crops. His mother, however; encouraged academic pursuits.

Willis, with his mother's blessing if not his father's, began reading the few books the family owned, often around a potbellied stove and accompanied by his sisters. The surrounding hills and valleys were still untouched, at least beyond the farming lands and orchards. These pristine regions ripe with unexplored mysteries called to young Willis, and he investigated their secrets every chance he got. His hunger it seems for learning and inquisitive nature seemed to spark a certain burning curiosity in the young man, ultimately forging his destiny. Nevertheless, the physically demanding farm work he grew up with also seemed to make its mark on him, inspiring a diligence, dedication, and thoroughness he would later bring to any project he undertook.

As a teenager, he had an opportunity to attend a new Normal and Scientific school in Vacaville where his studies included science courses and even field trips in Botany. In 1889 he rode the train to Berkeley to take an entrance exam for admission to the University of California and later he joined that year's freshman class and then graduated four years later. He began keeping a diary at the beginning of his junior year, an activity he carried on throughout his life and which eventually turned out to be his legacy. He initially called this his student notebook but later dubbed it his *Field Notes* of which volumes have been preserved at the Jepson Herbarium Archives.[95]

11 Certainly, there were no slugs, snails or other predators present or there would not have been a Council Madrone to write about.

He never returned to farming as a vocation and remained the rest of his life in academia. He became a protégé of Professor Greene the Chairman of the Botany Department, later he entered the university's graduate program. Willis was appointed as an Assistant Professor in Botany in 1891. His work included field trips into the surrounding region, during which he would gather specimens and label, describe, and categorize them. This ultimately resulted in longer summer trips around the California countryside involving more extensive field work. He published his first paper in 1891 describing one hundred and ten species. The following year he joined a small, exclusive group including John Muir which became a precursor to the Sierra Club.

Willis grew to be about six feet tall, a strikingly handsome man. In the field, he had been photographed [96] [94] carrying a special case for transporting specimens. He appears rugged, sporting a well-worn brim hat, a kerchief tied around his neck, a wrinkled denim shirt, and well-conditioned jeans. His expression is one of intense curiosity as he gazes into the distance, in some ways resembling a cowboy in a western movie. Keep in mind that the photograph was taken in the early 1900s, and he was the real deal. Later in his career he would acquire the sobriquet "Botany Man" [94].

Travelers in the west in the late 1800s and early 1900s got around by way of stagecoaches, wagons, horses, or their own two feet. Roads were mostly dirt, sometimes mud, and bridges were often nonexistent. Telephones were still exceedingly scarce and lodging in short supply and anything but luxurious. Field trips therefore involved only the most very basic means of travel and camping. In Jepson's book *The Trees of California* [97] there is a picture of him in a canoe beside two swimming pack mules crossing the Trinity River . Willis seemed to be a firm believer that the best way to discover new foliage was on foot or horseback.

Although throughout his career Willis reported on hundreds of various types of plants and trees, he seemed to harbor a special fondness for the Madrona tree. In his book he writes how he is always struck by joy when he encountered one. How its color, its demeanor and surprising variations always enchanted him. He also states that many people just passed it by but some, poets and artists have tried to capture this magic lure.

We now pick up the trail with Willis in his travels in the field of Trinity and Humboldt counties. We walk and ride with him in his now *legionary* **Field Books** [95], to see what he discovered. (I will cite the specific volume and page numbers where he makes various assertions, so the reader can travel with him on this discovery in Willis's words if they choose.)

On July 8, 1902, while traveling in Trinity County, he refers to the Terra Cotta bark of a Madrona beginning to peel with green color under it. (Vol. 8, p. 94). Later on, the 29th of that month he describes a trait of the Madrona that he observed, and I have described years later as the *cordiality* of the tree. He writes how a Madrona yields to an oak. They started growing together but while the oak did not give an inch the Madrona bent, yielding and reaching around the oak seeking and following the sun and finally snaking its way up to find some sun between the oak and a pine tree. (Vol. 8, p. 168) Again in August 5, 1902 (Vol. 9, p. 18) he noted when traveling through miles of untouched forest of Oak, Madrona and Spruce how the Oak and Spruce grew straight to the sky while the Madrona would ultimately reach the same height but their trunks would snake in various directions as they rose vertically to the overstory.

Willis' travels in the cited field notes were in an area very conducive to tree growth bordering on what is today the Redwood National Park, home to the world's largest trees. This perhaps helps to explain some of his findings. Finally, in 1902 he discovers a tree which became to be known as the famous *Council Madrone*! (vol 9 19-21)

He states: "*This is a tremendous tree. Undoubtedly the largest Madrona in California.*" A few lines later he writes: "*The Madrona stands in a little promontory at the near end. Leading down the ridge one is wonderfully impressed. I rubbed my eyes. I thought it must be an oak, a Maul Oak maybe, so big and round. When we got near – and the tree is within 60 ft. of this road one sees that it is the largest Madrona tree in all California,*"

He then goes on to record that it was growing on a hay field of the French & Pixton homestead. He spoke with a woman at the Ranch house, presumably Mrs. French, who knew about the tree but didn't know it was the largest Madrona in California! She said locally it was used to mark the corner between districts that were managed by different supervisors.

We turn now to Fig. 26 of Jepson's 1908 book [97] to continue our trail. Here you can find a picture of this large Madrone tree and he calls it the "Council *Madroña*". The black and white photograph there shows a fully developed crown which is both symmetrical and rounded. He reports the crown as being ninety-nine feet in diameter and seventy-five feet in height. The trunk, moreover, stands seven and a half feet in diameter at a height of four and a half feet from the ground.

Why did Willis call it the Council *Madroña*? According to the biography of Willis by Beidleman, [94] The prefix *council*, was given because interior and coastal Native Americans used to meet there. Others in the more current literature seem to echo a similar explanation. However, I have found no direct evidence in the literature to support this supposition but did obtain confirmation that Indians had dwelled there.

The trail of the Council Madrona continues into the twenty-first century, but only just. Numerous people visited and probably photographed it throughout the previous century. Frederick Coe, in his article on *The Madrones*, provides measurements made in 1975. [99] (Figure 9.1) He reports a circumference of 33'(25m), a height of 80'(25m), and a crown breadth of 125'(38 m). Coe then remarks on measurements of the one main trunk that comes off at a prominent angle: at the point where it exits from the main tree, it is 14' (4.5 m) in circumference. (Figure 9.1B) Moving out on the branch 19' (5.6 m), the circumference is 9' (2.5 m). In other words, the branch itself is bigger than most Madrona trees in their entirety!

In May 2017, I was able to find Dr. Coe's phone number, he had retired from a medical practice. I talked to his wife.[100] She said Dr. Coe will be ninety-nine years old in October and has difficulty hearing when talking on the phone, but would be happy to correspond by letter. Subsequently, he told me that he had visited the tree in 1971 and later in 1974 with his son. He had observed some decay in the large limbs at their bases in 1971, but otherwise, he told me, the tree had looked healthy. He then kindly sent me the photographs of tree that appear here. One outstanding characteristic of the tree is the large branch that juts out almost 90 degrees from the main trunk (Figure 9.1B). This long, protuberant limb, I believe, is the one that Willis Jepson had described when he wrote that the measuring tape went over the top at four and a half feet above ground. (Vol. 9, pp. 19-21). A similar picture appears in an internet publication. [101]

On March 20, 1975 the Council Madrona and a surrounding area were obtained by the Save the Redwoods League (SRL) in order to ensure its preservation. The SRL later passed on these lands to the California Department of Parks and Recreation. [102]

On the third of February 2000, just knocking on the door of the new century, a terrible event occurred. The tree, after perhaps five centuries of life, was completely torn in half and demolished. How did this happen? One source implies an incident involving unusually wet snow [101]; another blames a rare, excessive windstorm [102]. Certainly, these theories have a certain initial plausibility: the weight of wet snow can be very detrimental to the stability of a tree's structure, as my own son discovered in 2017 during a rare, wet snowfall near Portland, Oregon, where the main branch of a Madrone tree he had in his yard was torn off by the weight of the snow. Peter Wohlleben, in his book *The Hidden Life of Trees* (2015), discusses the weakness of trees with split structures, i.e., those whose trunks branch off in a sharp "V" shape near the bases. [103] However, plausibility aside, all of these implications are actually incorrect, as I learned early in 2017.

I was able to locate the phone number of the French Ranch. In a phone conversation with Mrs. Sally French, I learned several interesting facts. Her husband, Richard Lee French, who turned eighty in 2017, is the great grandson of James Edward French, the man who homesteaded the property around 1890, this being the French & Pixton ranch mentioned by Willis. Sally and Richard have three children. One day, one of their sons was working near the big Madrona (Council Madrone) tree and he heard it fall. It was a calm day. Sally said the tree had grown rotten in the region where the side branch merged from the main trunk. Apparently, the tension of the large branches became too great and it snapped, thus causing the whole tree to tear apart and topple.[104]

I have not personally seen the living or the fallen tree, but I found a website by Don Bain quite interesting. He photographed and produced panoramic views of many sites and posted them on the web. Included are quite specular panoramic views of the devastated Council Madrone taken April 26, 2004. Clearly the two massive trunks are split, almost in opposite directions. The remains of one trunk shown lying on the ground are higher than a woman standing in the picture. The earth must have shaken when these trunks came smashing down. No doubt that is why Sally's son heard the crash. The tangled, broken limbs toward the crown, as shown in Bain's pictures, confirm the force with which it must have struck. In one view, the remnants of the outer, scalloped bark near the bases of the trunks remain while the rest of the trunks look bare, save for some moss growing in certain areas. The tree seems quite dead.

Mrs. French also said that she thought it was true that the Council Madrone was a place where the Native Americans used to meet. There was a schoolhouse nearby and her husband had attended school there. The children used to go out in the adjacent plowed field and look for arrowheads and other artifacts. The area of the school was known as a place where Natives had stayed. Mrs. French went on to say that one of Sally's most romantic moments was when Richard, then single now her husband, took her up in the tree on the big side branch and showed her the various acreage around the area. She added that there have been numerous weddings held under the tree over the years and, at some point, even a style had been built for going over the fence to take part in the ceremonies.

The trail of the Council Madrone has come to an end with its destructive fall in 2000 – or has it? Carefully examining the pictures mentioned above (taken by Bain), one notes that, at the distal end of where one trunk fell, a tree is blooming, and it may well be a Madrone tree. The blossoms are white and hanging like a Madrone, and the time of is right for Madrones to bloom. Furthermore, this is probably the second tree which appears off to one side of the Council in the photograph in Frank Coe's article. If so, this tree must be an offshoot of the Madrone, either by roots or by seeds, since the Council lived well beyond the life of any other nearby trees.

Of course, Madrone trees are known for regeneration from their stumps, particularly after a fire. Perhaps, it is just wishful thinking, but just perhaps, the Council back in the twentieth century, its fifth century of life, had already begun preparing a replacement, a daughter tree. It would of course require a visit to the site to confirm or reject this hypothesis. Nevertheless, we can hope that this is part of the Council (or at least a direct descendant thereof) and that perhaps, in another five hundred years or so, it will be every bit as big as its parent.

Figure 9.1 Photographs of the Council Madrone kindly provided by Dr. Fredrick Coe, that he recorded in 1975. C. View of the entire tree, A. Closeup of the base of tree in C, B. A view that displays the prominent large branch that many people have stood on at various times. A brief case is shown in this photo near the base for size contrast. This style of brief case was about 3.5 inches thick.

Chapter Ten:

A California Immersion – Gustafson's Tree

The trail of the majestic Madrone trees continues taking us about 125 miles south of the deceased Council Madrone and 70 miles north of San Francisco CA on a sunny day in the early spring of 2017. Here at the Gustafson Family Vineyard was a living Heritage Tree estimated to be three hundred years old. Yes, Darlene and I were on a quest to see this famous tree which was probably the biggest *living* Madrone in Sonoma County, in California, and perhaps in the world.

On this day, I dialed the telephone number I had before me of the wine tasting room for the Gustafson Winery. This was located away from the vineyard in the town of Healdsburg CA. However, the phone just rang again and again. It seemed strange that no one would answer, as it was during business hours. I left my number when the answering machine came on. Well, what should we do? We had driven from San Luis Obispo yesterday, some three hundred miles, just to see this tree. We had today and part of tomorrow before we had to leave for the San Francisco International Airport to fly to Seattle. We were concerned that if we drove the seventeen miles to the vineyard without first having contacted someone there, we might not be able to get in. I was very anxious to view and photograph this Madrone, it was one of the few such living manifestations of nature, perhaps the only one! I think, however, Darlene would have been happy just to spend the afternoon by the pool at the condominium we were staying at.

Nevertheless, I convinced her we should go directly to the wine-tasting room in Healdsburg to see what we could learn. The town was small, so we easily found our way. Above the door of the wine-tasting room a sign announced Gustafson Winery and in smaller letters Tasting Room. We knew then we were at the right place, but to our dismay the doors were locked. Fortunately, we found a note posted which read: "Closed till 3 P.M. for staff training." I suggested to my wife that we gamble and drive to the vineyard in hopes we could get in. We entered the address into our GPS and it traced out the directions. The route resembled an exceedingly long *worm*, straight for quite for some distance and then curling sharply, indeed, almost folding back on itself in several places.

Once on the road, we immediately started passing row upon row of sleeping grapevines. In some cases, each bush stood isolated but as part of a precise row. In others the bushes were linked by a wire with vines clinging to it. Still others included a water system. The vines, always aligned from each angle, reminding me of the precision with which graves are situated in a military cemetery. Rolling hills were dressed in these vineyards, as were flatter regions of the valley, often bordered by trees. Intermingled along the way were tasting rooms and signs displaying the names of the parent wineries. This region was known as the Dry Creek Valley Appellation, with over nine thousand vineyards, seventy wineries, and one hundred forty years of grape-growing history. [105]

As the vineyards and tasting rooms faded in our rearview mirror, we slowed to go through a park at the base of the Sonora Dam, which turned out to be the site of a fish hatchery. A sign proclaimed that steelhead were now returning and could be viewed at the fish ladder. Maybe we would stop on the way back, Darlene and I agreed. The road now began to climb rapidly in elevation and assume more serious curves. Abruptly we came out on a vista with the Sonora Lake spread in front of us. We stopped, looked at the lake, looked at the GPS map, and then saw we had just missed a turn. Backtracking, we shortly resumed our trek along the GPS *worm*, noticing for the first time that it was really starting to *wiggle*. We began to see Madrone trees drooping toward the road from either side, reaching skyward, absorbing the sunlight. They were of various sizes, with bare and twisting trunks, dressed in darker, scalloped bark near their bases. The hills rose and fell on either side of us as we crested one slope after another, but the overall trajectory of the terrain was ever upward. At one point the road very nearly doubled back, the lower valley left far behind us now. Large oaks with monstrous trunks adorned the hillsides, their yet-leafless branches silhouetted against the freshly greened slopes, contrasting with the dark, definitive green of the leaves of the Madrone trees. We were able to steal periodic glimpses of the lake to our right before it disappeared entirely behind the next rise. The road wound upward still farther, until we sure we had climbed as far as we could – only to encounter a brief dip and then yet another incline. Finally, around a turn a gate with a large sign bearing the moniker *Gustafson Family Vineyard*, came into view. But much as we'd feared it might be, the gate was closed and locked.

I tried the intercom at the gate several times but there was no answer. I walked along the fence and could see the top of a large Madrone, but some young olive trees blocked most of the view. I then climbed atop a wall adjacent to the gate. Alas, even that didn't help much. Incidentally, a very nice Madrone with a diameter of about forty inches grew alongside the fence roughly fifty feet from where I stood. Clearly, this was big Madrone country.

Looking at the time, we decided to just head back to Healdsburg, as the tasting room should be open when we got there. Sure enough, it was, and there we met Steve Spinella and Tara Albertson. Tara said she had received my message but just hadn't yet had time to answer. Steve said he would be at the vineyard tomorrow and we were most welcome to come. We agreed to meet up at nine-thirty the next morning, and then we moved on to more serious business, sampling their vintage wine. They offered an excellent variety: Riesling, Sauvignon Blanc, Syrah, Cabernet Sauvignon, Cabernet Franc, and two Zinfandels. I liked the Estate Heritage Tree Zinfandel the best, perhaps I was prejudiced, in that the vines grew on an eastern slope in front of the Madrone tree. I liked the slight sweetness and mellowness of the wine, and I could almost taste the Madrone blossoms and berries in it – or was that merely my imagination? We left a little more *enlightened* than we'd come, and with a bottle of that Zinfandel wine, to boot.

The next morning, we were packed to travel and winding our way up that snaking road with no need now for GPS navigation. The gate was open and we traversed our way down the hill to the winery, inhaling the inaugural view as we went. The winery itself was architecturally pleasing, open glass windows, real chains hanging in place of rain chains and big oak barrels stacked along its perimeter. Between its flat-beam projecting structure, blended landscaping, and backdrop of a valley punctuated by rolling, tree-covered hills, in some ways it felt reminiscent of a Frank Lloyd Wright creation. A beautiful guest house stood behind the winery, enjoying the view (Figure 10.1).

Emmett Reed, the winemaker and vineyard manager, was moving wine barrels with a forklift. He greeted us with a smile, said the Heritage Madrone was back up the hill off the road, and, yes, we could look around first. "There is a path to the overlook just the other side of the main entrance," he told us. Stepping onto the compost trail, we followed the path he had mentioned. We were at once struck by the rows of descending grape plants. The plunging field terminated in a row of trees and hills partially obscuring the distant Sonora Lake. (Figure 10.1 A) Madrones decorated the hillside, and a picturesque little bench conveniently awaited us. The day and scenery were so pleasant, we easily could have spent the rest of the morning there. But, all the while, the Heritage tree was calling me.

Back up the road and a short walk was the Gustafson Tree with its arms splayed wide, as if expecting an embrace. It stood like a sentry over rows of Zindandel grape vines and the valley below, soaking up the morning sun, as it probably had been doing for some three hundred years. (Figure 10.2B) We got an up-close look at three massive branches, each in itself more than thick enough to serve as a trunk to most trees, protruding from the truly enormous main trunk at three distinctly asymmetrical angles. These emerged a few feet above the ground and reached far out, capturing a separate space for the sunlight. The main trunk climbed up perhaps six feet or more before beginning to divide itself into additional smaller trunks. The total height and breadth of the crown of the tree I estimated to be, respectively, 59ft (18 m) and 66ft (20 m). The diameter of the main base had been recorded at 11.5ft (3.5 m) see Figures 10.2A & 10.3.

The tips of many of the evergreen branches were starting to show their preparation for later blossoms. (Figure 10.4A) Part of the main trunk and many of the secondary trunks were covered with green moss, reflecting the effects of the fog that often moved in from the Pacific Ocean sixteen miles away and 1,771 ft (541 m) below the elevation of the tree. Unfortunately, near the base (Figure 10.4B) there was signs of rot beginning in one section. Hopefully, this won't ultimately lead to the demise of the tree. Nevertheless, the base and multiple trunks, were largely covered with denser, scalloped gray bark to about thirty feet up them. It was almost completely absent at elevations above forty feet. After that bare and twisted branches were exposed, revealing their characteristic peeled Madrone style, until they reached the green foliage, whereupon they disappeared into the leaves. The tree seemed to hold a certain enchantment, something others also had felt. [106] This was indeed an extremely extraordinary tree.

Finally, we tore ourselves away and returned to the winery, where we chatted further with Emmett and Steve Spinella, whom we had met the previous day. It was revealed that the owner of the vineyard, Mr. Gustafson, had been a landscape architect in Minnesota for thirty years, and had more recently completed a real-estate development in the local area. While traveling the back roads one day, looking for places to open a vineyard, he noticed the giant Madrone tree. The property at that time was a sheep ranch. He recognized that the type of soil that was good for growing Madrones was also good for growing grapes. Consequently, he purchased the land in 2002 and commenced the long process of creating vineyards, the winery, the guest house, and bringing to the market his wines. Emmett joined him in 2007 and has helped carry along the vision. [107]

I declined a taste of the wine because we had to drive to San Francisco, but we did take a final photo and one last sip of the view. Stopping at the fish hatchery down the road, we witnessed the end of the long upstream swim and battle of the steelhead as they followed their natural drive to spawn where they were born, reminding me in many ways of the journey of the Gustafson Family Vineyard.

Later, pinned back in my seat by the acceleration of the plane as it took off for Seattle, I felt a deep satisfaction at our mission's having been accomplished, and anticipated enjoying in the future a glass of the Estate Heritage Tree Zinfandel wine that we had packed in our luggage.

Figure 10.1 Views at the Gustafson Family Vineyard located at 38.6703° N 123.0333° W. A. North view of Sonoma Lake with grape vine rows in the foreground. B. East view from the winery with stacked wine barrels, 3/3/2017.

Figure 10.2 Westerly views of the Heritage tree at the vineyard. A. Darlene standing beside the tree providing perspective of its size. B. Spreading wide its branches at the head of the rows of Zinfandel grape vines.

Figure 10.3 Closeup views of the tree. A. Northwest view with a bottle of Zinfandel wine at the base. B. The same view as 10.2A but much closer.

Figure 10.4 A. The foliage on the upper branches revealing red peeled branches and centrally the buds for the coming blossoms (March 3, 2017). B. Even closer view of Figure 10.3A, revealing a rotted section in the right of center of the photo.

Chapter Eleven:

Gulf Island Appeal - Thetis Island Trees

I cut back the throttle on the *Sea Overture* as we entered Telegraph Harbor on Thetis Island, in August 2016[12]. As our boat slowed, the wake rushed in to meet her stern, rolling in on itself before diminishing to small, receding wavelets. We slipped past Dayman Island, a small, ten-hectare (twenty-five acre) wooded island about three thousand meters off to our port side and isolated against the sea. It didn't particularly draw my attention at the time but would come to intrigue me later. Meanwhile, the tip of Foster Point reached out on our port side, while the northern reach of Kuper Island closed in on our starboard side. Both were dressed in evergreens reaching to the sky, and in some cases, out over the water. Boats of various sizes and forms, anchored or connected to buoys, witnessed our arrival without salutation, except to nod briefly in reaction to our wake.

Reducing our speed further, we closed in on the first marina and fuel dock on our port side. I recalled a bit of local history about the area where the marina is. In a letter Rosamond Anketell-Jones, an early pioneer to Thetis Island, wrote to her daughter in 1980, she revealed some detail about a colorful piece of family history. [108] Around 1885, her uncle (Rosamond's father), Harvey Stillwell, had purchased the parcels of land on the south and west sides of Telegraph Bay, the area Darlene and I were now passing. After acquiring the tracts, Sitwell had immediately began clearing them to build a farm for himself and his family. In 1889, his father, Reverend Sitwell (Rosamond's grandfather), and two of Harvey's sisters from England, came to visit and to see how things were progressing. They were disappointed to find that the new house thus far consisted of just four walls and a roof, so the daughters took over the old house with mud floors while the men set up camp in the new house. Rev. Sitwell later rowed to Chemainus and purchased materials with which to make curtains that could be used to divide the new home into makeshift rooms, so that the entire family could live in it while construction continued. Harvey's friend caught one of the daughters' eyes and later became Rosamond's father.

The voice of a dock manager at the second marina brought me back to the present. Under his direction, I maneuvered the *Sea Overture* into a spot on the dock. This marina had several Madrone trees, perhaps I should say *Arbutus* trees as that is what the British Columbians call it. (For the remainder of the story, I shall refer to Madrones as *Arbutus*). A prominent one was on the way to the office leaning heavily on an evergreen tree. A sign over the Telegraph Bistro's office advertised ice cream and other delights. Near the marina was Canoe Pass, an east-west canal dug in 1905 to facilitate passage through a natural high-water conduit, which separated Thetis Island on the north from Kuper Island on the south. [109] A road led about a quarter-mile to the west from the marina, where it met the main island road. At that junction a vegetable stand stood with other sumptuous staples such as freshly baked pies. In the summers, there was often a farmer's market there, where we had once bought a nice *Arbutus*-wood bowl from a local artisan. A short walk from there takes one to a shop which roasts coffee beans and sells them both ground and whole.

The other marina has a pub, with outdoor tables at which to eat on warm days or anytime, really, if you don't mind braving the elements. Darlene and I have stayed at both marinas – at one of them inadvertently - due to a certain map's incorrect matching of phone number and location.

---

12 Thetis Island is located six miles northeast of the town of Chemainus on the east side of Vancouver Island B.C, Canada which itself is about 50 mile north along the coast from Victoria, B.C. This island is linked by a thirty-five minute ferry ride to Chemainus.

After securing our boat, I was eager to get off on the mission I had been planning for some time. We were traveling with our boating friends, who had already moored their boat. It was our turn to host dinner on our boat that evening. We settled on 5:30. While the others made plans for their afternoon, I gathered my camera, tape measure, rope, and inclinometer. I had some unfinished business to attend to, so I set off on my own. Darlene, knowing me well, reminded me that I needed to be back with plenty of time to help prepare and set up for dinner. "You are barbecuing, you know," she reminded me.

"Of course," I replied.

What was this mission I had in mind? The story can be traced back to 2014, two years previous. Darlene and I had taken folding bikes on our summer boating, and had decided to explore some of Thetis Island, as it didn't seem to have too many hills. We had ridden west past the vegetable stand, and at the first junction steered our bikes onto North Cove Road. There we'd discovered more hills than anticipated, so we reversed our direction and soon passed a schoolhouse and community center. Arriving back at the junction, we'd continued to Foster Point Road and shortly passed the turnoff to the ferry terminal serving Chemainus. This ferry had brought changes to the island since the time when Reverend Stillwell and others had had to row or take private boats back and forth. The regularity of the ferry reminded me of the tide, bringing visitors in and then carrying them back out again.

We pedaled farther down Foster Point Road until, suddenly, we saw a large, remarkable tree leaning out over the road. As we drew closer it became apparent that this wasn't just any ordinary tree. On the contrary, this was an *Arbutus* tree! We parked our bikes and began examining it. We were amazed at the size of its base, and at its large, impressively tall trunk. So tall that even craning our necks, we couldn't see the crown: obscured by the tree's foliage, it might well have disappeared in the heavens. We of course took several pictures of the base and as much of the trunk that fit in the images both with and without each of us standing in front of it. We then went on exploring the rest of the road and, finally, strolled down a path to Foster Point. (Figure 11.1)

Figure 11.1 Large *Arbutus* on Foster Road, Thetis Island, B.C. A. The tree as viewed from the road looking north, B. A closeup of the base of the tree, C. A closer view of the upper branches.

In the winter of the next year, 2015, while searching the internet for information about the *Arbutus* trees, I came across a site claiming the largest *Arbutus* tree in British Columbia was on Thetis Island. [110] Reading further I realized it could not have been the one we had seen on Foster Point Road as it was reported to be near the community center where we had biked past the previous summer. The site provided measurements of the tree, as well as a photo of it, but the picture was not very clear, showing only an outline amongst other trees. I could not find any report of the other *Arbutus* tree we had passed on our bikes. That was when I hatched the plan to see and measure both trees the following summer, when we scheduled to boat there. So here we were in 2016, and that was my mission for the afternoon. I knew I had better hurry to ensure I would be back in time to help with dinner as it was a fairly long walk to both of the trees.

Somewhere past the vegetable stand alongside the road, I found myself distracted by numerous beautiful *Arbutus* trees reaching out into the bay. They looked as though they had been waiting for me to photograph them. Catlike, they seemed to be stalking the sun and open space, inching forward, twisting and turning, capturing each ray. They shed bark along the way, exposing nakedness, and raising their leaves to the light. Well, I thought to myself, I'll only be a minute while I record this. About twenty pictures later I was on my way again. (Picture after the Table of Contents)

After huffing and puffing up the hill, I came upon the community center. It was silent and no one was around. At the back, a fairly dense forest embraced it. Someplace in the woods behind the center was supposed to be the tree. With some hesitation, I stepped into the understory, pushing aside sword ferns, which were over my waist. I watched for holes in the duff as well as the big tree. I had progressed about two hundred meters when I saw an encouraging mass slightly to my left – there it was. (Figure 11.2B)

I was surprised. I had anticipated a tall, straight tree, but instead it divided quickly from the ground with the branching complete at about one and a half meters above the base. Each of these branches was quite enormous in and of itself; factoring in the main trunk, the whole structure was truly immense. Gray, scalloped bark covered the main trunk, and was present well up the tree on both of the two large branches. The bark at the bottom of the tree was overlaid with green moss (Figure 11.2 A).

I worked my measuring cord around the circumference, below the bifurcation at a height of about fifty-four inches, and pulled it tight, marking it where the length encompassed the tree. Removing the cord and laying it on the ground, I measured this length and found it to be 266 inches (or, rounded, 6.8 meters). This was close to the value of 6.64 meters reported on the internet, measured in 2009 [118]. Repeating the process, I measured a circumference of 9.4 meters at ground level and 7.4 meters, at a height of one foot. As I went around the tree, I found a hole under it on the north side, about 1.4 meters deep. It may have been home to some critters from time to time. The east side featured a burl, which accounted for the much larger measurement at ground level. After taking numerous pictures, I started to exit the woods, toward the south. I stopped at about fifty meters into my departure and looked back at the tree. The tree seemed to be dead: all the leaves hanging on the branches were shriveled and brown, with no sign of life about them. Oh, no, I thought. Is this the end of this majestic tree? This could not have happened very long ago; the dead leaves were still clinging to the branches. (Figure 11.3) At the base of the tree on the north east side was a burl and green spouts were waving at me. (Figure 11.3 A) The tree was trying to regenerate itself. The big question was whether herbivores would find and ultimately destroy them. I look forward to returning perhaps in 2022 when travel across the border is again possible to see if they have continued to grow, offering a regeneration of this ancient tree.

Looking at my watch, I saw I couldn't ponder the matter any longer. I still had the Foster Point Road tree to measure. I hurried back down the road past a farm on my right arriving shortly back at the junction. With no hesitation, I struck out on to Foster Point Road, hastening by the ferry landing, and continuing down the main road, past another junction on my left which led to the other marina with the pub. It seemed like I just kept walking and walking, anticipating seeing the tree at any time, but we had been riding bikes when we saw it before, so I realized it might be a lot farther than I had estimated. Small roads, presumably leading to private properties, disappeared into the woods at various points along the way, but where was that tree?

As I hurried along, I was greeted by the aroma of evergreens. Then I saw it, looming above the other trees like a watchtower, its longest branches spread out over the road: the *Arbutus* itself, just as I remembered it. Snapping pictures along the way, I arrived at the base of the tree and began sorting out my measuring tools. At the time, I had not yet learned about measuring a tree using the standard DBH (a height of four and a half feet for making diameter and circumference measurements, a standard developed by foresters). So, I measured the circumference at one, two, and three feet above the ground, finding, respectively, circumferential measurements of 8.2, 6.9, and 5.9 meters.

While I was obtaining the measurements, a woman came by and asked what I was up to. She was interestingly dressed, in a long black skirt, and said she lived nearby. After I explained what I was doing, she told me how a huge branch had torn off the tree the previous winter and landed on the road, splintering into pieces. She pointed up along the trunk to the spot where the branch had been ripped loose, presumably by snowfall or a strong gust of wind (or both). I talked her into letting me take a photo of her in front of the tree, but unfortunately, the focus was off, I discovered later. She insisted on taking my picture by the tree, and hers turned out much better than mine.

The next task was to measure the height of the tree. Using the rope, I measured its total length, then laid it down, marked the location of the end, and repeated the process until I was 246 feet away from the tree. Using my inclinometer, I aimed along it to the top of the tree and observed the angle to be twenty-three degrees with respect to the ground. Then, using the tangent of the angle and the measured distance from the tree, I calculated that the tree itself stood at a height of 105 feet, or about thirty-two meters. Scribbling all this information in my notebook, I began packing up my tools, then glanced down at my watch. As usual and just as Darlene had warned, I'd lost track of time! I had to hurry, or else I'd be late to help prepare dinner for our guests and that would not be good.

The return trip was much faster. I jogged as far as my body would let me (not terribly far, I'm afraid) before tapering to a light stroll to catch my breath. Moving at a brisker clip, I quickly reached the other side of the cove, scurried past the leaning *Arbutus*, and broke into another jog as I came up the walkway of the dock. I stepped onto our boat, causing it to sway. My wife looked up at me with that expression she reserves for just such occasions and gave me the usual, gentle scolding: "You're late… again."

"Not to worry!" I reassured her. I was dripping with sweat from the trek. I hurried to the bathhouse for a one-loonie shower. Meaning, I put a Canadian dollar coin in the slot inside the shower stall, which bought me about three minutes of hot water. I quickly dressed and returned to begin setting up the barbecue, chairs, and table for hors-d'oeuvres and wine. When our guests arrived, everything was under control (even my heart rate), and we sat down to talk about everybody's afternoon activities and enjoy the summer evening ambience on Telegraph Harbor.

We returned to Thetis Island the next summer. I was eager to see if the tree near the community center had recovered, or if it was indeed dead. This time I went straight to the tree. Sure enough, it appeared quite deceased, with most of the dried leaves gone from all of the branches. As I stood in front of the base with its forked trunks, I felt a sense of awe and reverence, even affection of a sort. It was perhaps akin to the feeling one might experience when visiting the grave of a long-lost friend, or while standing before the Lincoln Memorial in Washington, D.C., reflecting on the historical giant whom it honored. Lacey leaves of a cedar tree drooped down to my line of sight, underscoring that mystical, almost transcendental quality that defined the moment.

I paused long enough to examine the two branching trunks that formed the tree. The north diverged from the vertical by about 10° and had a circumferential length of 3.78 meters at its base, while the south one diverged at 30° and had a circumference of 3.6 meters where it joined the other trunk. There were cedar trees surrounding it except on the west side, all of which had circumferences around 16 inches (0.41 meters). There was a Douglas Fir about thirty meters to the north and another 15 meters to the southeast. Otherwise, it appeared that trees had been cleared away at some point. However, as I moved farther away, I found an *Arbutus* at about 90 meters to the south with a circumference of 8.92 meters at a standard measuring height of four and a half feet (DBH), with a smallish maple growing just 6/10 of a meter away. The maple had a DBH circumference of 2.4 meters. As I progressed further, I found another big *Arbutus* which had a circumference of 3.5 meters. These *Arbutus* trees were easily overlooked because their bark that was readily visible was the denser type that looked a lot like the bark of maple trees.

Figure 11.2 The large *Arbutus* near the Community Center on Thetis Island, B.C. the pictures taken 8/12/2016. A. An easterly view of the base of the tree with its two large divided trunks. B. The base of the tree when I first found it partial hidden by the foliage of cedar trees.

The bright sunshine didn't penetrate the understory much here, which was probably why these trees preserved their heavy bark and had not peeled. This was true all the way up the trees as far as I could see, a view that lasted until they disappeared into the branches of the adjacent trees.

Suddenly I was struck by an interesting thought. The size of these *Arbutus* trees indicated that they were well over a hundred years old, which meant the parents that fostered them were even older. Therefore, it was very likely that they were daughter trees of the big *Arbutus* that had died. If so, then the heritage of the big tree was assured, not all had been lost with its death.

Epilogue

The origins of Thetis Island's name are the subject of some debate. Some believe it is named after H.M.S. ("Her Majesty's Ship") Thetis, for surveying the island. However, the H.M.S. Thetis was a thirty-six-gun frigate with three masts, and not particularly suitable for survey work. Three letters written by Captain Augustus Kuper, the captain of the H.M.S. Thetis, to Rear-Admiral Moresby describe the cruises in the Vancouver Island area of the frigate between April 1852 and February 1853. [111] They included no report about surveying in the region of the island.

Steamships had become common by this time and were proving much more practical for surveying. According to Andrew Scott, in his The Encyclopedia of Raincoast Place Names, Thetis Island was named by Captain George Richards in 1858 in honor of the boat H.M.S. Thetis.[112]

An adjacent island about a quarter mile southwest of Thetis Island also has some interesting history. This island has the name Dayton honoring one of the officers on H.M.S. Thetis. Since being settled by its earliest visitors in the 1890s, the island has been privately owned by a long succession of sequestered loving and sometimes eccentric individuals. The first in this line was probably Henry Burchell, an early pioneer who came to Thetis Island in 1890. [113] One of the more notorious owners was Al Hubbard, who built a hangar on Dayton for an airplane that he flew and a slip for his yacht; he sold it in 1968 under financial pressures. These details and other entertaining writings concerning Mr. Hubbard and his exploits with LSD (a psychedelic drug) are given by Fahey (1991). [114] Since that time, it has continued to be privately owned.

In his book *Giants - The Colossal Trees of the Pacific North America* [92], Audrey Grescoe describes how on Dayton Island, in 1993, he was shown the biggest *Arbutus menziesii* he had ever observed. It grew among conifers and was not located in an environment where most *Arbutus* trees tend to grow. The tree rose straight up, about forty-five feet, and then topped off at about eighty to a hundred feet.

I went around the island in August 2017 in my dinghy, hoping to find someone of whom I could ask permission to look for the tree. I didn't see anyone, or any boats at the two docks. I observed many smaller *Arbutus* trees growing along the shore, but I could not see any evidence of a tall inland *Arbutus*. I hope to be able to visit at some future time to investigate the report of the tree.

In retrospect, a thought, perhaps a theory hit me. I was pondering why some large old *Arbutus* trees, such as the one just described or the one along Foster Road on Thetis Island, grew straight up among the other tall conifer trees around it. In contrast, I have seen other *Arbutus* trees growing in the woods snaking their way up to the overstory? I believe in the case of the large *Arbutus,* those trees had been growing before the adjacent trees had grown tall, so they did not need to hunt for breaks in the overstory for sun. Perhaps even, the trees adjacent may had been cut for lumber years early on but the *Arbutus* not offering good lumber material had been saved. In such a case, the ones I now saw were replacement trees that grew much faster than the *Arbutus* only now reaching the same height as it. Opposite to this trend, are the younger snake like *Arbutus* I have seen in the forest. I believe these had begun growing when other much taller conifers were already present. Therefore, these *Arbutus* trees would have to had hunt for breaks in the overstory as they grew, hence their sinuous growth pattern.

Finally, one must bear in mind; my observations were just moments or snapshots in time of the life of the trees. Consequently, the trees' forms or structures were a record of what had happened years before in their history. Yes, a history of their struggle, an account that is informative, if we can only properly read it.

Figure `11.3 A. A southern view of the base of the tree 8/2/2019 showing the presence of a burl with green *Arbutus* sprouts present there. B. Northern view of the upper trunk and branches of the tree demonstrating that is dead with no green foliage. I had observed no green foliage in 2016, again in 2017, and lastly 2019.

Chapter Twelve:

Love at Home - An Anacortes Tree

The trail to this tree was very short, no cruising, no airplane trips. It is found right here in Anacortes where I live, alongside a busy thoroughfare. I must have passed it a hundred times when I used to live outside Anacortes, yet somehow never noticed it, perhaps because 32nd Street is the main west-east access road into the commercial area. Nevertheless, once I finally recognized it for the botanical treasure that it is, I asked myself how I could have been so oblivious. After all, this magnificent expression of nature towers over the power lines and the Victorian home in whose front lawn it grows.

The tree's trunk splits at eighty-five inches above the ground into two huge trunks, each meandering skyward and forking into multiple branches, as of if each had its own idea about how best to capture the sunlight. (Figure 12.1 C) The character of the tree seems to reflect the very quaint but flamboyant Victorian-style house where it grows, as well as the character of the owners, particularly Mr. Russell L. Hibler, the patriarch of the home. The environment of both the home and the tree itself must promote longevity. Mr. Hibler died in 2015 at the age of 101. Mrs. Hibler passed away at age 90 and the 124 year-old tree, my estimate of its age, still remains and looking healthy in most ways. [115]

Russell and his wife Ethel moved to this home from Virginia in 1947, with their two sons Harry and Cranston. Russel was a welder by trade and had worked in Anacortes for two different businesses before opening his welding and machine shop, which used to sit on the site of what is now Seafarers' Memorial Park. His hobby revolved around steam engines. He built two steamboats from 1959-1995 which could be seen at various times around the San Juan Islands. The last one, which he called *Letha*, was later bought by W.H.G. Schlager, who kept her at Lake Whatcom and renamed her the Whatcom Princess. [116] This name was quite fitting, as she was indeed a very classy little boat, what with her enclosed cabin, protruding smokestack, white stripping running from bow to stern, and generally perky look. After retiring in 1995, Mr. Hibler shifted the focus of his hobby to steam cars, first building a 1/3 scale radio-controlled model and then a full-scale Loco mobile. He would meet regularly with a group of men at a local restaurant in Anacortes, always sitting at a table reserved for their enthusiastic discussions. I recall seeing Russel there a time or two, but I didn't personally know him. His son, Harry, often lent a hand in the construction of the steam cars in Russell's shop, located just behind the Hibler home. I speculate that the men's passion for the craft may have mysteriously inspired an extraordinary pace of growth in the Madrona in their front yard. How else, after all, could its diameter have increased (as I calculated it to have) at a rate of about one-half inch per year?

I determined this utilizing a photograph Harry had sent me of the tree in front of the house, with his dad standing on a ladder resting against the house. [117] I estimated the tree diameter to be about half the height of his father in 1958 (about thirty-five inches). In January 2017, I measured the diameter at a height of four and a half feet and found it to be sixty-four inches, its circumference to be a bit over thirteen feet, and its height to be approximately sixty-five feet. Assuming the diameter had increased just under two and a half feet in 59 years gave me the above estimate of ½ inch per year, a healthy growth rate. The unobstructed southern exposure provides the tree plenty of sunshine, most likely the nutrients and water for the lawn have been beneficial. I recently learned that an underground stream may be flowing there which certainly would add more hydration.

Harry told me that when they were young, he and his brother used to climb around in the tree. I asked if his mother was ever concerned about this and he said no, she seemed to trust that they wouldn't fall and hurt themselves. One time Harry said they noticed what looked like a tree growing out of their roof. It was on the north side, where two sections of the roof form a "V." They had to assemble a scaffold to get up there, and, once they had, found that a tree had started to grow in the debris that had collected from fallen leaves and bark. He didn't say what kind of tree it was, but it could well have been a Madrona, as I suspect Madrona berries fell regularly on the roof every fall.

The property had been for sale for a while after Russell's death, but Harry told me that a buyer from Seattle had recently purchased it. What would the new owner do? Would they let the tree keep on living, would they remodel the house, or would they both fall to demolition and new construction as many old houses had? I certainly hoped that would not happen. As the months and then three years went by, whenever I passed it, I was relieved to see the tree growing and the house still looking as stately as ever.

It was October again and I was once more happily observing the bright red clusters of berries appearing on the Madrona trees. They complemented and contrasted with the red, orange, and yellow leaves of the Maple and other deciduous trees which were dressing in their fall colors. As I drove past some of these, I suddenly had an inspiration. Wouldn't it be fantastic if I obtained berries and thus seeds from the stately big Anacortes tree? That spring I had luck in starting two seedlings from the berries I had acquired the previous fall from a big tree in Port Angeles, WA. (This famous tree I describe later in chapter fifteen). Encouraged with this small success I thought maybe I could start seedlings from this marvelous Anacortes tree. I turned on to M street and headed towards the former Hibler house. Pulling to a stop by the house I parked the car and started thinking how should I do this? I noticed there were lights on indicating the owner was home. I decided it would be best to ask if it was okay to pick berries rather than just blundering ahead and doing it. The clusters of berries on the tree were too high to reach without a tool but the wind had blown many off. Donning my mask because of the COVID -19 virus pandemic, I stepped onto the first rung of the stairs to the door with a touch of trepidation unsure of what greeting I would receive. I noticed a sign over the door stating, White House. Interesting, I thought, I had not noticed that before, but I also noticed it did not say welcome!

Nevertheless, the two-panel glass door beckoned with a white sash hanging on the inside. As I approached, I saw a woman coming towards the door, like she was expecting me. Depressing the doorbell, I heard it chime, and she indicated to me to come in. I lowered my mask so she could see I was not a desperado, if so at least one willing to reveal my face. Raising it back up again I opened the door. She was interestingly dressed in a colorful and intriguing designed top. Her brunette hair with hints of curls was long but above the shoulders spread to each side of her face. I later noticed she had a comb in her hand so I must have interrupted her. She had a smile almost like she was expecting me perhaps thinking I was a different person. Stepping inside, looking around, I saw the home was delightful, everything restored to the Victorian style, it reflected the external architecture of the dwelling. To the left as one enters, was a formal sitting and dining parlor with a charming tapestry hanging on the far wall depicting two white swans and a young couple. A black wrought iron bar wrapped with white curtain supported and accented it. The original brick fireplace now painted white completed the room to the right. To the left, a bay and two side windows faced the street. Two matching but not identical couches offered visitors a place for leisure conversation. Returning to the entrance, to the right of where one enters, was a more casual room beckoning with a couch for relaxing by the window. However, looking to the center, a straight staircase immediately embraced me which seemed to climb forever, topped with a Nautical Chart mounted on the far end wall.

I explained to her that I was interested in her tree and wanted to obtain a few berries from it. She said my timing was particularly good as she was putting her house up for sale that very day and she initially thought I was the real estate agent coming to put a lock box on the door. She clarified that she had had a stroke sometime before and could not keep the house maintained any longer. As our conversation progressed, I learned that she had been a realtor in Denver for many years and had a Victorian style house there. Several years ago she had sold it and moved to Seattle. Later she learned of this house in Anacortes, purchased it, and she and her husband moved here. They fit well into Anacortes with their love of the old house and boating in the adjacent sea with their 28ft Aspen Cat. However unfortunately, her husband became ill, then later died and she was left alone.

Since the listing for the house had just been published, she anticipated people would be coming that day to view the house and based on her real estate experience she wanted the house to be welcoming including having all the lights on. However, because of her stroke she needed help to turn them on. She asked if I could turn on the lights upstairs, in the basement, downstairs and in the garage. I guess I did not look or sound like a desperado for her to trust me to do this. This request gave me an unprecedented opportunity to visit the house and the shop where Mr. Hibler had kept his machine tools and conducted his hobby work. It also gave me a chance to snap pictures of the various rooms, and to see the Madrona tree from the eyes of a person living in the house looking out. I was particularly impressed with the many bedrooms that were upstairs. There was a little kitchenette with a refrigerator included which I later learned Mr. Hibler had set up for a caregiver during the latter years of his life.

Through many windows one obtains a view of the Madrona tree. Many hefty branches hung adjacent to the decks, particularly the upper deck. It was easy to see how these *chariots to the sky* would call young boys, begging them to be climbed and so had the young Hibler boys succumbed to that call. When I remarked to Carol Ann, the current owner, that the son, Harry had told me about their climbing, she said that the other brother, Cranston, had been killed in the Vietnam war. I did not know, but later learned he died from multiple fragmentation wounds in the Thua Thein Province on March 30, 1970. He was in the 501st Infantry. The Thua Thein Province is a central region in South Vietnam along the coast where the ancient Imperial City is located. In fact, we had visited that city in 2005, but had no idea of the sad event that had occurred to the Hibler boy years before. It is strange how the pathways of lives may intertwine with others like branches of a Madrona tree. These upper decks were a favorite of Carol Ann and she referred to them as a widow's walk or widow's watch. In fact, she said she often would step out on them and talk to her deceased husband when she felt lonely.

After turning on the lights upstairs I proceeded to the back of the main floor where there was a modern kitchen with a delightful breakfast nook with a view of the morning sun. Out the back of the kitchen a door opened to another deck with steps descending to the garage. It was an L- shaped configuration that probably evolved as an add-on when Mr. Hibler's moved in his machine tools and set up a work area. It now was of course empty of all his tools and had been replaced by other odds and ends of the current owner. I turned on all the lights as requested, went back in the house to complete my task by going down to the very roomy basement. Returning to the main floor Carol Ann was standing in front of a mirror applying a curling wand. I thanked her and said I would get out of her hair now, figuratively speaking, but I would be back in a few days to obtain berries from the Madrona tree. She smiled, perhaps professionally, having to deal with all kinds of customer humor in the past, but she said most genuinely that I was indeed welcome to return anytime and obtain as many berries as I desired.

A week later I did revisit, a For-Sale sign adored the front lawn, and almost all the berries were gone from the tree branches due the strong south winds of the prior week. However, there were plenty of berries scattered on the lawn and front walk. I picked up several bags full selecting the ripest ones. The next time I paused by the house it was January 4, 2021, the lights off, the For-Sale sign gone, and the listing on the realtor website said the sale was pending. What will happen to the house and tree when the new owners take over, I pondered? I did feel concern again but since I had berries from that beautiful tree in my refrigerator, undergoing cold temperature striation for spring germination, I was more confident of the tree's legacy. I anticipated in the new season, new babies, new seedlings, and start of a new generation.

However, living stories never end they just progress. Therefore, in October of 2021 I returned to the house to obtain some more berries. I was encouraged by my earlier acquisition as I now had two seedlings about one and half inches tall growing from those berries picked the previous fall. There had been some changes in the yard as the new owners had added a partial fence. As I was walking around the front yard peering at the lawn looking for berries the door opened, and a man stepped out asking if he could help me. I explained what I was doing, and he introduced himself as Kevin Harris the new owner. He happily discussed the history of the tree and the house of which much, he already knew. Then he took me on his porch where we had a south-east view of the tree and showed me a big crack that had formed in the tree (Figure 12.1B). This development was justifiably of concern to him. He had talked with someone from the city's Park Department and the recommendation was to do nothing just wait to see what the natural outcome would be. Kevin certainly didn't want to take any drastic steps to the tree which was of course a favorite to many people, including themselves. He said he would just follow that advice for now.

Unfortunately, I must leave the reader in suspense, as I am also uncertain, pondering what will happen to the tree. The story is yet to be written. However, I did acquire a bag of berries from that beautiful but hurting tree. I will use these in spring planting, perhaps as insurance for more seedlings. If something terrible happens at least there will be children to carry on the legacy of this one hundred twenty-something-year-old majestic Madrona tree.

Figure 12.1 Views of the Anacortes Madrona at 32nd and M streets I estimate to be 124 years old in 2016 (see text). C. Picture of the tree in front of the Victorian style house. A. The base of the tree in 2016 looking northwest with its prominent trunk division. B. A southeast view of the tree in 2021 showing the split that had developed.

Chapter Thirteen:

A Sunshine Coast Affair - Savary Island's Tree

The engine hummed evenly. The bow dipped, rose, hesitated, twisted slightly, dropped again, like a slow waltz. The water's surface was placid, almost as if it were glued together, cohesive and without ripples from the wind, yet it rolled and wobbled as disturbances from passing boats moved through it, lifting and dropping the bow. The surface was thus continually active, with light and dark regions changing places. The tachometer sat steady at 2300 RPM, the bearing at 316 degrees, and the surface speed at 8.2 knots, indicating a current of 8/10 knot in our favor. The northern tip of Harwood Island slowly gave ground off our port side as we plowed north.

After a week or more of fires in British Columbia's mainland, the sky remained a blanket of mist and smoke. The sun, when observable, was a deep, fiery orange. Looking back, I saw that periodic waves were receding at an angle of perhaps thirty degrees on each side of our stern, about five wavelets, before collapsing into froth. Immediately behind the stern, the water rolled out with turbulent foam churned by our propeller, paralleled by two frothing lines, trailing each side of the boat. All these sights diminished and finally disappeared into a gray curtain of fog and smoke. The autopilot kept us locked on our bearing, except when I occasionally disengaged it to take waves from passing boats at a better angle.

Looking forward, I noticed a slight shadow of an island, Savary Island, emerging from the gloom. Glancing at the chart plotter, I perceived that it, resembled a big banana, tips curled northeast and northwest. I munched on a sandwich. The time was 1:01 p.m., approximately five hours since we had departed Pender Harbor.

Savary Island, becoming more distinct now, was named in 1792 by Captain Vancouver, according to Andrew Scott. [112] It is unclear to maritime historians exactly who Savary was. In any event, the island is home to a large *Arbutus menziesii* tree measuring 5.58 meters in circumference, as reported in 1984's BC Big Tree Registry. [118] The tree is also noted in Anne & Laurence Yeadon-Jones' book. [119] In the book, it is described as a giant. This tree I hoped to see the next day, but for the moment I had to concentrate on the boat as we pulled into Lund to secure moorage.

That evening, we sat around a table with our friends, discussing how we should get to Savary Island. One of the options was to take a water taxi, as it was only a few miles away. The taxis ran every half-hour, I recognized them by the big wakes they left behind as they exited or returned to the harbor. However, if we opted to ride on one of these boats, we'd have to be back by noon to check out of the marina – something we couldn't be sure was feasible, since it would require leaving early in the morning on the taxi and thus missing a leisure breakfast at the nearby café, famous for its huge, scrumptious cinnamon rolls.

Everyone voted against that option. Every year, when we came this way, having breakfast at the café was a tradition to which we all very much looked forward to. Another possibility was to leave the marina with both of our boats and travel to the northeast side of Savary Island and anchor there. Once anchored, we could use both or one of our dinghies to go ashore. However, this idea didn't sound particularly appealing, either, since the shore slowly tapers into the ocean. Grounding the dinghy with several hundred feet of tethering line would be necessary to prevent its drifting off to sea as the tide came in. We didn't have that much line readily available. Of course, we could always use a dinghy anchor (I didn't have one myself, but our friends might have). This would avoid the need for the long line, but, if the tide were to come in, it would require swimming in freezing cold waters in order to get to the dinghy upon our return. Unsurprisingly, no one appeared quite willing to volunteer for that job.

Suddenly our friend Denny piped up: "Why don't we take our boats, but then instead of using dinghies, use our kayaks to go ashore? We could easily pull them up above the high-water line."

"Wow." I thought. That seemed like a great idea and promised a bit of adventure. We are all in our seventies now, so our *adventures* are no longer quite on the order of Mt. Everest expeditions.

At noon the next day, we departed for Savary Island. It was quite a sight as we arrived: small boats tethered to buoys, small runabouts grounded on the beach, and many boats coming and going. Float planes were also arriving and departing; they would land in the bay, and then ease right up to the edge of the shallow water. Their passengers would then step out into the sea with their luggage and trundle up the beach, then do the same when they departed. In a similar manner, the water taxis were unloading passengers before picking up a new set. There were, as well, small private runabout boats powering up as they prepared to coast up onto the sandy shore. People who had already arrived at the beach one way or another were enjoying the sun as they lay about the sand in their swimming suits. It looked as if we'd arrived on a Canadian holiday! We later learned that indeed we had, British Columbia Day, to be exact!

Dropping and securing our anchor, we unloaded our two single-person kayaks. I held my wife's kayak in place against our boarding ladder, and steadied it while she got in. As I released her, she paddled off like a duckling swimming away from its mother. Next, I secured my kayak to the boarding ladder, gathered my camera and other gear, and stepped into the kayak with as much dignity as I could muster in the face of considerable waves rolling in from other boats, and given my seventy something age and less-than-perfectly limber body. Releasing the kayak from the ladder, I, too, paddled off like a duckling from the mother boat.

Incidentally, the addition of the boarding ladder to our boat was something which, after an awkward situation earlier that summer, we had learned to treat as a strict necessity. While attempting to climb out of the kayak and back into the main boat, I had tipped, unceremoniously, over and spilled into the sea. I had left myself with a hopelessly, and potentially tragically, inadequate remedy for this sort of situation: a looped rope hanging into the water. Although my brain had assured me that I should be able to pull myself out with this rope, my muscles apparently disagreed. Indeed, but for the heroic and compassionate assistance of some people who came by in another boat, this book would not be in your hands.

Back to our Savary Island adventure. Once in the water with our kayaks, we looked around and found our friends to be in their own double kayak, heading our way. We were soon joining the people on the beach, tugging our kayaks up above the high tide point. On the way, I noticed a little girl in her tiny bathing suit, she was perhaps all of eighteen months, crying her little heart out. Her mother was venturing into the shallow sea to greet her family, who were arriving in a water taxi. This must have been a frightening sight indeed to the young girl: her mother leaving her and going into the ocean. I didn't watch long, but I am sure she was soon consoled by her returning mother. This was just one of the many sights along the beach, including the seagulls and the scalloped sand.

Leaving the kayaks, we emerged onto the dusty road which paralleled the beach. We looked around, knocking off the sand from our shoes and feet as best we could. People were being collected and transported to their cottages at various locations on the island. The cab service seemed to consist of pickup trucks rather than cars. These trucks were loaded with people and their traveling gear; they reminded me of the transport services in Guatemala. As we walked up the road toward our destination, I kept checking the navigation on my phone. Glancing around, I observed to my surprise large *Arbutus* trees growing along the road, some at least three feet in diameter.

Moving along the road, up a hill, we steadily drew away from the hubbub of the beach. The farther we went, the more the beach sounds were muted by the large trees on either side of the road. Soon we could hear almost nothing except our own chatter and the noise of an occasional passing vehicle. Spiraling Douglas firs and *Arbutus* trees crowded the sky along the road. In many places the trunks of the firs were four feet in diameter. The main road was called Vancouver Boulevard. It climbed up from the beach and became the backbone of transportation for the island.

Huffing a little, we passed a bike rental shop, a closed pub, and a small but active store selling ice cream. We agreed to stop on the way back. We then turned up a side road, heading south toward the center of the island. Meandering through a residential area, we observed cabins and other, more elegant homes. Some had been there for ages, some were new, and others were still under construction. We chatted with a couple who were out walking with their dog. We asked them if they knew where the big Madrona tree was, but they didn't seem to understand. Then we remembered that we were in Canada and rephrased the question accordingly: "Do you know where the big *Arbutus* tree is?" Ah, now they had it!

"Yes," they said, "you are very close. You can go either right or left at the next junction, but right is the shorter route."

Excited about seeing the tree, I quickened my pace down the shorter route. The others followed. In a few minutes we came to another junction, at which a sign declared: Arbutus Lane. Turning left, we followed the GPS instructions, but it didn't seem to end at any big tree. Instead, it led to the middle of a big Salal (*Gaultheria shallon*) patch. There were some other nice *Arbutus* specimens nearby, but clearly no heritage tree. "Well, now what do we do?" seemed to be the common thought. We heard someone running a power motor off behind a house to our left. I headed in that direction and found a man in his backyard operating a saw. When I asked him where the big *Arbutus* tree was, he retorted, "It's just down the road a few houses, towards the bluff. The house has a For Sale sign in front of it." Oh, I thought, I know where that is, as we passed it earlier.

We stopped at the site and looked around. The top of a large tree could be seen above the house, toward the bluff. As we were standing in the road debating our next move, we saw a woman working in the adjacent yard. We started a conversation with her, and, yes, she said that this was indeed the location of the big *Arbutus*. It was on the property next door to hers, which her son Richard Warring owned; however, he wasn't home at the moment. She told us that her name was Lorraine, and that she had lived there for quite some time. When we asked her if we could come into the yard to see it, she kindly obliged us.

Rounding her house and stepping onto her back porch, we saw it at once: the giant *Arbutus* tree, leaning slightly away from us. (Figure 13.1A) It was perhaps the most unusual of its kind I had ever seen. In some ways it looked like a sculpture, rather than a living tree. Or, put another way, the main trunk somehow seemed both dead and alive. (Figure 13.2) A large, wide red region ran from the base up the tree, wrapping slightly to the right and following a large diverging branch. The live red region contrasted with the obviously dead areas, which looked rather like bleached driftwood. My eyes trailed up the large right diverging branch of the tree, to the point at which it divided into a dead branch on the left, and a live, twisting and peeling large branch on the right. (Figure 13.1A) The right branch continued up in a serpentine manner, until it dove into multiple branches with green foliage. These were the limbs we had seen above the roof of the house from the street. Returning to the first bifurcation, to the left of it was a large trunk which rose a short distance, terminating at a point where it had clearly been truncated with a saw. Lorraine revealed that this section had been excised after the more distal portion had been dead for a long time and needed removal.

Most of the large, now removed section lay in the yard, principally hidden by vigorously growing Salal bushes. Toward the far side of this truncated region, a much smaller branch appeared to still be alive, rising up before corkscrewing to the left and ending in green foliage. The typical heavy and tile-like bark, found near the base of most *Arbutus menziesii* trees, was present in the form of patches throughout the dead and living regions. In the deceased regions, it overlaid the dead wood, and in the living regions it abutted the red bark. Whether the bark underneath the live region was green, as is typical, I could not tell. There were a few small, healed cankers near the base of the tree in the red area. Several of the upper branches offered intriguing shapes when viewed from different angles. (Figure 13.3) The tree is about a hundred feet or so from the south bluff of the island, with no obstructions to deflect the ample sunlight it must receive. The soil was quite sandy and well populated with Salal bushes.

Before we left, Lorraine related a story about a fellow named Jim Spilsbury, a genuine legend on the island and, indeed, along the entire British Columbia coast. He was born in 1905, in Findern, Derbyshire, but emigrated with his parents to Canada as a child. He grew up in British Columbia, mainly on Savary Island. He was a Renaissance man one could say, who became an expert in marine radio and founded a successful radio communications company in which he visited clients by boat, up and down the British Columbia waterways, solving their radio communication needs.[120] In World War II, because of the difficulty in obtaining gas for boats he changed to a small seaplane for this function. That later mushroomed into a commercial airline. Starting with just this one plane, he and his partners developed one of the three largest carriers in Canada. The company was sold in 1955 at which time it had thirty planes in its service. He also authored several books and was an avid photographer and painter. Many of his adventures can be read in several books [121, 122] and are described in a wonderful YouTube movie [123] .

In 1992, his daughter had brought him over to Lorraine's house. He sat on their deck, relaxing and looking at the big tree. He declared that it hadn't changed one bit since his childhood!

Lorraine further revealed that the tree had attracted a lot of attention over the years, not all of it desirable. She said that, one time, a group of women had come and surrounded the tree, holding hands, presumably to gauge its circumference. She didn't explicitly say so, but I got the impression that she'd half-expected them to break out in some type of mystic's chant. However, they had turned out to be harmless *tree huggers*. Continuing, she exclaimed that people used to come right into the yard without asking. She would often find them standing on the deck at all hours of the day and night. Finally, the Warrings built a fence near the road to keep people from popping in uninvited.

As we had already observed, there were a lot of big *Arbutus* trees on the island. However, we soon learned that even more large trees could be found nearby. In fact, a quite husky tree grew just east of Lorraine's deck. (Figure 13.4) It was a very healthy specimen. We measured the circumference of this tree fir heights of three and a half feet and then four and a half feet from the base. We found, respectively, circumferences measuring 13'4" and 12'9" (4 and 3.9 m). By contrast, the big *Arbutus* was 18'10" and 17'11" (5.7 and 5.5 m) at the same respective heights. This second tree leaned out over Lorraine's house and was probably about two and a half times the height of the house. However, it was difficult to gauge its actual height and breadth because its branches were intertwined with some conifers. This tree must have been a daughter tree of the big *Arbutus*, itself probably more than 150 years old. The big *Arbutus* was several hundred years old, most likely already there when Captain Vancouver named the island. Lorraine showed us several infant *Arbutus* trees that were shooting up. She said they tended to sprout often but didn't seem to survive very long.

We thanked Lorraine, then bade her good-bye and headed back toward the beach. When we got to the store, we stopped. It was time to celebrate our little adventure with some ice cream cones. These creamy delicacies were explored with our tongues and greedily devoured as we headed down the road. Returning to our boats, Darlene and I secured the kayaks, and I started the engine, pulling forward to raise the anchor. As we looked north, we saw that our friends were already well on their way and headed toward Desolation Sound, a hazy shape disappearing into the smoky horizon.

Figure 13.1 A. The Savary Island Heritage *Arbutus* tree seen from Lorraine Warring's deck.
B. The smoky view from the back of our boat as we approached Savary Island.

Figure 13.2 Closeup of the base of the Heritage tree.

Figure 13.3 Views of the upper branches of the ancient tree.

Figure 13.4 An attractive and sizable *Arbutus* growing next to Lorraine's deck.

Chapter Fourteen:

The Grand Slam – Heritage Trees in Victoria, Crofton, and the Islands Salt Spring and Galiano

The winter of 2018 was receding when sitting at my computer I scanned the list of large heritage *Arbutus* trees on the University of British Columbia's Big Tree Registry. [124] I realized I had seen and photographed three of the twelve but there were still nine trees listed that I had not had the pleasure of meeting.

As the spring progressed the Madrona trees bloomed and then the green berries appeared. In other fields the spring athletic sports had advanced towards their summer phase, baseball leading the pack. In Seattle, the professional team the Mariners were on television almost every day now. My feet were getting itchy not to play baseball but to see the remaining heritage *Arbutus* trees. Studying the geographical distribution of them: six on Vancouver Island; two on Salt Spring Island; and one on Galiano Island an idea struck me. I could hit a home run with the bases loaded, A Grand Slam! That is, Darlene and I could take a three-day trip and visit all of the remaining trees in one sweep, that is of course, if she would agree. I thought: "How to propose it to her?" So, I casually suggested: "How about taking a little travel adventure?"

She perked up, always ready for an adventure, then stopped and looked at me with suspicious scrutiny, holding it for several moments she said: "Are there Madrona trees involved in this adventure?"

Well of course I had to confess. However, the warming days seemed like a stimulant to traveling and I think she was eager to do something. After thinking about it for a minute she then turned to me smiling and exclaimed: "It could be fun."

The first tree on our list was at the Royal Canadian Naval Force Docks in Victoria, a secured area. I hadn't known whom to contact to obtain permission to enter the base. I started by calling the Harbour Master there, a few days before our trip. He answered, his tone perfectly cordial, but he wondered what *Arbutus* tree I was after, since there were a lot of them on the base. I referred him to the website listing the big *Arbutus* and he gave me the number to the PR department. I would need to contact someone in it, he said, to make arrangements to come on the base and see the tree in question. After a few more calls, I'd managed to persuade the folks in charge to let Darlene and me visit the dockyards. Rodney, a PR representative, would escort us to the tree. We would meet up around one o' clock the following afternoon, at the entrance to the base.

After packing my equipment into the car, Darlene and I headed out on the morning of June 12, 2018, at around quarter of seven. Our aim was to catch the early ferry from Anacortes to Sydney, British Columbia. Arriving in Sydney at about half-past eleven we had time for a quick lunch before driving down to Victoria. While eating, Darlene and I struck up a conversation with a gentleman seated at the next table. As I remember him now and consider how best to describe him, the words seasoned and salty leap into my mind. Particularly, salty as having long experience with boats.

Upon learning of my interest in the *Arbutus* tree, he told me how the wood used to be exploited on boats for commercial purposes. The wood was first fashioned into blocks using heavy machining equipment, then drilled and employed as bearing blocks for the propeller shaft. All boats with interior engines and propeller shafts protruding from their hulls require bearing blocks in order to prevent an influx of water while permitting the shaft to pass outside the boat and provide a low-friction support. Being impermeable to water, the *Arbutus* wood had worked very well in these early days. It was very hard and therefore durable, lasting far longer than boats with bearings made of less sturdy materials. By drilling a hole, the size of the shaft and adding a grease or oil port perpendicular to the shaft for lubrication, the boats might easily last for a decade or more. Eventually the *Arbutus* wood used in the boats was replaced by rubber-based bearings. Nowadays, even more sophisticated technologies and hardier materials are put to use for this purpose.

Finishing our lunch and heading for Victoria, we were soon at the dockyards' gate and there met Rodney. After loading my equipment into his car, he drove us to a large *Arbutus* tree. It was gorgeous, with big, exposed red branches. I began snapping pictures. But soon a gentleman came along, who turned out to be, of all people, the Harbour Master I had spoken to by phone before our trip. "You must be the fellow from the University of Washington. You're taking pictures of the wrong tree" he grinned. "The one you want is around the other side of that building."

Sure enough, we could see the upper branches of a large *Arbutus* peeking over the building he'd pointed to. "Ok" I thought to myself, I lowered my camera, thanked him for the tip, and we drove around the building.

Skirting the structure, a spectacular and astonishing tree came into view. It had multiple large trunks spreading out from its ancient and distorted base. As I got close, I could see it had four major trunks, each were imperfectly aligned with either the north, south, east, or west directions. The diameter of the north trunk was about one meter, as was that of the east trunk. The west and south trunks were slightly smaller (0.9 meter). It was difficult to obtain accurate measurements, however, because the trunks weren't straight at all; rather, they twisted and curled at sharp angles (Figures 14.1, 14.2, & 14.3).

The trunks' lower halves were covered with a heavy bark, as was typical of *Arbutus*, but the upper trunks were exposed, with a thin, predominantly reddish bark not yet peeling. Later in the season, I anticipated, they would begin to exfoliate, and the bark underneath would most likely be smooth and green in color. Overall, the tree was quite complex in form. I measured the circumference below the bifurcations as best I could and found it to be 28 ft (8.6 m). I followed the contour to get the best estimate. The maximum diameter of the main trunk was about 10 ft (3 m) in the east-west directions and roughly 4.4 ft (1.3 m) in the north-south directions.

There were some fuel barrels on one side of the tree, which served nicely as qualifying photography markers, each one-half meter in diameter and just a under a meter in height. I used these markers for scaling a photograph, from which I later estimated the height of the living tree to be about 43.7 ft (13 m) and the width of the crown to be about 51 ft (15.5 m). Two central branches, taller than the rest, were utterly dead, entirely devoid of leaves. Curiously, however, the rest of the tree appeared quite healthy. The tree was surrounded by asphalt, except for the area immediately around the base. This tree must have been here at this very location around the time the harbour was first discovered by the Spaniards, in the late eighteenth century. One of the brick buildings bore a sign declaring the year of its construction, 1894, long after the tree had sprung up.

While I was recording the sundry measurements, several people came by. Many of them paused for a moment, some even longer, curious about what I was up to and about the tree itself. Most of them had walked right by it every day for months or years now, but of course few, if any of them, had ever paid much attention to it, simply regarding it as just another tree in spite of its beauty. When I had finished taking all my measurements and photographs, we drove with Rodney back to the gate. We thanked him for the courtesy of letting us onto the base, our thoughts already turning to the next tree on the list.

Figure 14.1 Heritage *Arbutus* tree at HMC Dockyard Esquimalt west of Victoria, BC Westerly views: A. Base of the tree, B. the total tree.

Figure 14.2 Views of the base of the Dockyard tree (June 12, 2018) A. Looking south, B. looking north.

Figure 14.3 Views of some of the upper branch structure of the Dockyard *Arbutus*.

It, too, was located in the Esquimalt area, and so was fairly close by. We arrived shortly at the given latitude and longitude coordinates, which, as it happened, were near the entrance to Witty's Lagoon Regional Park. However, my phone's GPS showed that the tree was situated in a stand of bushes. I was certain we were in the right spot, but there was no sign of any *Arbutus* tree. I pondered what our next step should be. I spoke to a family that was just starting off on the trail that weaved its way through the park, hoping they might be locals or at least tourists more knowledgeable about the area than we. I asked them where the large *Arbutus* tree was located. They didn't seem to know, but they did say there were a number of large trees on the other side of the park, near the lagoon, and suggested we get there via the west entrance.

Back in the car, we drove about a quarter of a mile, soon arriving at the parking lot adjacent to the west entrance. I began to walk down the trail and almost immediately came upon the tree. It was very recognizable, because of a large bulge protruding from one side of the main trunk. (Figures 14.4) This prominent feature was quite unusual. It is a type of burl, usually if present, found at the bottom of the tree at the start of the roots. A number of other smaller protuberant regions emerged from the tree at various points along the main trunk. I had no idea what caused these swellings. Overall, the tree was large and seemed to be quite healthy.

I proceeded to photograph and measure it as best I could. It was difficult to get accurate height and breadth measurements of the crown of the tree as it merged with the foliage of its immediate neighbors. At the vertical midpoint of the bulge, the height was 4.5 ft (1.4 m), a circumference of 14.6 ft (4.5 m). The bulge extended below its midpoint 2.5 ft (0.76 m), and there the circumference was just over 11.5 ft (3.5 m) with a diameter of 4.9 ft (1.5 m). A large branch projected from the main trunk about 9.8 ft (3 m) from its base, in such a way that it was almost perpendicular to the tree itself. The tree was located just off the trail, which was composed of gravel packed from the many people that had walked along it.

It was finally time to move on to the third tree, as it was getting rather late in the afternoon. While this one was also nearby, it was situated on private land and no definitive directions or coordinates were available. So we decided to skip that one for the time being and instead move on to the fourth on our list.

Once again relying on my phone's GPS for guidance, we worked our way through the five o'clock, rush-hour traffic to McDonald Park. Somehow, we just missed the coordinate location by our first drive-by, mostly because there was no place to stop and the traffic was thick with evening commuters. About eight hundred meters further down the road there was a turnoff, from which a trail emerged and crossed the highway. Pulling off there, we were surprised to see a large *Arbutus* tree standing right in front of us almost saying, "Hello!"

Could this really be the one we were after? This spot did not lie anywhere near the coordinates indicated for the tree to be located. Confounded, I set out walking along the road in the direction of record. As I drew closer, it soon became evident that there was, in fact, no large *Arbutus* anywhere within sight. I didn't yet give up all hope, however, since the given coordinates did place the tree quite a way from the road, toward the beach area. But even after scanning the small valley below, I still didn't see any big *Arbutus* tree. In fact, there was a large depression indicating that a slide had occurred here relatively recently leaving a cliff dropping thirty meters or more to the beach area. The tree had been recorded in the Big Tree Registry in 1993; plenty of natural phenomena (winds, rain, storms, floods, etc.) might have transpired here in the interim. There were several *Arbutus* trees of fairly good size distributed along the road adjacent to the cliff, but none of especially remarkable size.

Returning to the big *Arbutus* near our car, I decided that I would measure and photograph it; perhaps it was the one on the list, after all, or at least genetically related to it (Figure 14.5). The circumference was about 14.7 ft (4.5 m), with a diameter of 4.9 ft (1.5 m). The tree remained straight for about 20 ft (6 m) after which trunks emerged diverging quite dramatically. On the side of the road there was a cavity in the tree which, would perhaps ultimately prove detrimental to it. However, the tree did at the time appear to be perfectly healthy. The bark, like that of most such trees, was heavy at the base and thinner near the upper branches, where the thick cork began to taper into a lighter, less dense material reddish brown in color. None of this higher-up bark had begun to peel yet, but I imagined it would a bit later in the season, when the weather was bound to grow hot.

Hopping into the car we set off for the fifth and final tree of the day. This one lay north of us, rather near the Swartz Bay Ferry terminal in Sydney. The GPS routed us along several remote, and at times somewhat rough roads, but eventually led us to within a stone's throw of our destination. There was no tree immediately at the side of the road, but the coordinate mark indicated it was only about a hundred meters away.

I climbed out, gathering my equipment, and crossed into the woods, doing my best to beat back the thick foliage impeding my passage. Soon a tall, particularly handsome *Arbutus* emerged from the understory (Figure 14.6). It rose straight from the soil for about 3.9 ft (1.2 m), at which point it split off into three distinct trunks. The largest one was almost a 3.3 ft (1 m) in diameter, the others just over one-half that. The overall base was approximately 7 ft (2.1 m) in diameter, the circumference just over 20 ft (6 m), and the height an impressive 131 ft (40 m). This last measure struck me as rather implausible, until I remembered that the tree was situated in a grove of conifers, which essentially forced it to reach vertically to compete successfully for sunlight. The tree seemed healthy and peaceful in this quiet location buried deep in the woods. Incidentally, there was a tennis court not far away located in a small, cleared area in the woods, although, by the looks of it, it was seldom if ever used. After I'd completed my photography and measurements, we left for the hotel.

Figure 14.4 An unusual and large Arbutus at Witty's Lagoon Regional Park west of Victoria, BC near the west entrance. B. At a distance it is almost hid by the adjacent trees. C. The large growth on the trunk is visible with a closer view of it in A.

Figure 14.5 A substantial size Arbutus tree along the McDonald Park road, easterly view. Note the cavity at the base more visible in the close up of B.

Figure 14.6 A noteworthy size *Arbutus* along the Hillgrove Rd. west of the Swartz Ferry on Vancouver Is, B.C. (Lat. 48.68835°, Long. -123.442833°). A. See the carrying case 2 ft. (61 cm) long for a tripod for a camera is shown at the base of the tree for perspective. North view. B. Eastern view of the base with some minor branching, C. However, looking up the tree its immensity dwarfed me.

In the morning, feeling fresh, we left for the sixth tree, embarking on a trip which turned out to be something of a wild goose chase. First, we missed the ferry. Had we caught it in time, we would have shortened the driving distance considerably and avoided much of the morning traffic. Nevertheless, driving south, we did finally reach the Canadian One Freeway. It took us due west, then north along Vancouver Island. About an hour and a half later, we passed Nanaimo before continuing north toward the location the GPS had divulged. Getting as close as we could to the tree with the car, I finally cut the engine and, my legs more than ready to go back to work, I climbed out with a sigh of relief. Darlene said: "I will stay here and wait for you, don't get lost."

I noticed she was back reading her book before I had departed. I hiked back along a road where the tree was supposed to be, but either the coordinates were wrong or else it had been cut down for some reason. The tree had been registered some sixteen years prior, I remembered, so any number of explanations were possible for its absence. The location was right in the middle of an open area totally devoid of trees. All that grew there was Scotch Broom, an invasive species that will cover a clearing within a short time. I thought to myself, reluctantly accepting the fact that, by all appearances, Tree #6 was now history.

I returned to the car and we headed south to catch a ferry to Salts Spring Island, home to the next two trees on our list. The ferry in question departed Crofton on the Vancouver Island side and docked at Vesuvius Bay on Salt Spring Island. It made this trip eight times a day, taking about twenty minutes for each crossing.

Arriving at the ferry we waited in line. I almost immediately noticed the large *Arbutus* tree adjacent to the loading area (Figure 14.7). I had read about it on the internet some time ago. It wasn't listed in the Big Tree Registry, I recalled, but somebody had posted some information about it on a blog back in 2012, along with some photos of it. Included in the blog was a plea from Charronne, an anonymous tree hugger to save the tree. [125] The impressive size of this *Arbutus* was far from the only unusual thing about it. Indeed, I seemed to recall from the internet photograph, it was comprised of two major trunks emerging from the same root region. In the posted pictures, both trunks had appeared quite healthy, so something must have happened in the previous six years or so. The trunk nearest the road had been cut off around 11.5 ft (3.5 m) above the ground, along with many of the associated major branches. As for the remainder of the tree, the northeast trunk was flourishing, its numerous branches spread very widely, almost like open arms welcoming travelers to the ferry. I further noticed that the remnants of the spring blooming were unusually prominent, indicating there would be a heavy berry production.

Arriving at Salt Spring, we proceeded to the site of Tree #7. The year before I had tried, to no avail, to find this tree while boating to Salt Spring Island. After a long walk I had arrived at the coordinates, but there was no tree there just a vegetable farm. Later, I'd looked again at the tree listing and I'd noticed that a street address was also given, it seemed be at a location across the road from the spot in which I'd searched initially. Unfortunately, at that time it had been too late to go back and try again. This time, though, we drove straight to the road and proceeded down it slowly, toward the address provided, keeping our eyes peeled for the tree. No one was home at the house corresponding to the address, but two dogs did startle us with a rather vociferous greeting. As we drove back along the lane, we noticed a beautiful *Arbutus* standing just on the other side of a long fence, at most sixty meters from the edge of the road. *Perhaps this is the one?* However, since it sat on private property, I didn't want to risk getting in trouble by simply hopping the fence. We tried a second time later in the day but once again we found the home occupied by only the two dogs. Despite their threating barking, I taped a note to the door explaining who I was and what I was after. I included my phone number hoping to hear from them.

We stopped in downtown Ganges, made a reservation at a hotel, and then went to the visitor center. I inquired there about a large *Arbutus* tree (Tree #8) that was located near or in the Mount Maxwell Provincial Park. They were very helpful, and a woman there told us about going on a hike in the park, earlier in the spring which involved very difficult *bushwhacking*. Their group had encountered a huge *Arbutus* tree along their trek. Someone had told her it was the largest such tree in all of British Columbia. (Tree enthusiasts often make that claim so I have learned to take such statements lightly.) The tree in question did appear, though, to lie within our general vicinity, going by the coordinates provided in the Big Tree Registry – and, as it happened, was the second tree on our list of the Salt Spring Island collection.

We were unsure where exactly this tree was located, however: according to the GPS, it seemed to lie right along a road well up on the mountain. This didn't seem to correlate with the tree described by the woman at the visitor center. Nevertheless, we decided to simply drive as best we could to the given location. Shortly, out of Ganges a road led off the main motorway. We followed that, but the asphalt soon ended and became gravel. Continuing to deteriorate, further, it became dirt and gravel mixed. We wound our way up a steep hill. It had rained that morning, so much of the dirt had turned into mud. Large bumps and deep ruts began to appear along our path. I had to maneuver our little, initially clean, black Prius very carefully to avoid getting hung up on the large swells or dropping into one of the canyon like ruts. It reminded me of the driving trips in Baja Mexico and the Canary Islands, where I'd ventured off the thoroughfare seeking the remotely located *Arbutus* trees. I think Darlene was getting a little uneasy, not saying anything but fidgeting in her seat.

We followed the passage through the woods until we came, finally, to the location corresponding, we thought with the GPS coordinates. As I'd suspected, we found ourselves at the start of the Provincial Park, rather than the actual location of the tree. A series of trails appeared to originate there. After a moment's all-too-familiar discussion, I decided to park the car and simply follow the most promising-looking trail. It traveled first along the top of a prominent hill populated with Douglas Fir which seemed to become increasingly denser. It was obvious this was not the terrain where *Arbutus* grow. Since we had no definite coordinates and the park was extremely large, I knew it would be difficult, if not outright impossible to hunt down the tree absent additional information. The lady at the visitor center had suggested that, if necessary, I contact the group of hikers with whom she'd stumbled across the tree. Once a year they hike in that general area, she'd explained, usually in the spring. She'd recommended that I arrange to visit the park at that time and tag along with the group. I said we'd certainly make every effort to do so.

Turning back down the mountain, we jounced along toward Ganges, the site of our hotel. I would just have to cross the tree off my list for now. After dinner I decided to drive back out to where tree #7 was located and see if the owner(s) of that house might be home now. By this time, Darlene was tired of the adventure and ready to investigate the bed and the television in the hotel instead.

So back to and down the road that I felt quite familiar with, I went. As mentioned earlier, I was again greeted by the disharmony of barks, but this time, when I knocked, someone appeared. Leaning through an open window, he asked if he could help me. I explained that, if possible, I would love to see the big *Arbutus* tree up close, take some measurements and snap a few photos of it.

"What tree is that?" he replied. I pointed down the road to the spot in which the tree stood, inside the field. Following my finger and line of sight, he added: "Ah, I see. That's not on our property, I'm afraid. It belongs instead to our neighbor". He then directed me to the road that led to their house.

So off I went in pursuit of the neighbor. I knocked on the front door, and was soon greeted by a very warm, cordial woman. Her name was Valerie. Her face lit up as I explained who I was and what my purpose was in being there. As it turned out, she was as enthusiastic about *Arbutus* trees as I was! She agreed with me that it was a very beautiful tree indeed, and that its foliage was very full compared to that of most others of its kind. In fact, she said, she planned to marry her fiancé under that tree on the first of August of that very year!

She accompanied me to the tree, and we walked around its massive trunk, admiring it. (Figures F.14.8) It sat in a wide-open field, allowing the very bushy growth, and thus also yielded ample occasion to take several long-distance measurements of it, including a triangular measurement of its height. Looking east the tree was almost 5 ft (1.5 m) in diameter rising to about 9.8 ft (3 m) where it split into 3 trunks. (Figure 14.8B) Looking north, the largest trunk was just about 3.3 ft (1 m) in diameter, the second and third trunks about three-quarters of that. (Figure 14.8A) The circumference measured just over 17.4 ft (5.3 m) the height a remarkable 105 ft (32 m) and the breadth of the crown approximately 65 ft (20 m) (Figure 14.8C).

Amazingly, Valerie had told me that her neighbor also had a big *Arbutus* tree on *his* property. The neighbor in question, was the fellow with whom I'd chatted with earlier. He hadn't told me about his own *Arbutus* tree, but then I hadn't asked. She explained that this second tree was located behind her neighbor's house, situated in a grove, hence not visible from the front of the house. After completing my measurements of her tree, I debated whether to go back to the first house. I'd noticed several cars now in their driveway and parked along the side of the road by their front yard. If he was hosting a party of some kind, I mused, perhaps this wasn't the best time to bother the man about a tree. It was getting quite late in the evening, anyhow, so I decided to leave it for another time. Incidentally, the tree I measured that day, the one belonging to the lovely neighbor, was smaller in circumference than the one in the Registry by a full meter, but considerably taller. Perhaps, then, I ought to consider making another trek there sometime to try again at getting a look at the *Arbutus* we'd originally intended to see.

Seeing the final tree on my list (Tree #9) for this Grand Slam tour required taking a ferry which stopped at two other islands (North Pender and Mayne) before arriving at Galiano Island. This meant getting up quite early in the morning to catch the ferry that would afford time to find the tree on Galiano and yet still catch the later ferry to Tsawwassen on the BC mainland. We could then drive home to Anacortes from Tsawwassen, which was south of Vancouver, without further ado. Still half-asleep, we waited for the ferry. It was quiet, the morning early, it was sparkling with the activity of the birds and the aura of moisture in the air. The smooth glossy water lapped the rocky shore. When the boarding gate opened, we drove into the ferry, parked, and clomped up the steps seeking out first coffee and then the breakfast line.

By the time we arrived at Galiano, I was wide awake and very excited. Darlene with less enthusiasm would have preferred more time in bed. We had visited this island many times by boat but never had an opportunity to explore it with a mechanized vehicle. We drove off the ferry and onto the web of roads slowly, wanting to take in the gorgeous scenery and savor the view from the harbor, before proceeding across the island in pursuit of the last, hopefully most beautiful *Arbutus* yet.

On the way, we passed the Hummingbird Pub, which reminded us of the many trips we'd taken on the Pub Bus there. This bus makes round trips daily from the marina in the summer, located in Montague Bay. We often anchor or tie to one of the Provincial Park buoys in the bay. The Pub Bus is an old, colorful school bus converted into a vehicle serving less strictly academic purposes. Its driver, equally colorful, has a box full of CDs loaded with classic '60s tunes like Blueberry Hill. These he plays at a very loud volume, with a bus full of happy riders on the way home from the Pub who often provide accompanying backing vocals. Occasionally, a couple will try to dance in the aisle to the music. Their swaying is usually somewhat exaggerated, either due to the speed at which the bus rounds the turns or the overindulgence in the wide variety of libations on tap at the Hummingbird.

According to the coordinates listed for the tree, it was located almost at the end of the road at the northwest point of the island. Along the way, we stopped at a little turnout adjacent to a small park called Lovers' Leap. Indeed, it would be the last of the lovers if they leapt off the cliff there. My wife and I declined to volunteer, as we've spent too many seasons together to end the marriage so foolishly. Several, very pretty *Arbutus* trees were growing there, some quite petite. This side of the island faced the southwest, so it was an ideal environment for them, with plenty of good sun exposure. It also afforded an excellent view of Wallace Island, situated just across the waterway; we had boated there many times.

Before long we arrived at the coordinates of the final tree. Ah, yes! There it was, standing along the side of the road in all its unassuming glory - completely dead! (Figure 14.9)

The small branches at the very tip of what was left of this unfortunate colossal elder likely hadn't boasted any green foliage in many seasons. On the waterside of the tree there was a huge cavity about 7 ft (2 m) in height and 3 ft (0.9 m) wide. When I poked my head in there, I saw that the inside of the tree was completely hollow. In fact, it looked as if at one time a fire might have smoldered there. There was no sign at the base of the tree of any young sprouts one might expect to find of a burnt tree, if there had been any, they had long since disappeared.

Across from the tree there was a residence. I knocked on the door and an elderly, very pleasant woman answered. I told her who I was and what I was doing, and she replied that, while she and her husband had lived in the house for only thirty years, they had bought the property almost a half-century earlier. Before building their home, they had used a small cabin initially as a summer retreat. She was now ninety-two years old and had lost her husband a few years earlier. Her son lived with her now. She had a daughter who also lived on the island nearby. She said the tree had always been there. *A quiet and reliable neighbor I thought to myself.* She wasn't sure when it had finally met its demise. She had noticed there had not been much greenery on it for several years.

We ended our Grand Slam trip late in the day by catching the ferry to Tsawwassen. Waiting in line I did some mental arithmetic. We had set out to see nine trees. Two we'd crossed off the list; one we couldn't find; two may have been the wrong trees; and one we had added, the Crofton ferry tree. We had therefore seen seven large trees, and even if a couple of them hadn't been on our list, they had been unique enough that encountering them had been worthwhile.

Fairly satisfied, we boarded the ferry and about an hour later found ourselves at Tsawwassen. Exiting, we soon passed the road to Point Roberts, that peculiar little piece of the United States *stuck* in British Columbia on the south side of the Tsawwassen peninsula. I made a mental note that we ought to go there sometime and check it out.

Arriving home around nine o' clock that night, the sun was just beginning to sink over the San Juan Islands painting the sky a mixture of orange, red, and pink hue, a changing blend of colors. Our trip had also been a blend of surprises, awe, unanticipated events and fascinating findings, all the source of intrigue that motivates us researchers.

Figure 14.7 This nice *Arbutus* tree grows near the Crofton Ferry Terminal, BC. A. Southern view of the tree. B. A close up of the base of A., C. The view is looking west towards Salts Spring Island.

Figure 14.8 This elegant tree is on Salts Spring Island BC, east of the End Road. I call it *Valerie's Tree*. A. Northern view of the base with the 2 ft. (61 cm) tripod carrying case on the ground for perspective. B. Eastern view, and C. The total unusually bushy tree again looking East.

Figure 14.9 The reported Heritage tree on Galiano Island, BC. looked quite dead (southern view).

Chapter Fifteen:

Love Across the Water - The Remarkable Madrones in the Ports of the Olympic Peninsula

Two days before Halloween of 2019, undeterred by the looming threat of ghosts, goblins and black cats, Darlene and I drove about seven miles to the south from Anacortes to the Coupeville - Port Townsend ferry terminal. As we approached the entrance, I observed choppy waters in the terminal bay. A boater myself, I naturally felt some alarm at this sight. Once aboard, however, we were relieved to discover that the turbulence was due, not to the wind, but rather a local tidal eddy arguing with the incoming tide. The channel ahead was smooth and so was our trip, at least we thought it would be.

As the ferry cruised toward Port Townsend, we enjoyed a spectacular view of the Olympic Mountains, complete with snow-skirts around their peaks. A clear blue sky served as a picturesque backdrop to the waterfront of Port Townsend. Disembarking, we found our way to Fort Worden State Park and Alexander's castle. This brick edifice, shaped like an inverted T, has a centrally located *keep*, a windowed three-story tower with ostentatious battlements at its rectangular top. It is a castle only by American standards, too young and perhaps too small to qualify by most Europeans' definition. Nevertheless, it offers unique and rather comfortable lodging, available by reservation for those seeking a weekend getaway but tired of the region's more conventional lodging.

The castle was constructed by Reverend John Alexander in 1883, originally intended as an Episcopal rectory and marital home for him and the Scottish woman he planned to marry. Unfortunately for the reverend, when he arrived in Scotland to wed his betrothed, he was too late; she had already tied the knot with another suitor. A few years after returning from Scotland, Alexander resigned his ministry but maintained the castle as his private residence while turning his attention to other pursuits.[126-128] All of this I was to learn only later, however; the moment we arrived at the castle, my eyes were drawn north to an open field, where there stood a large tree I recognized at once as a Madrona, or *Arbutus*, to our Canadian friends. (Figure 15.1C) I had read about this tree on the internet and that was why we were there.

I began snapping photos of the tree as I approached it, and then, once closer, as has become my custom in such situations, continued to do so while circling it. It quickly became apparent to me that the tree was not a single Madrona! In fact, it was a whole *group* of Madronas! More precisely, a ring of them, all of which appeared healthy and had reached great heights. They were laden with red berries, many in large clumps. As I circled again around the trees, I counted eight main trunks, and all appeared to be growing from a common base. (Figure 15.1B) The outside circumference of the ring measured just shy of 30 ft (9 m). In the center of the ring was a depression of about 5 ft (1.5m) in diameter and 1ft (0.3 m) deep, a concave hollow, in which nothing appeared to grow save some remnants of a tree stump, a bit of organic debris, and some black material. (Figure 15.1A)

Making a third pass around this cluster of impressively sized specimens, I paused to measure what was clearly the largest of the trees. Situated on the southeast side of the group. I found its circumference to be 8.8 ft (2.7 m). At an early point along its path of ascent, it split into three separate trunks, each of significant size. While I'd been thinking of this specimen as a tree unto itself, I soon realized that it might not be a self-unit, after all. Instead, it maybe just one of several trunks which had initially sprouted from one still larger, long since defunct giant tree. This tree may have been cut or perhaps had been disposed of by fire. Such action would account for the cavernous recess in which the trees were anchored and the black material I had noticed in it, most likely charcoal left from the fire. It is well documented that Madronas will sprout new growth from burnt stumps. [129]

Had there been an accidental fire, perhaps, or was the tree instead cut down long ago and then deliberately burned in order to dispose of the stump? Later researching the history of Fort Worden, I could find no mention of a fire save in the context of what has become known as the *Triangle of Fire.*[13] However, the fire alluded to here is cannon fire, for the protection of the entrance to Puget Sound against naval invasion.

Concern for such defense dates back to the mid-1800s and construction of the twelve-gun batteries at Fort Worden commenced in 1897, spearheaded by the Army Corps of Engineers. Land was cleared; large chunks of the terrain re-arranged; and huge amounts of cement, gravel, and sand were brought to the site. One can easily picture the beehive of activity and in the rainy season: men sloshing about in the mud; roads being forged; horses and vehicles pulling supplies up from the beach; cavities being dug for emplacements; rocks being blasted; and laborers generally swarming all over the site.

It is important to remember that, at the time, trees were either a hindrance to construction or a source of building materials. Although the Madrona's wood is not particularly well suited for lumber, a specimen as large as whose remnants I had discovered, was not likely to have survived the action. Something, anyway, had happened and we could only speculate as to what it was. Well we had lingered long enough and needed to continue our journey.

The next stop was to find and visit a fellow by the name of James Causton, a certified arborist who lived about ten miles east of Port Angeles. Back in the 1990s, Mr. Causton had become concerned about the health of a particular huge Madrona tree in Port Angeles. [130] The specimen had been estimated to be about 400 years old! It was indeed, a very special member of its species. [131-133]

The tree nearly perished during the commercial boom of the mid-to-late '90s. At the time, plans had been laid to construct a building in the lot adjacent the big tree. The building would be situated directly under the drip-line of the tree's crown; of further concern was the tree's branches extended way out over the street, and the sidewalk passed within eighteen inches of its base. While this commercial posturing was taking place, I imagine the poor tree must have been thinking, if trees *can* think[14]: "Excuse me, people, but I was here first!" In fact, this mammoth Madrona predates even the founding of Port Angeles itself by more than *two centuries* and has spent the bulk of its unobtrusive life in the total absence of streets, houses, and to a large extent, non-indigenous human beings.

As of 1990, there already stood a building on the property in question, namely, a ceramics-crafting operation. Mr. Causton felt sure that this building had, and would continue to have, a significant impact upon the tree. Furthermore, he knew, the new building then still under construction, would undoubtedly cause some root loss. Worse yet, he predicted that water would likely leach from the concrete used for the foundation, possibly altering the acidity levels of the soil. Along with the already-present cement sidewalk and the asphalt of the street which covered a portion of the tree's normal root span, this would guarantee further deterioration of the tree's natural environment.

Mr. Causton voiced his misgivings to various civic groups and government agencies, with the hopes of raising both awareness of the threat the new construction posed to the tree and the funds necessary to combat it. Some of his warnings were published in various newspapers, which publications acknowledged Mr. Causton for his efforts. Having read some of the relevant articles, I wanted to meet with him and hear him tell his story firsthand. I had obtained his address and phone number and tried to call him several times to no avail, so I figured we'd just stop by his house, it was on our way to our next destination, and hope luck was on our side. As it happened, it was.

---

13 Location of three forts for the defense of the naval entrance to the southern part of Puget Sound, Admiralty Inlet: Fort Worden, on the west, Fort Casey, on the east on Whidbey Island; and, Fort Flager, to the south, on Marrowstone Island. [126]

14 Plant biologist Lincoln Taiz of University of Santa Cruz, CA doesn't think so and says he has seen no evidence of any type of nervous system in plants. I must say his view is scientific but very unromantic. (L. Sander, Plants Don't Have Feelings or Consciousness, Science News, Nov 9, 2019, p. 5, www.sciencenews.org).

Figure 15.1 Madrona (*Arbutus menzeisi*) at Fort Worden, Port Townsend, WA. D. The group of trees in the middle of an open area, loaded with red berries at the time. B. A closer view illustrating that is was a group of trees not a single tree. A. At the base of the group was a depression and the trees formed a ring around the edge of the depression.

We turned onto his country lane and jockeyed our car into a parking spot beside one of his vehicles. Off to our right I saw somebody standing near a shed, a pile of logs, and some sections of split wood. He apparently was splitting logs. I strolled down the lane and, as I approached, a big black dog suddenly blocked my path, voicing with a series of loud, sharp barks its displeasure at my unannounced visit. Startled, I breathed a sigh of relief when I saw it was constrained by a rope, albeit one of generous length, tied to a nearby tree stump.

The fellow cutting wood was just finishing up, by the looks of it, and appeared to be wearing sound protection earmuffs. Noticing me at last, he leaned over and killed the power on his log splitter, removed the devices from his ears, and approached me. He seemed both puzzled, naturally, and quite affable. "May I help you?" his expression seemed to be asking as he came within a few feet of me.

I introduced myself, inquiring if he was the man I was after. He confirmed that he was James Causton and gave my hand a vigorous shake. He was about five-foot ten, slender, with a bushy white beard, gray moustache, shoulder-length gray hair, and a warm, disarming smile. He appeared to have spent a lot of time outdoors and, though clearly in the sunset of his life, appeared healthy and fit. Quieting his dog, who had remained pretty agitated, despite his owner's clear welcoming of my presence, he invited me to stay and chat. Of course, I happily accepted his offer.

The sun was spilling through the trees in such a way as to form a nice, warm spot just a few feet from where Mr. Causton had come to greet me. So, improvising, he pulled up a couple of boxes and we sat down to talk. He confirmed some of the things I'd read in the papers and elaborated on his various crusades regarding the imperiled Madrona. He clearly harbored some residual antagonism toward the city of Port Angeles in connection with the saga.

Historically, the city had been a logging town and still received much of its financial backing from the logging industry. This industry is by definition interested in trees for their commercial value and are not fond of tree huggers. Mr. Causton confirmed for me that, in 1999, a woman named Virginia Serr had purchased the lot on which the tree sat in order to save it from likely destruction at the hands of future construction. Her husband, Ted, had passed this tree daily as he'd traveled from their home to his place of work. Following his death, she'd decided that purchasing the property and saving the tree would serve as a fitting memorial to him. In fact, she has installed a sign on the property which reads: "Welcome to Ted's Tree Park." (see Figure 15.2D).

Much has happened since then, much of which has been reported in Port Angeles's local newspapers. In 2000, Mr. Causton received an award from the Pacific Northwest Chapter of the International Society of Arboriculture for his efforts in the preservation of the four-century-old Madrona. A summary of these efforts, drafted by Causton himself, was published by the Northwest Arborist and Associates. [130] As we sat in the sun that mid-autumn day, Mr. Causton shared with me some personal reflections on, and updates to, the events he'd written about in the article.

Shortly after Mrs. Serr had purchased the property, she had made arrangements for the existing building to be demolished and removed. Unfortunately, a large excavator was brought in to do this and, ironically, the use of heavy equipment caused incidental damage to the tree's roots. Mrs. Serr had initially intended to have the leftover wood from the demolished building ground up and used as a mulch to fertilize the production of new grass. However, she canceled this plan when Mr. Causton had raised concerns that, there was a likelihood of a substantial lead presence in the paint that had been applied to the wood, the resulting mulch might ultimately do more harm than good. Instead, Mrs. Serr elected to simply have the debris hauled away.

Mr. Causton also told me that a number of volunteers had additionally removed about forty cubic yards of various debris which had accumulated over the years. They replaced it with a clean organic composite consisting of horse manure and wood chips. Following application of the new mulch, the surface was inoculated with a fungi known to foster symbiotic relationships with the roots of trees which improves the trees acquisition of minerals and nutrients from the soil. This fungi is called *Mycorrizal*; [134] Mr. Causton obtained a supply from a fungus expert named Mike Amaranthus, who pioneered its use in 1995 for plants in general. Amaranthus since founded a company in Grants Pass, Oregon which is still in operation today, producing and distributing a wide array of Mycorrizal fungi intended for different types of plants.

Following application of the fungi, a four-inch layer of Douglas Fir chips was spread to promote healing, restoration, and further growth. In 2003, Amaranthus published a paper which included two photographs, both furnished by Mr. Causton himself, displayed in a before-and-after arrangement. [134] The second photo showed the state of the tree about six months after it had been subjected to the fungi-treatment. The improvement in the tree's overall health was both obvious and remarkable, in particular the distinct greening of its foliage. How much of this improvement was directly attributable to the fungi itself, as opposed to the mulch or some combination of the two, is of course a matter of speculation.

Mr. Causton further informed me that the sidewalk over which branches had extended had subsequently been removed, replaced by a sidewalk which was routed around the tree giving it a wider berth. As seen in the photograph (Figure 15.2C), this project did eliminate the parking along the street in this small area but provided more space and protection for the tree.

About a year later the health of the tree appeared to improve. Since then, however, it has deteriorated considerably. Mrs. Serrs had brought in other experts and consultants, periodically seeking advice on how she might help reverse this troubling trend. At one point it was determined that certain large diseased branches should be excised from the tree. This procedure was ultimately performed. Mr. Causton upon learning of it later was concerned that the cutting open of large cross-sections may have rendered the tree itself more susceptible to further invasions by insects, disease, and fungi. Finally, additional mulching and inoculating with what was thought to be beneficial root fungi was also performed at some point, though Mr. Causton wasn't privy to the details. However, at the time of our visit this diligent concern seems to have been dropped as grass was growing all around the tree for the purpose of having a nice lawn.

On the whole, I must say that Mr. Causton seemed pessimistic about the tree's prospects. Not just for this particular Madrona, but for trees generally in our ever more artificially altered and crowded modern landscape, where the preeminence of commerce, vehicular travel, and human habitation are often in direct collision with the preservation of nature, yes, even beautiful, four-century-old trees. I'm afraid I concur with the Mr. Causton's assessment.

The afternoon was slowly giving way, so we ended our chat. Darlene and I had to get on to Port Angeles to see this famous tree for ourselves.

Arriving in town, we traveled west along Eighth Street. Soon we were able to make out in the distance a large tree which jutted out over a portion of the street. I said to Darlene, "That must be it." She agreed. Another few blocks along and our suspicion was confirmed: this was indeed the tree that had become the subject of so much local notoriety back in the '90s. (Figure 15.2C)

After finding a place to park, I got down to business with my camera and a tape measure, not wanting to lose any of the afternoon that was left. The tree was undeniably a magnificent specimen, but the branches were not full of green foliage, as I had anticipated. As I craned my neck to study the high-up branches, I could see there were still some red berries scattered throughout them, with small tufts of green growing adjacent to them. Several large clumps of berries were growing on a few of the easternmost branches, about twenty feet above street-level. (Figure 15.2A) Despite these superficial signs of life, the tree was clearly distressed. Many leaves were dry, some branches completely bare, unlike the lush foliage found in a healthy tree.

Nevertheless, it was obvious that the great tree was making a valiant effort to perform the functions that all trees are ordained for, propagating itself (specifically, its DNA) via production of fruit, in this case berries. Experts in the field believe that such acts require a significant expenditure of energy, which could instead be harnessed in the service of self-preservation. It occurred to me that, trees do this in the same way human mothers do when they sacrifice huge amounts of time, energy, attention, and other resources in the care of their young.

Standing under this superb and imposing Madrona specimen, I couldn't help but be awed by its sheer size. It reminded me of some of its equally magnificent relatives such I have seen in British Columbia, and in Sonora County in California. A heavy bark surrounded its trunk all the way up to a height of at least twenty feet or more the height of the average two-story home, for example. Above these, I spied branches with exposed bark, the reddish exterior having peeled away earlier in the year, as part of the tree's natural shedding cycle. Some moss appeared to be growing on its north side, as is often observed among large trees. (Figure 15.3)

There were a few passersby as I snapped my photos, took my measurements, and performed my routine inspections. None of them paid me or the tree much mind, they'd all doubtless seen the tree dozens if not hundreds of times, and I'm sure I wasn't the first person to show an academic interest in it. It was regionally famous, after all. Some children came to the fence dividing the lot from that of the childcare center next door appropriately named Madrona Children's Academy, curious about what I was up to. Though I answered their questions as I laid out my yellow tape measure and prepared to determine the tree's circumference and diameter, they continued to pepper me with questions: "What are you doing? Why are you doing that? What is that yellow thing?" I circled the tree again, taking pictures from as many angles as possible before crossing the busy street to snap a few final shots, all while negotiating the evening traffic. There I timed my shots to avoid vehicles appearing in them.

Glancing at my watch, I saw it was time to head home if we were going to catch the ferry at a reasonable hour. Fortunately, I realized, we'd probably seen all we were going to see on this trip, anyhow. In retrospect, I now realize I should have given the tree a last goodbye hug.

As our car bumped over the on-ramp of the 6:45 ferry, I sighed wistfully. Darlene and I had enjoyed many exciting adventures during our pilgrimages to various Madronas over the past couple of years, both within and well beyond our native Pacific Northwest, and while I took a great deal of satisfaction in having now checked off the last of the trees on my list, I also felt a little sad that our adventures had ostensibly come to an end.

Then I thought to myself: *Unless, of course, I learn of another big one someplace new....*

Epilogue

That thought hung in the air for two years to almost the same day, October 29, 2021. I was sitting in my living room scanning the internet with my Ipad when a headline caught my eye: "Ted's Tree One of the Largest in the State, Dismantled." written December 9, 2020 in the Peninsula Daily News.

I was shocked! I continued to read and see the pictures of it being cut down and with pieces of its enormous branches lying on the ground. I had just been talking to Darlene about taking a trip to Port Angeles to obtain more berries from that tree. I had been delighted with my limited success of having two baby trees growing from berries I picked off the ground from it two years previously. The largest was now 11 inches tall growing in a pot. I had felt I needed insurance, so to speak, more Madorna starts, to help carry on the legacy of this famous tree. Alas too late. I wanted to run outside and hug the two that I had, telling them: "Sorry your Mother has died." But no, I am afraid to touch them I don't want to ruin or smoother them. I suddenly felt paranoid, I must keep them growing.

All things considered I still had an urge to go and see the tree, if there was anything left to see. The article in the paper had indicated that there might be a large section of the tree left as the owners were unsure what to do with it. A picture of Jackie Miller, a daughter of Virginia and Ted Serr was shown in the paper. She discussed with the reporter a few options they were thinking about for the tree. One included leaving a section that could be turned into a tree house for the adjacent Madrona Children's Academy. The article had been written eleven months previously, so I pondered whether the tree remnants were still there.

I decided if it all possible I would try to talk to Jackie Miller. After a little detective work, I found she had retired from a local school where she had been the financial advisor. Of course, they wouldn't give me her phone number, but they would take mine and pass that onto her, thus she could call me if she wanted to. After a second attempt at reaching her in this way I was delighted to get a call from her.

Figure 15.2 The Port Angeles, WA, giant Madrona (*Arbutus menzeisi*) tree. C. This westerly view shows how the tree branches hang over the street and how the street curb was moved away from the base. D. An expanded view of the sign, *Ted's Tree Park*, erected by Mrs. Ted Seer to honor her deceased husband, Ted. A view looking north from across the eighth street. A. A view of ripened berries growing on one of the tree's branches.

Figure 15.3 Two northerly views of the 400-year-old tree. A. a closer view of the base. The diameter of the tree in east-west direction was 10 ft. 11in (3.33m), diameter in the north-south direction was 7ft (2.1m), and the circumference at 3ft above ground was 23 ft (7.1m).

She was very friendly when she learned who I was and what my purposes were. She then relayed the story about the tree and her parents which were similar to what I've already heard. However, she gave the family's personal version of it. After her mother had bought the property, she had tried to give it to the city to make it into a park. The city declined to accept it for reasons undisclosed. Virginia, not to be deterred, decided to make it a park herself and she called it: Ted's Tree Park. Jackie went on to describe how her mother used to go down every day to the tree, with a chair and sit there for several hours. Sometimes she would do a little cleanup around the park, trimming the grass and bushes and pulling weeds. Of course, later she couldn't do that and had succumbed in late March of 2020. Rather dramatically, six weeks after her death the tree also seemed to die. Its remaining green leaves just started turning brown and shriveling up. Yes, the long, perhaps 400 year life, struggling in later years to survive just seemed to be over when Mrs. Serr's struggle also ended.

Thereafter, concern arose about dead branches falling off the tree onto the sidewalk, street and/or the neighboring school and someone being hurt. Jackie said that after all the paperwork and arrangements were made for cutting down the tree, they decided not to make any announcements about cutting it. They were afraid something similar to what had happened in another park might occur there. Some *tree huggers* had come and chained themselves to the trees to prevent them from being cut down. This was not a headache that the family wanted! The cutting took place over a weekend with some of the wood donated to the Strait Turners a group of artisan wood workers and some ended up as firewood.

I asked what was to happen to the remaining part of the tree? She said: "Well the family which there were five members involved, decided to sell the property since they couldn't care for it anymore. What the buyers will do with it she didn't know?

I expressed the scientific value it would be to obtain a cross section of the main trunk, if it was to be cut down. The growing rings could be counted and the actual age verified. Also, the yearly spacing between the rings would provide climate history of the local environment over the previous 400 or so years. She indicated I could track down the new owners probably and ask them.

Since I had now learned that most of the main trunks of the trees were still present, I decided I would go and see it. I made reservations for the ferry to go to Port Townsend and return later in that day. Darlene declined to go on this little adventure with me. Perhaps because it was rather rainy and didn't sound too exciting to her. "This is a dead issue." she said. I choked; she was starting to pick up my type of humor.

Since I would have time, I decided to contact some former friends I had worked with who lived near Sequim which was on my way. We would meet for lunch. Sequim is a small town that many like to retire in because it is in the rain shadow of the Olympic Mountains. However, I didn't witness that the effects of that shadow that day, my windshield wipers had a steady workout. Arriving there around noon, I met them, and we enjoyed getting reacquainted.

Saying goodbye and stepping out of the restaurant I advanced to my car and suddenly looking down I saw one of my tires was flat. Not what I wanted. Opening the trunk, I realized that there was no spare tire as this was a recent enough model where the car only included a kit to temporally seal and re inflate the tire. After reading through the manual a couple of times I was able to apply this equipment and inflate the tire. The pressure seemed to hold. I then drove the prescribed three miles to ensure the sealant was spread completely around the inside of the tire and reconnected the compressor in the kit to determine if the pressure was to still at the prescribed level. It was, but nevertheless I talked to a local tire repair place and found out it would be two hours or more before they could help me. The tire looked good, so why not gamble and just go the rest of the way to Port Angeles? I could see the tree and then retest the tire.

Arriving at the site of the tree I was of course disappointed when comparing to what I had seen before. It was appalling to see this magnificent tree stripped, naked, standing with only its truncated structure. Nevertheless, even in its current state it was a magnificent monument. (Figures 15.4) Taking as many pictures from various angles that I thought would document the situation I turned to head back towards Port Townsend. First, checking the tire, it seemed be still good, so I hurried on.

Fortunately, the tire remained inflated and as the car banged off the ferry ramp at Whidbey island. I dialed Darlene: "I will be home in about one hour."

Happily, I entered the door and was greeted by Darlene. We then shared our day's experiences while we enjoyed a late dinner.

Yes, it did seem like now all our big tree adventures were over – maybe.

Figure 15.4 Views of the Pt. Angeles tree after it had died, and large branches had been removed. A. Westly view like 15.2C. B. Northern view like Figure 15.3. Pictures taken November 4, 2021.

Chapter Sixteen:

Closure

Although a romance can go on a lifetime, Darlene and mine for 57 years, writing about it must end. Nevertheless, the beautiful Pacific Madrone remain, bending out over the rocks, reaching to the sunlight over the water, the leaves capturing the energy and the CO_2 and producing the carbohydrates the tree requires. The flowers bud and bloom, the old leaves are replaced by new, the bark peels in the summer and the red berries appear in the fall.

We were particularly drawn to this yearly dance as we boated the Salish Sea. I recall one bay in Desolation Sound where we had anchored several summers. The bay was partially surrounded with captivating geological formations of huge rock steps. It was the home to Madrona (*Arbutus* for our BC friends) and other evergreens. I leave you with my impressions:

Tenedos Bay

Where the rock and trees
Share the sun.
The leaves seize each ray,
As if for fun,
Activating chlorophyll,
No motion – everything still.

Madrona and fir
Share the slopes.
Rising straight, the conifer.
Twisted, the Madrona from copes
With wind and shade.
Peeling naked their trunks
A mystery yearly obeyed
As ritual as praying monks.

Their bodies, crooked winding
But reaching towards the sky.
Roots grasping, holding, binding
Seeking their nutrient supply.

Giant rock steps randomly inter-placed,
Draped with green and dried moss,
Faces cracked, lifted, and displaced,
Platforms running diagonally across.

The sanctuary of these entities,
Salted with the sea and rain,
Washed with struggles and mysteries,
But steady, still, patient they remain.

The setting sun contrasts
The bared trunks and shadowed rocks.
The colored light casts
Tranquility on these jagged blocks.

We visit for a day
Cathedrals sublime.
A moment of survey,
A dot in time.

Appendix A: An Intimate Involvement - Qualitative and Quantitative Comparisons of Several Arbutus

The Flowers

Carefully cutting several slits with dissecting scissors in the one continuous sepal of the white blossom of the *Arbutus* flower, I gently ripped the region between these cuts towards the calyx, the base of the blossom. A viewing window into the depth of the flower was suddenly open. Positioning it under the binocular microscope, adjusting the focus, the inner heavenly constituents became visible, in fact they jumped out at me. Lustrous fluff was present near the base of the flower. Focusing further I zoomed the magnification; I saw that this was angelic like hair surrounding each stamen filament shining in the exposing light. I was awed by the beauty. It reminded me of looking out the window of an airplane as it climbed up through the clouds to break into sunshine with large puffy clouds above and below.

This was my first successful microscopic forging into the beauty of the blossoms. This excited me, enticed me, and drew me on, not only in microscopic exploration but in Botanical learning to understand what I was seeing. I had to struggle to get there, but that was okay, it was a romance after all.

The beauty of the intact blossoms starts with the way they dress the trees, hanging in single, small, or in large clusters. Although the blossoms of the Western Hemisphere *Arbutus* species are white, pale to gleaming white, they still stand out from the green foliage and are immediately apparent. This is true of the Eastern Hemisphere *Arbutus* as well, but they have also developed some beautiful exceptions that are pink or ruby in color. First there is a variant of the *Arbutus undeo* that apparently originated in Ireland called *Arbutus undeo* f *rubrica* (Figure A1C*)* but the true history of its origin seems to be unknown. There are some bushes that were transported and planted a few decades ago at the Washington Park University of Washington Botanical Garden. Further, some of these have been propagated by humans to Medina, a city located on the east side of Lake Washington, where I took the photograph. These blossoms can vary from white to pink and even ruby color depending on the seasonal and environmental conditions. This is compared in Figure A1B of a photograph of the beautiful hybrid, *Arbutus* 'Marina' discussed earlier in Chapter Five. Perhaps the species that most consistently offers the pink to ruby color is the Canary Island *Arbutus canariensis,* Figure A1D, I took in Tenerife and the Figure A1A in San Francisco. At the San Francisco Botanical Garden there are two *canariensis* trees that have been translocated decades ago. Rather surprisingly, these bloom in the spring rather than the fall as the *canariensis* do in their native homeland. I am unsure why this is but must somehow reflect the difference in the climate.

Figure A1 Pink and ruby colored flowers. A. *Arbutus canariensis* San Francisco Botanical Garden, B. *Arbutus* 'Marina' San Francisco Botanical Garden, C. *Arbutus unedo* f *rubrica* Medina, WA, D. *Arbutus canariensis* Tenerife, Canary Islands, Spain.

On site study of blossoms and/or their berries is desirable but challenging since maturations occur only a short time during the year, only one to two months. It is therefore helpful to live near where the species grow otherwise it is necessary to establish contacts in the appropriate area and convince someone to send samples to you. Transport by mail has its disadvantages, even by reportedly rapid delivery, as specimens may not arrive in good shape. Traveling there of course, is an option for the investigator but that can be expensive, and it requires careful planning to arrive at the proper time. Transporting bulky microscopic equipment adds to the complication. If interested in both flowers and berries, most species flower at a different time than when their berries are ripe, a double complication. Fortunately, some species like the *Arbutus unedo* bloom in the fall and have berries that are becoming mature at the same time. Happily, these grow around where I live and so also do the *Arbutus menziesii*. I have studied the *menziesii* blooming in the spring and in the fall their ripened berries. I was also lucky enough to time my visit to the *Arbutus peninsularis* in Baja Mexico when those trees were blooming. Similarly, I visited the Canary Islands in the autumn when the berries were mature and I also saw a few flowers, but at that time I had not realized the potential of studying them. I corrected that oversight when I visited the Golden Gate Botanical Garden in San Francisco in the spring, where both the *Arbutus canariensis* and *Arbutus* 'Marina' were blooming. Regarding the Texas, *Arbutus xalapensis*, I received both flowers and seeds most kindly from a colleague in Austin, Michael Prochoroff. Finally, I was tipped off concerning the existence and locations of the *Arbutus undeo* f *rubra* by Daniel Mount, a regional trained botanist, consultant and designer of gardens. It was only a short drive to see and photograph these.

Returning to my microscopic studies I stumbled around when I first began both in equipment and technique. I first tried to add a magnification lens to my Iphone camera, that didn't work very well. Next, I tried a microscope with fixed magnification lens I could swivel in and out for different amplification. It was workable but cumbersome and then finally I obtained a binocular microscope with zoom magnification, adjustable lighting, and with a camera attachment.[15]

One of the biggest challenges for me was how to carefully dissect and position the blossoms optimally for photographing. It took me several flowering seasons to learn. I initially tried using various clamps to grasp the blossom or its stem. I built an x and y micro adjustment table with a rotating holder; I even acquired a miniature suction apparatus normally used for holding micro circuit components and I attached that to the adjustment table to suck and hold the blossom. But always during a procedure turning a certain way might apply too much stress and the flower would fall off the holding mechanism. I tried super glue but that didn't work either. I needed a method for holding the flower for dissecting and then positioning it without damaging or misaligning some of the individual components in the flower. Nothing seemed to work well. The septal of the flower is delicate easily bends, tears, and breaks. Most of the septal needs to be removed to get a clear viewing of the inner components of the flower and this is not easily performed without disturbing the anthers inside.

In the end, I accidentally stumbled on a simple and reliable way of holding the flower for my purposes. This happened when I was sitting at my table with various flower components scattered on it. I was eating my lunch. Fortuitously that day I had a peanut butter sandwich. Out of nowhere the thought struck me, would the blossom stick to peanut butter. I tried a small blob of the butter on a piece of paper and placed a blossom against it. Eureka, it stuck very nicely! Wow! I forgot my sandwich and rushed to my microscope with dissecting scissors and tweezers. As I tried dissecting the septal the blossom stayed in place beautifully. I then maneuvered the paper to various angles and thus the blossom. Pressing lightly on the blossom I could change its angle without dislodging or damaging it. Looking through the microscope I could respectively adjust the blossom for the best photographing positions. Is this just a fluke? I grasped another blossom, more peanut butter, and under the microscope I again dissected it easily and again could position it where I wanted it. It worked so well I knew this was not a onetime accident it was a fool proof technique! I didn't check my pulse, but I know it must have been quite elevated since I completely overlooked my lunch that afternoon. I found it when I was about to go home still spread on my table.

I later switched to using black paper as the base for the peanut butter because it provided a better photographic background for the blossom. I also found other viscous gels like Vaseline could work too. I still like to use peanut butter, though. I thank the peanut farmers, Jimmy Carter included.

Once a blossom was positioned and dissected (Figure A2) I could adjust the zoom and focusing controls of the microscope to examine each intricate component of the blossom. Of special interest is the stamens in the blossom, there are ten in each *Arbutus* flower distributed around the female pistil with its green ovary and its long style and bright shiny stigma. These are the male components of the flower. They lie "hugging" the style of the pistil closely in an immature flower then pull away from it when the flower matures and opens. Each stamen is composed of an anther which has two sacs each with an intriguing spur. The anther is supported by a filament that attaches it to the base of the flower. (Figure A3) This filament increases in size from where it attaches to the anther to just before it attaches to the base of the flower. Small hairs originate from it. When the sacs open, they release pollen that has developed in them. White powder particles (Figure A2) which I later learned were pollen (each grain 10 micrometers in diameter), were sprinkled in the mouth of the sacs, and distributed along the inner wall of the sepal captured in short fibrous hair, and some grains of the pollen stuck and were being absorbed into the stigma.

15 I recommend the latter to any interested beginner but have a camera attachment that feeds directly into a computer.

Once the stigma receives and absorbs a pollen grain, a pollen tube begins growing down the style to the ovary of the flower. Some pollen tubes are visible in Figure A4C. This picture is of a flower that is late in the flowering state and has thus been pollinated and several tubes are present. As each pollen tube arrives in the ovary it starts the impregnation process. It takes a number of pollen grains to fill the ovary and hence the resulting beery with seeds.

The photographs of Figure A4 A & B demonstrate what the blossom of an *Arbutus menziesii* looks like before and after being dissected. The cusps at the base of the flower are more transparent than the those of the other species. Micro hairs are present on the magnified view of the stem (Figure A4D).

The purpose of the spurs (Figure A2 & A3) is unclear but may help cause the sacs to disperse pollen if a pollinator (bee, hummingbird, butterfly, moth) introduces its tongue or beak into the flower to obtain nectar, in the process bumping the spurs shaking the sacs and distributing pollen. The spurs are one part of the inner flower that has some variation among the different *Arbutus* flowers. The spurs are shorter and stubbier in the *Arbutus* 'Marina' and the *Arbutus canariensis* than in the others. In the *A. unedo* for example, the spurs are much longer and often partially curved, and I even found it completely curled in few instances.

Figure A5 D & C provides a more detailed look at the pistil itself. In photo Figure A5 C, the light had glistened from the sticky surface of the stigma giving it a glossy look. Because of the adhesive nature of this surface a pollen grain immediately attaches itself to the stigma if it encounters it. Figure A5B show a magnified view of the ovary with a dotted line illustrating where a cross-sectional cut was made to reveal the inner part, shown in the Figure A5 A. Walls, sepals between the ovals are apparent. Each of these ovals will grow into a seed if pollenated.

Returning to the blooming tree, if one happens to look at the ground below it after it has been flowering for some time one may notice *shells* of flowers scattered there. Looking closely these shells are blossoms without the pistil, but still with all the male components in them. The pistil remains attached to the stem on the tree. It appears once the ovaries are pollinated, the strength of the base of the blossom weakens and any disturbance by the wind will shake this shell loose from the stem. It is like the tree says: "I don't need you anymore and I now will concentrate only on the ovaries promoting the development of the berry with its seeds." These ovaries develop soon into small green berries as shown in Chapter One, Figure 1.4 B.

Figure A2 Dissected *Arbutus unedo* blossom.

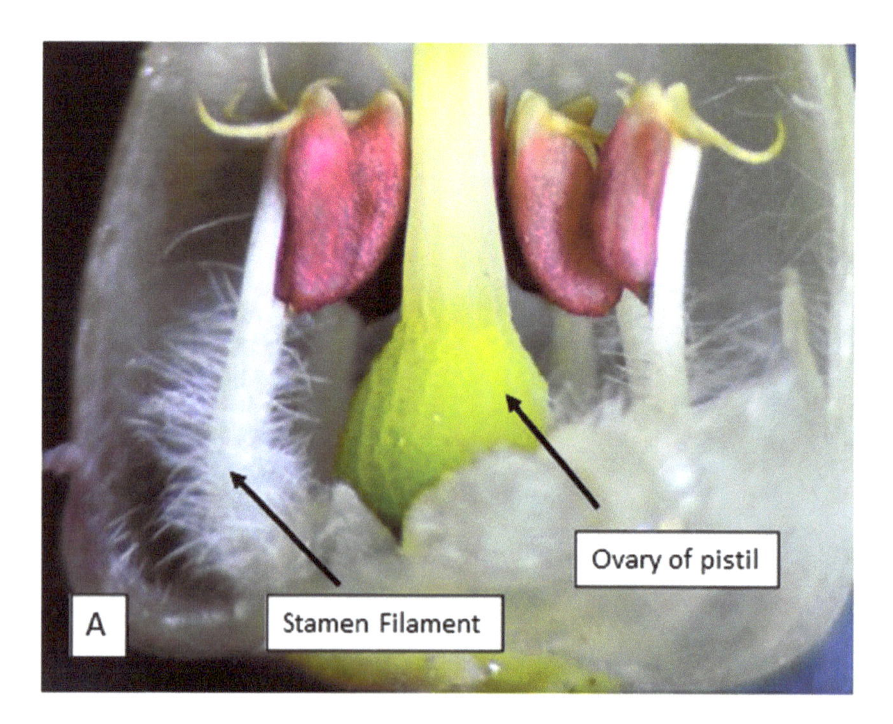

Figure A3 Another dissected *Arbutus unedo* blossom. C. Illustrates how each stamen is aligned around the pistil. B. Several of the stamens have been removed for clearer view of the stamens. A. An enlargement of B to see more detail of the ovary and stamen filament.

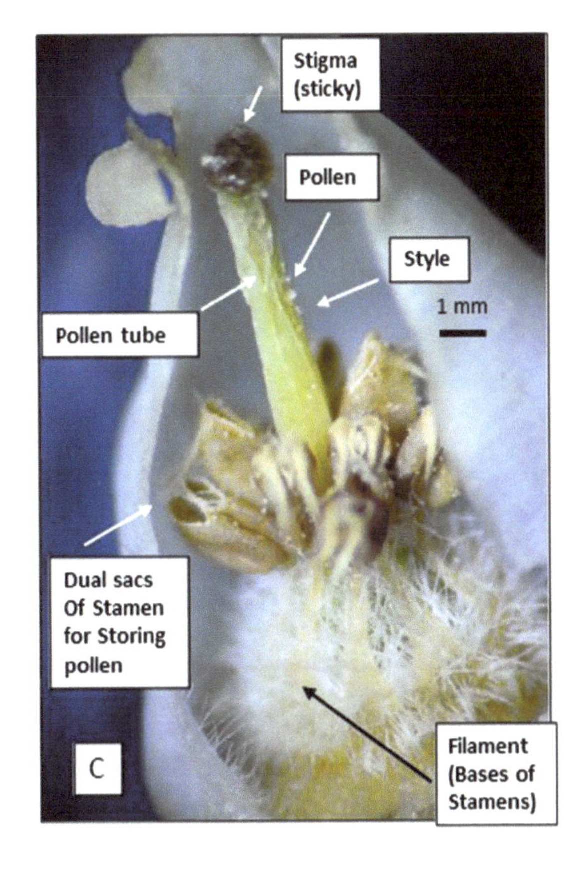

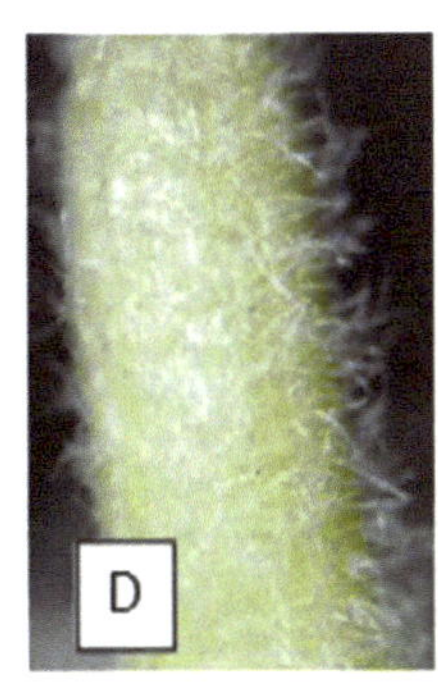

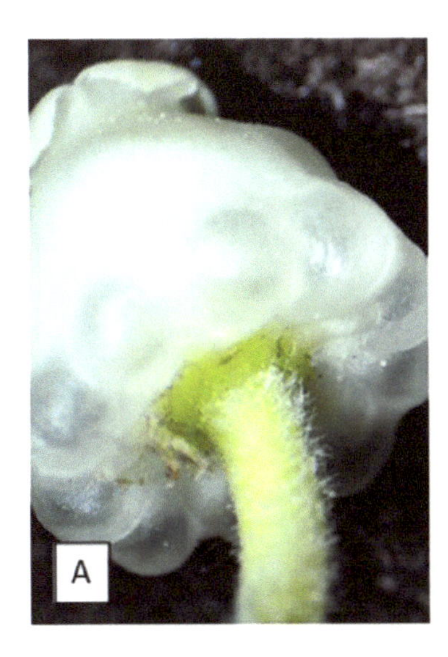

Figure A4 D. A cut away view of an *Arbutus xalapensis* blossom with components labeled. Note: Pollen tubes are visible in this specimen because it is at a late stage of maturity with the stigma well pollenated. A, B. &D *Arbutus menziesii* (Pacific Madrone) A. view of the flower from the stem illustrating the almost transparent cusps, B. Cut away view of the same blossom in A. D. An enlarged view of the stem with short fibrous hair present on it.

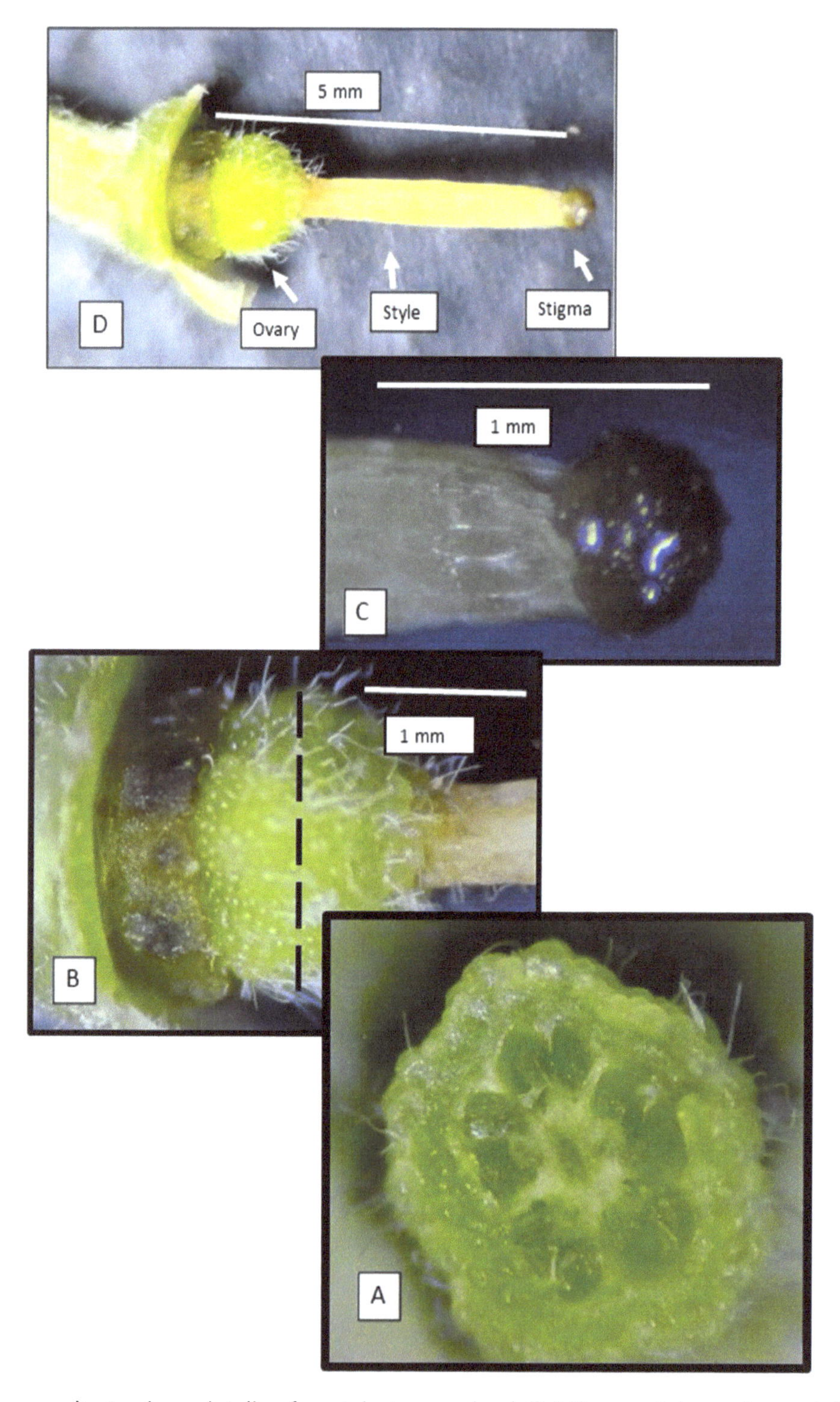

Figure A5 A composite to show details of an *Arbutus unedo* pistil (stigma, style, and ovary). D. The stamens have been removed for visualization. C. An enlargement of the stigma showing pollen tubes near the surface of the style. B. An enlargement of the ovary with a dashed line showing where it was cut to reveal the cross-section view of it. A. Cross section of the ovary, showing septal walls which divide where the seeds form.

Berries and Seeds

The berry size is quite significant between the *Arbutus* species of the different hemispheres. The upper photograph of Figure A6 demonstrates this difference between a Western Hemisphere, *A. menziesii* and the Eastern Hemisphere, *A. unedo*. The surface of the *unedo* is covered with small pyramid protrusions which are hard in contrast to the rest of the fruit body. It also turns red when it is completely ripe. It is tasty at that point but soft, it quickly loses its firm texture and will fall off the tree shortly. It also is the stage best for making jellies or alcohol products because of its high sugar content. (see Chapter Two) The Western Hemisphere berries are rarely eaten by humans although I have seen one report of the indigenous people eating them. [93] The photograph (A6C) shows a cross-section through an *unedo* berry. Seeds are visible as well as the septals or septums that divide the fruit, reminding of a similar structure observable in a sliced tomato or orange. All the Western Hemisphere *Arbutus* berries I have seen are similar in size to the *A. menziesii* shown in Figure A6. Since the berries are smaller than the *unedo*, the seeds are more concentrated in the space. The size of the seeds themselves are only a little less than the *unedo* seeds (Figure A7B).

A more quantitative comparison of berry size, seeds per berry, and seed size are given below in Table A1 for four *Arbutus* species. The number of seeds per berry vary considerably. The *canariensis* by far had the largest, with an average of 71 seeds/ berry compared to the others which ranged between 10-36. The number of samples for the *canariensis*, however, were only four so it does not representative of a statistical population. Bear in mind that each seed requires a single pollen particle to be captured by the stigma. Therefore, if the pollinators were small in one growing area or season one anticipates the seed number will also be small. The environmental conditions during the blooming period are important. If it is rainy and/or windy the pollinators present are most likely reduced. I have pondered the effect of rain on the blossoms themselves, regarding the possibly of washing the pollen out of them. Most likely this does not occur because the blossoms tend to bend down preventing rain from running into the flower. Wind may increase the self-pollination because of the shaking of the blossom. It is worth noting that some seeds in the berry will not germinate. It has been found that if seeds are put into a container of water, non-fertile seeds will float but fertile seeds will sink. [135] In my limited study, I found the Eastern Hemisphere seeds to be longer and wider than the others, but again the number of samples of each are not large. (Table A1)

Table A1: Quantitative Comparison of 4 Arbutus Species (Average ± 1 Standard Deviation)

Arbutus:	***menziesii***	***xalapensis***	***canariensis***	***unedo***
Berry Diam. (mm)*	10.0 ± 0.8	11.3 ± 0.9	22.1 ± 2.0	20.0 ± 4.1
No. samples	40	21	13	20
No. Seeds/ Berry	10.3 ± 9.0	11.5 ± 7.0	71.2 ± 26.0	36 ± 22.0
No. samples	20	16	4	5
Seed Size)				
Length (mm)	2.5 ± 0.3	2.4 ± 0.4	3.2 ± 0.3	3.7 ± 0.4
Width (mm)	1.7 ± 0.2	1.4 ± 0.1	2.0 ± 0.1	2.0 ± 0.2
Length/Width	1.5 ± 0.2	1.8 ± 0.4	1.6 ± 0.2	1.8 ± 0.2
No. Samples	16	11	11	18

Nectar

A key component of almost all flowers is the nectar they produce. The nectar is a sweet tasting liquid which attracts insects and even hummingbirds. A 2005 paper on the analysis of nectar in *Arbutus unedo* [136] perked my interest, since nectar is a key in the pollination cycle and in the trees' propagation. The authors reported obtaining on the average 3.6 to 7.1 microliters of nectar/blossom between October and December of 2004 in southern France. They had used 20 micro liter capillary tubes to probe in the blossom to draw out the nectar.

In April of 2019, I decided to see how much nectar I could find in the *Arbutus menziesii*. I used 3 and 5 micro liter capillary tubes and initially tried to employ the rubber suction adapter that comes with the kit. I found the suction plugged the capillary tube by drawing in part of the wall of the flower. After experimenting I found that just by probing with an empty capillary tube around the base of the stamens, I could recover nectar. Just the capillary action would draw fluid at the tip of the tube into it. The volume is measured by the length of fluid column in the tube and the volume of the tube. After experimenting I found I was most successful when probing an almost mature blossom that had not opened yet by slipping the tube in through the immature *mouth* of the blossom. They were still slightly green. Furthermore, I more recently, November 2019, studied some *Arbutus unedo* the same way. Blossoms at three stages of maturity were studied: the *menziesii* open, open but green, closed and green, for the *unedo* the three states are shown in Figure A7A. The results are recorded below in Table A2

Table A2 Comparing the Nectar of Two Species

Arbutus menziesii **(microliters of nectar)** ***Arbutus unedo***

	Mature	Green	Green		Fig A11B-1	Fig A11B- 2	Fig A11B- 3
	Open	Open	Closed		Open	Closed	Closed
Mean	0.66	1.87	1.74		0	1.67	0
STD	0.60	0.83	1.26		0	.93	0
N=	17	17	11		33	14	8

STD= standard deviation and N = the number of specimens sampled

The findings illustrate that the blossom that is almost mature but has not opened has the best chance of having nectar. Once it opens, probably some pollinator has withdrawn nectar. This was always the case of the *A. unedo* studied but not always the case in the *A. menziesii*. In the latter case, for blossoms that were just open but still quite green I found considerable nectar. Nevertheless, my volume findings with the *A. unedo* are much less than the findings in the above cited paper. Why is this? I don't entirely have an answer.

However, according to Thornburg [137] 2007 flowers secrete nectar continuously until the pollination process is complete. His studies were conducted with an ornamental tobacco plant which has large nectaries making it easier to study them in the laboratory setting than other flowers. In the wild it is not easy to isolate blossoms to prevent pollinators from visiting them. Further, I believe it would be difficult to repeatedly sample *Arbutus* blossoms without knocking them off their attachment to the tree. In my studies I had to remove the blossoms to sample them thus destroying the ability for the tree to continue providing nourishment to it. Therefore, my sampling was a one-time measure in the blossom's life. Do the *Arbutus* continue to produce nectar during their pollinating cycle? We can only infer that they do based on the studies of other flowers. If a pollinator does not visit the flower will the nectar fluid keep building up in it? If so, sampling late in the pollinating cycle would give larger amounts of nectar present or if repeated sampling of a viable blossom would provide a larger total. It seems that more intriguing questions are inviting further study.

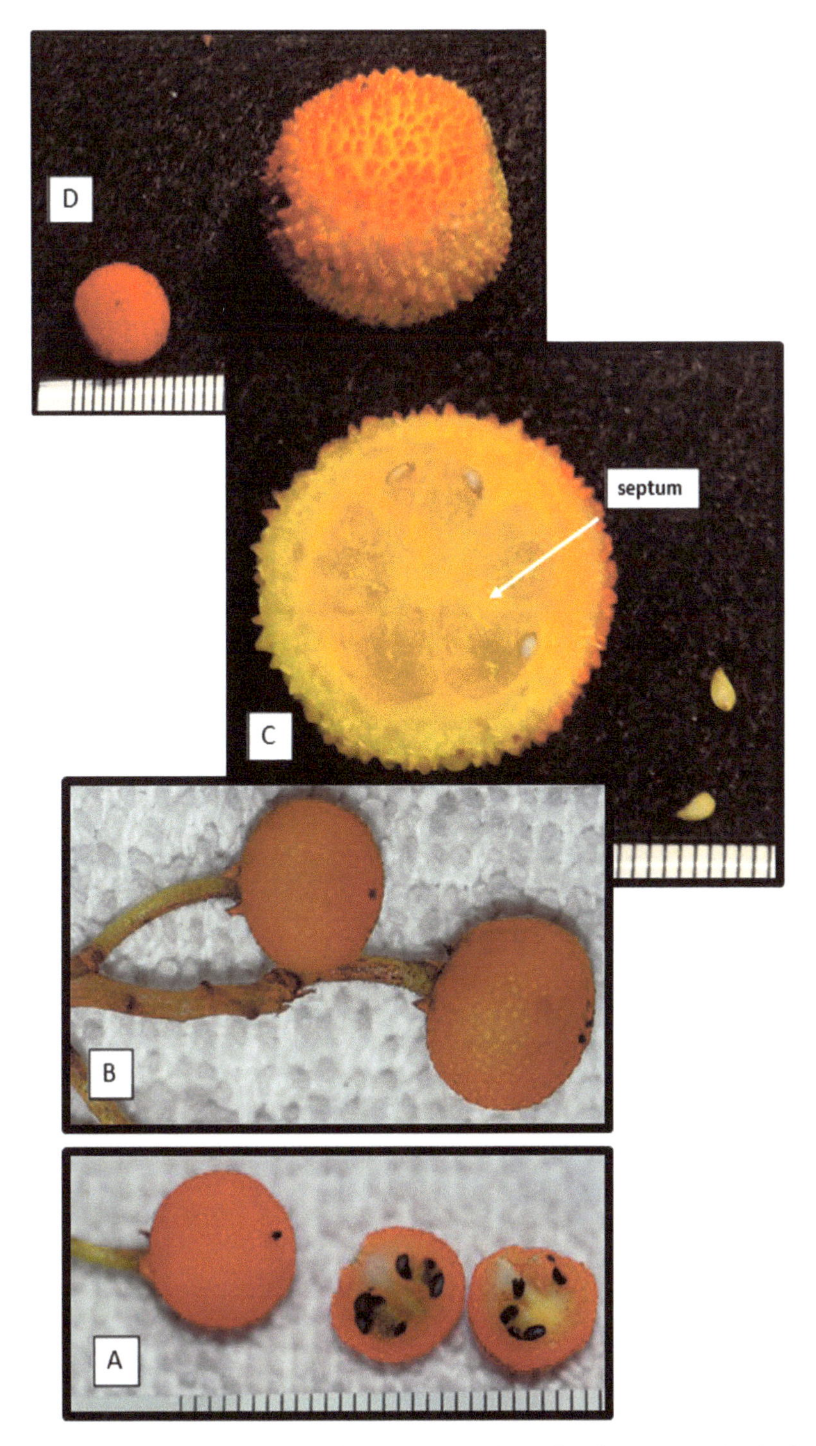

Figure A6 Comparison of berries and seeds of *Arbutus unedo* and *Arbutus menziesii*. The small divisions in all the scales are 1 mm. D. Both berries are shown, illustrating the size difference. C. A cross sectional cut through a *unedo* berry shows the septal divisions and two seeds. B. Two *menziesii* berries. A. One *menziesii* berry and a cross-sectional cut showing both sides of the cut berry with seeds inside.

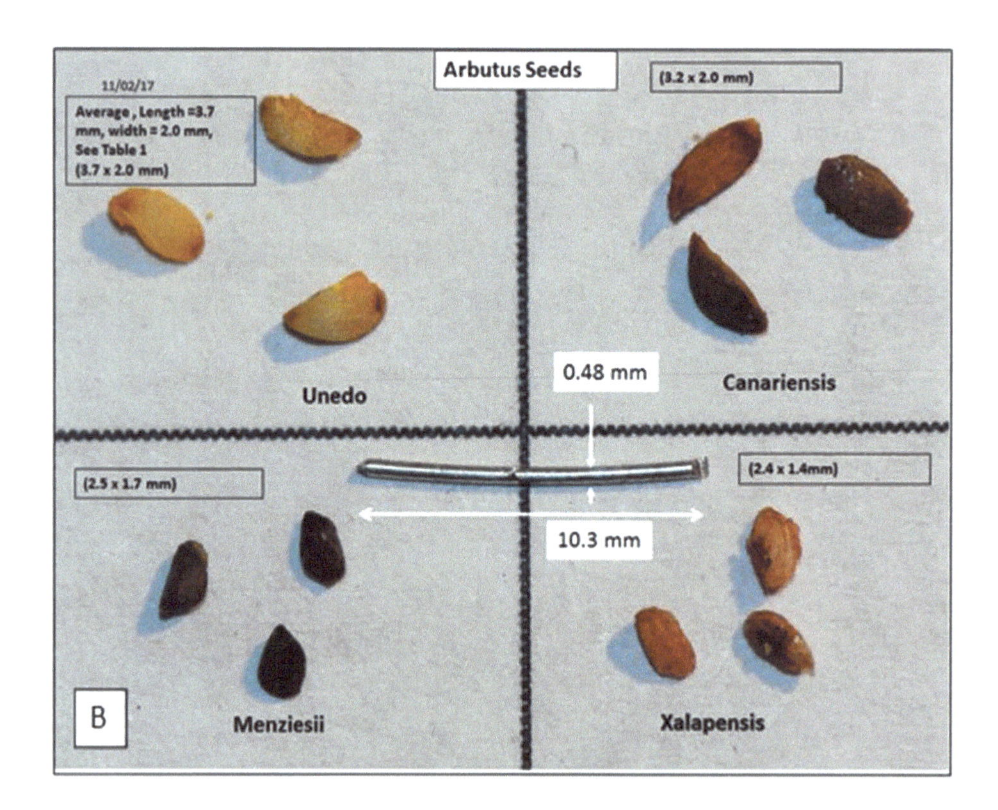

A

Arbutus unedo Blossoms" Progressively from the top down:
1. Mature opened
2. Mature not opened
3. Immature not Opened
Scale: small division 1 mm.

Figure A7 B. Comparisons of the size of seeds in the upper part of photo of Eastern Hemisphere *Arbutus* (*unedo and canariensis*) and lower part of two Western Hemisphere *Arbutus* (*menziesii* and *xalapensis*). A. Three stages of maturity of an *Arbutus unedo* that were studied for their nectar.

Leaves

In Chapter one I discuss that one of the first features noticed about trees is their leaves. Botanists often provide considerable technical detail about the leaves when they discover and describe a new species. The length, width, and the ratio of the two are sometimes reported. Quantitative comparison of leaves is given in Table A3. However, one must be careful when comparing the leaves because the size of the leaves will vary depending on the dryness and heat of the climate. Large leaves will be found in more damp or rainy environments with less sun and more shade. In contrast, small leaves will be found in the dryer and sunnier climates. The same species will respond in these ways depending on its location. I have observed large leaves in the *canariensis* which grew at high elevation on Tenerife Island where fog occurred often whereas smaller leaves were present in a tree located about 200 feet above the ocean where it was much dryer, even requiring supplementary watering during part of the year. Serrations are sometimes present around the edge of the leaves particularly in young trees, perhaps to try to repel herbivores.

Table A3: Quantitative Comparison of 4 Arbutus Species (Average ± 1 Standard Deviation)

Arbutus:	***menziesii***	***xalapensis***	***canariensis***	***unedo***
Leaves				
Length (mm)	101.9 ± 27.8	70.7 ± 13.5	147 ± 35.0	69.5 ± 11.8
Width (mm)	49.8 ± 14.1`	30.6 ± 9.2	50.6 ± 24.0	24.3 ± 5.0
Length/width	2.1 ± 0.3	2.4 ± 0.4	3.0 ± 0.2	2.9± 0.3
Serrated?	Some	None to little	Fairly to highly	Fairly to highly
No. Samples	25	9	4	40

Bark and Tree Structure

I conclude by discussing the bark and structure of the *Arbutus* trees. First, the seasonal peeling thin bark is an attractive feature of the *Arbutus* that I have well demonstrated in photos and discussion throughout the book. Its occurrence, when, and where on the tree it appears relates to the amount of exposure to the sun it receives during the season. The color of the under bark after peeling also relates to the sun exposure and perhaps the heat of the summer: presenting a white bark in the *xalapensis* (Chapter Six), almond to bone color in the *mensiesii* (Chapter Two), and even some yellowish tint in the *canariensis* (Chapter Four). The heavy bark present at the base of the tree and sometimes ranging to the upper branches or even the entire tree, is very different from the peeling bark. This heavy cork is more like most other types of trees but only about one-quarter to one-half inch thick. The *unedo* seems to offer this bark over the whole tree with limited peeling. This was a trait I also observed in the *arizonica* but there peeling did occur on the small branches towards their tips (Chapter 8). This heavy bark has a rough, mild fractured appearance. One of the *arizonica* trees had a rattlesnake skin like pattern. An irregular checkered structure was apparent in some of the *peninsularis* trees (Chapter Seven). Overall, the *Arbutus* bark offers a mystery that has yet to be resolved.

The structures of the *Arbutus* trees are also characteristics that attract the eye and give them special charisma. The trunk twists and turns in some cases and others it grows straight up. This initially puzzled me. I discuss this at the end of the Epilogue to Chapter Eleven regarding some the ancient Heritage trees, early in Chapter One regarding the cordiality of the *Arbutus* an observation I relearned 125 years after Willis Epson

(Chapter Nine). It is not rocket science, but when we observe a tree, it reflects the history of it growing from a sprout struggling for sun exposure with its neighbors until it has reached the size that we observe. If it is twisted and torturous it illustrates how it had to bend and reach over the years to capture sunshine through gaps in the branches of adjacent bushes and trees. If it is tall and straight it grew up when initially it was not being shaded by other trees, then perhaps overtaken by faster growing trees later in life. Usually, the very old and large trees I have observed have grown in areas where they received a lot of sun and the other nutrients they needed without much competition. In such cases they seem to be broadly spread out with lower branches almost competing with upper branches by growing way out from the main trunk. Many of these heritage trees have large branches that split off not far off the ground, four to five feet. Does that indicate that early in their life they had to start reaching out for sun in different ways because of perhaps competition from shrubs or other short foliage? Observing the other trees and the environment around a tree provides some clues as to why its structure is what it is. Bear in mind the age of the *Arbutus* tree and the age and how rapidly the adjacent trees grow. What has gone on twenty to fifty years ago there? In the case of the ancient ones, we can ponder what happened hundreds of years ago? Clearly, the environment and changes in the environment have been and will continue to be a major impact. However, the aggressiveness, carelessness, self-centeredness, and curiosity of humans probably has made even a bigger impact on most trees.

References

1. Sørensen P: Arbutus. In: *Ericaceae, Part II The Superior-Ovaried Genera*. Edited by Editor: Luteyn J, vol. II. New York: New York Botanical Garden Press on behalf of Organization for Flora Neotropica Stable 1995: 194-221.
2. Linnaeus C: Species plantarum., vol. 1. Stockholm; 1753.
3. Pursh F: Flora americae septentrionalis (A Systematic Arrangement and Descriptions of the Plants of North America). In., vol. 1. London: White, Cochrane & Co.; 1814: (specimen 355), Preface.
4. General Biology [http://www.reed.edu/biology/Courses/BIO332/plantfamily/family_info/Ericaceae.htm]
5. Gonzalez-Elizondo MS, Gonzalez-Elizondo M, Sorensen PD: Arbutus Bicolor (ericacae, arbuteae), A new species from Mexico. *Acta Botanica Mexicana* 2012, 99:55-72.
6. Wells D: Lives of Trees (An Uncommon History) In. Chapel Hill, N. Carolina: Algonquin Books of Chapel Hill; 2010: 303,304.
7. Simard S: Finding the Mother Tree: Discovering the Wisdom of the Forest, 2021, Alfred A Knoph, NY
8. Elliott M: A canker disease of Pacific madrone (Arbutus menziesii) caused by the fungal pathogen Fusicoccum arbuti (Botryosphaeriaceae). University of Washington, Seattle, WA,Dissertations: ProQuest Dissertations Publishing 2005
9. Map of San Juan Islands https://www.waggonerguidebooks.com/store/p306/elizabethpersonsanjuanislands.html
10. Gulf Islands BC [https://en.wikipedia.org/wiki/Gulf_Islands#/media/File:Gulf_Islands_map_2.png]
11. Desolation sound [https://mapcarta.com/Desolation_Sound]
12. Santiso X, Lopez L, Gilbert KJ, Barreiro R, Whitlock MC, Retuerto R: Patterns of genetic variation within and among populations in Arbutus unedo and its relation with selection and evolvability. *Perspectives in Plant Ecology Evolution and Systematics* 2015, 17(3):185-192.
13. Off the Beaten Path: hidden treasures of the arboretum the Pink-flowered Strawberry tree [http://www.mountgardens.com/wp-content/uploads/2018/10/mount_strawberry-tree.pdf]
14. Sealy J: Arbutus Unedo. *Journal of Ecology* 1949, 37(No. 2 (Dec)):365-388.
15. Paula S NP, Arce C, Galaz C, Pausas JG: Lignotubers in Mediterranean basin plants. . *Plant Ecol* 2016, 217:661-676.
16. Tappeiner JC HT, Walstad JD: Predicting Recovery of Tanoak (Lithocarpus-Densiflorus) and Pacific Madrone (Arbutus-Menziesii) after cutting or burning 1984, pp. 413-417, 32(3):413-417.
17. Mitchell F: The biogeographical implications of the distribution and history of the strawberry tree, Arbutus unedo, in Ireland. . In: *Biography of Ireland, past, present and future*. Edited by KS CMaK, vol. 2: Occ. Publ. Ir. Biogeog Soc 1993: 35-44.
18. Santiso X, Lopez L, Retuerto R, Barreiro R: Phylogeography of a widespread species: pre-glacial vicariance, refugia, occasional blocking straits and long-distance migrations. *Aob Plants* 2016, 8.
19. Santiso X, Retuerto R: Master of one trade: Arbutus unedo relies on plasticity to persist under habitats differing in water availability. *Journal of Plant Ecology* 2017, 10(5):869-881.
20. Sculpture bear and unedo tree [(en.wikipedia.org/wiki/Statue_of_the_Bear_and_the_Strawberry_Tree).]

21. Sandford J: Medronho Story - Algrave Stories In.: Praski Publishing; 2013.
22. Sadori L AE, Bellini C, et al. : Archaeobotany in Italian ancient Roman harbours. *Review of Palaeobotany and Palynology* 2014, 218:217-230.
23. Delaney F: Ireland, A Novel. New York: Harper 2005.
24. Painting Mermaid on Arbutus Tree [www.greenmonkeystudios.ca]
25. Afrin S, Forbes-Hernandez TY, Gasparrini M, Bompadre S, Quiles JL, Sanna G, Spano N, Giampieri F, Battino M: Strawberry-Tree Honey Induces Growth Inhibition of Human Colon Cancer Cells and Increases ROS Generation: A Comparison with Manuka Honey. *International Journal of Molecular Sciences* 2017, 18(3).
26. Lancellotti E, Iotti M, Zambonelli A, Franceschini A: Characterization of Tuber borchii and Arbutus unedo mycorrhizas. *Mycorrhiza* 2014, 24(6):481-486.
27. Rodriguez-Vidal J, al. e: Undrowning a lost world- The marine istope stage 3 landscape of Gibraltor. *Geomorphology* 2013, 203:105-114.
28. Vidal-Matutano P, Perez-Jorda G, Hernandez CM, Galvan B: Macrobotanical evidence (wood charcoal and seeds) from the Middle Palaeolithic site of El Salt, Eastern Iberia: Palaeoenvironmental data and plant resources catchment areas. *Journal of Archaeological Science-Reports* 2018, 19:454-464.
29. Kalamatianos Dance utube [https://www.bing.com/videos/search?q=kalamatianos+dance&&view=detail&mid=D7AEE62AF2E17FFA2F61D7AEE62AF2E17FFA2F61&&FORM=VDRVRV]
30. Bertsouklis KF, Papafotiou M: Morphometric and Molecular Analysis of the Three Arbutus Species of Greece. *Notulae Botanicae Horti Agrobotanici Cluj-Napoca* 2016, 44(2):423-430.
31. Wild Flowers of Israel -Arbutus andrachne [http://www.wildflowers.co.il/english/plant.asp?ID=212]
32. Davis P: Flora of Turkey and the East Aegean Islands, vol. 6. Edinburgh: Edinburgh University Press; 1978.
33. Markovski A: Morphological Characteristics of Greek Strawberry Tree (Arbutus andrachne L) Genotypes. *Acta Agriculturae Serbica* 2017, 22(44):193-206.
34. Serce S, Ozgen M, Torun AA, Ercisli S: Chemical composition, antioxidant activities and total phenolic content of Arbutus andrachne L. (Fam. Ericaceae) (the Greek strawberry tree) fruits from Turkey (vol 23, pg 619, 2010). *Journal of Food Composition and Analysis* 2012, 25(2):234-234.
35. Issa RA AF, Amro BI: Studying the aAnti-tyrosinase effect of Arbutus andrachne L extracts. . *Intern J of Cosmetic Science* 2008:271-276.
36. Bertsouklis KF, Papafotiou M: Seed Germination of Arbutus unedo, A-andrachne and Their Natural Hybrid A-andrachnoides in Relation to Temperature and Period of Storage. *Hortscience* 2013, 48(3):347-351.
37. De La Brocquiree B: Travels of Bertrandon De La Brocquiree 1432, 1433. London: H. G. Bohn; 1848.
38. Israeli history: it's all about roots [https://www.timesofisrael.com/israeli-history-its-all-about-roots/]
39. History on high at Mount Scopus [https://www.timesofisrael.com/history-on-high-at-mount-scopus/]
40. Bertsouklis K, Papafotiou M: Morphometric and molecular analysis of the three Arbutus species of Greece. *Notulae Botanicae Horti Agrobotanici Cluj-Napoca* 2016, 442:423-430.
41. Bertsouklis K: Discussion regarding A x andrachnoides (personal communication). In.; 2020.
42. The Scots who fought in the battle for Jerusalem [https://www.bc.com/news/uk-scotland-42263779]
43. Wade N: Before the Dawn. New York: The Penguin Press; 2006.
44. Arbutus canariensis -Victoria Australia [http://vhd.heritagecouncil.vic.gov.au/places/70757/]
45. Lamdin-Whymark S: Tenerife Nature Walks. Oxford, UK: Flintwork Publications,; 2013.
46. Lamdin-Whymark S: Communication about where Arbutus canariensis In.; 2017.
47. Schmincke H-U: IV. The Geology of the Canary Islands. In: *Biogeograpy and Ecology in the Canary Islands.* Edited by Kunkel G, vol. 30. The Hague: Dr. W. Junk; 1976: 67, 73-76.

48. Corne L, Quintero J: Canary Islands, 6th edn. London: Lonely Planet Publications Pty Ltd; 2016.
49. Schwidetzky I: II. The Prehispanic Population of Canary Islands In: *Biogeograpy and Ecology in the Canary Islands.* Edited by Kunkle G, vol. 30. The Hague: Dr. W. Junk 1976: 15-24.
50. Dugard M: The Last Voyage of Columbus. New York: Little, Brown & Company; 2005.
51. Treaty of Alcáçovas [https://en.wikipedia.org/wiki/Treaty_of_Alc%C3%A1%C3%A7ovas]
52. Vingiani S, Adamo P, F T: Lichen-rock interaction in volcanic environments: evidences of soil-precurso formation. *Geophysical Research Abstracts, EGU General Assembly* 2012, 14:EGU2012-7944,.
53. Pascual M, Acebes Ginove ́s J, del Arco Aguilar M, : Arbutus xandrosterilis, a New Interspecific Hybrid between A. canariensis and A. unedo from the Canary Islands. *Intern Assoc for Plant Taxomomy* 1993, 42:789-792.
54. Pen ́elas J, Filella I, Zhang X, Llorens L, Ogaya R, Lloret F, Comas P, Estiarte M, Terrada J: Complex spatiotemporal phenological shifts as a response to rainfall changes. *New Phytologist* 2004, 161:837-846.
55. Bertin R: Plant phenology and distribution in relation to recent climat change. *J of the Torrey Botanical Society* 2008, 135(1):126-146.
56. Tao Z, Wang H, Dai J, Alatalo J, Ge Q: Modeling spatiotemporal variations in leaf coloring date of three tree species across China. *Agricultural and Forest Meteriology* 2018, 249:310-318.
57. Demoly J-P: Nouveaux hybrids d'arbousiers. *Bulletin De L'association Des Parcs Botaniques De France* 2004.
58. Panama American Exposition InformationSources [https://www.huffingtonpost.com/thomas-gladysz/fair-reading-about-the-panama-pacific_b_7164460.html]
59. Demoly J-P: Communication Letter and email. In.; 2018.
60. Demoly J-P: "Les Cèdres": An Exceptional Botanical Garden. Paris: Editions Franklin Picard; 1999.
61. Mackenzie L: commuication email. In.; 2018.
62. Catt P: Communication by email. In.; 2018.
63. Briggs Nursery (history) [https://www.briggsnursery.com/about-briggs/history/]
64. San Marcos Growers [https://www.smgrowers.com/products/plants/plantdisplay.asp?strSearchText=arbutus&plant_id=158&page=]
65. The Days of DDt and Roses (see paragraph on Victor Reiter) [https://www.pacifichorticulture.org/articles/the-days-of-ddt-and-roses/]
66. Carla Reiter Obituary [https://www.legacy.com/obituaries/sfgate/obituary.aspx?n=carla-reiter&pid=165526001]
67. The legacy of the Saratoga Horticultural Research Foundation [https://www.pacifichorticulture.org/articles/the-legacy-of-the-saratoga-horticultural-research-foundation/]
68. Ritter M: A Californian's Guide to the Trees Among Us. Berkeley, CA: Heyburgh; 2016.
69. Sullivan M: Yearly Guide to the Trees of San Francisco, 2nd edn. Birmingham, AL: Wilderness Press; 2013.
70. Baldwin R: Correspondence by email, phone, and mail. In., San Marcos Growers director edn; 2018.
71. Flowering all year San Marcos Growers [https://www.smgrowers.com/info/arbmarflw.asp]
72. Guadalupe Mountains National Park - Pratt Cabin [https://www.nps.gov/gumo/learn/historyculture/prattcabin.htm]
73. Kunth KS: Nova Gener et Species Plantarum (quarto ed.); 1818.
74. Carl Sigismund Kunth Biography [https://en.wikipedia.org/wiki/Carl_Sigismund_Kunth]
75. Von Humboldt, Alexander Biography [http://libweb5.princeton.edu/visual_materials/maps/websites/thematic-maps/humboldt/humboldt.html]
76. Bonpland, A Bibliography [https://en.wikipedia.org/wiki/Aim%C3%A9_Bonpland]
77. Buckley SB Biography [https://en.wikipedia.org/wiki/Samuel_Botsford_Buckley]

78. Buckley S: Proc. Acad. Nat. Sci. Philadelphia: Academy of Natural Sciences; 1862. 1861.
79. Sørensen P. (Personal Communication).
80. Durand, E Biography [https://en.wikipedia.org/wiki/Elias_Durand]
81. Hileman LC, Vasey MC, Parker VT: Phylogeny and biogeography of the Arbutoideae (Ericaceae): Implications for the Madrean-Tethyan hypothesis. *Systematic Botany* 2001, 26(1):131-143.
82. Parker V. (Personal Communication) 2017.
83. Ortega A AL: Biological and Socioeconomic importance of the Sierra De La Laguna at Baja California Sur, Mexico. In: *Proceedings of the Symposium on Biosphere Reserves, 4th World Wilderness Congress* Edited by Gregg WP Jr. KS, Wood Jr. JD. Washington, D.C. : National Park Service and Forest Service Dept. of Agriculture, USA; 1987: 207-211.
84. Centeno-Garcia E: Mesozoic tectono-magmatic evolution of Mexico: An overview. *Ore Geology Reviews* 2017, 81:1035-1052.
85. Biospher Reserve Information, Sierra La Laguna, Mexicao [http://www.unesco.org/mabdb/br/brdir/directory/biores.asp?mode=all&Code=MEX+13]
86. United Nations Educational, Scientific and Cultural Orgaization (UNESCO) [https://en.m.wikipedia.org/wiki/UNESCO]
87. Rebman JP RN: Baja California Plant Field Guide. San Diego, CA: San Diego Natural History Museum; 2012.
88. Rose JR, Goldman: Studies of Mexican and Central American Plants—No. 7, Contributions from the United States National Herbarium 1911, 13(9):312.89.
89. Arriaga L, Rodriguez-Estrella R, Ortega-Rubio A: Endemic Hummingbirds and Madrones of Baja are they mutually dependent? *The Southwestern Naturalist* 1990, 35(1):76-79.
90. Sargent CS: *Arbutus arizonica* (A Gray) Garden & Forest, 1891 4:317.
91. Carder A: Forest Giants of the World Past and Present. Markham, Ontario: Fizhenry & Whitside; 1995.
92. Grescoe A: Giants-The Clossal Trees of the Pacific North America Vancouver, BC Raincoast Books; 1997.
93. Goddard PD: Life nod Culture of the Hupa.... Berkley, CA, : Berkley Press; 1903.
94. Beidleman RG: Willis Linn Jepson—"The Botany Man". *Madroño* 2000., 47(4):273–286.
95. Jepson W: Field Book of Wilson L Jepson. In., vol. 9. Berkley, CA: The University and Jepson Herbaria; University of California of Berkeley; 1902-1903: (selected pages included in text).
96. Jepson WL Pictures [https://ucjeps.berkeley.edu/main/archives/images_jepson.html]
97. Jepson W: The trees of California. San Francisco: Cunningham, Curtis & Welch; 1909.
98. Sylvan - Definition [https://www.merriam-webster.com/dictionary/sylvan]
99. Coe F: The Madrones. *Pacific Horticulture* 1983, Spring.
100. Coe F: Telephone and Letter communication In., telephone converstation with Mrs. Coe and letter communication with Dr. Fredrich Coe edn.
101. Council Madrone, Pacific Madrone Research [https://ppo.puyallup.wsu.edu/pmr/pacific-madrone-research-2/the-council-madrone/]
102. Pacific Madrone [americanforests.org]
103. Wohlleben P: The Hidden Life of Trees. Munich: Ludwig Verlag; 2015.
104. French S: Discussion about the Council Madrone. In., Telephone conversation edn; 2017.
105. Dry Creek Valley AVA [en.m.wikipedia.org]
106. The Heritage madrone, a bonus in the wine writer's life, for Shiloh. [https://wakawakawinereviews.com/2012/10/31/happy-halloween-or-and-now-for-something-completely-different-and-a-little-random-the-heritage-madrone-a-bonus-in-the-wine-writers-life-for-shiloh/)]
107. Gustafson Family Vineyards [gvvineyard.com]

108. Rosamond Anketell-Jones ~ some history & a memoir November 29, 2015written c1980 to her daughter: [http://www.thetisblog.net/history/2015/11/29/rosamond-anketell-jones-some-history-a-memoir.html]
109. Thetis Island [http://britishcolumbia.com/plan-your-trip/regions-and-towns/vancouver-island-bc-islands/thetis-island/]
110. BC's Biggest Arbutus [(http://www.waymarking.com/waymarks/WM79PP_BCs_Biggest_Arbutus)]
111. Lamb WK: Four Letters relating to the Cruise of the "Thetis", 1852-53. *The British Columbia Historical Quarterly* July 1942, 6(3):189-206.
112. Scott A: The Encyclopedia of Raincoast Place Names, A complete reference to coastal British Columbia. Madeira Park BC,: Harbor Publishing; 2009.
113. Kelsey S: The Lives Behind the Headstones. . Canada Copy Printing & Design Ltd. ; 1993.
114. The Original Captain Trips [http://www.fargonebooks.com/high.html)]
115. Russell Hibler Obituary
116. SBA Steamboat Register – Whatcom Princess, [http://www.steamboatassociation.co.uk/resources/register/html/what0611.htm]
117. Hibbler H: Telephone Discussions and Letter, and Photo. In.; 2017.
118. Arbutus Big Tree Registry [http://bcbigtree.ca/index_registrymenus.a5w?setViewPort=species]
119. Yeadon -Jones AY-J, L.: Desolation Sound of the Discovery Island, A Dreamspeaker Cruising Guide, vol. 2. Seattle,WA Sasquatch Books 2000.
120. Jim Spilsbury Obituary [https://www.legacy.com/obituaries/timescolonist/obituary.aspx?n=jim-spilsbury&pid=157463569]
121. White H, J S: The Accidental Airline: Spilsbury QCA (Spilsbury Saga). Madeira Park, BC: Harbor Publishing; 1988.
122. White H, J S: Spilsbury's Coast: Pioneer Years in the Wet West, 2nd edn. Madeira Park, British Columbia, CA: Harbour Publishers; 1991.
123. A wonderful Youtube of the life of James Spilsbury [https://www.youtube.com/watch?v=_FRhJ2i-Enc]
124. Vancouverislandbigtrees.blogspot [http://vancouverislandbigtrees.blogspot.com/2012/02/saving-ancient-crofton-arbutus.html]
125. Crofton ferry terminal big arbutus -blog [https://vancouverislandbigtrees.blogspot.com/2012/02/saving-ancient-crofton-arbutus.html]
126. Fort Worden Historical State Park [https://parks.state.wa.us/511/Fort-Worden]
127. St. George P: Fort Worden History; 2011.
128. Five Reasons to Stay at Alexander's Castle in Fort Worden, WA [https://smalltownwashington.com/five-reasons-to-stay-at-alexanders-castle-in-fort-worden/]
129. `McDonald P, Tappeiner II J: California Hardwood Resource: Seed, Seedlings, and Sprouts of Three Important Forest-Zone Species. aAlbany, CA United States Department of Agriculture Forest Service 2002.
130. Port Angeles Madrona [https://www.northwestarborist.com/madrona.htm]
131. Gawley B: Sign marks 400-year-old madrona tree. *Peninsula Daily New and Sound Publishing, Inc* 2006(September 7).
132. Dickerson P: State's largest madrona tree ailing, but help is on the way. *Peninsula Daily New and Sound Publishing, Inc* 2007(August 8).
133. Landmark madrona tree is dying. *The Columbian* 2013(September 27).
134. Amaranthus M: Bridging the Gap withy Mycorrhizae. *Arbor Age* 2003(January).
135. MacDonald P: The Manual of Plant Grafting. Portland, OR: Timber Press, Inc.; 2014.

136. Rasmont P, Regali A, Ings T, Lognay G, Baudart E, Marlier M, Delcarte E, Viville P, Marot C, Falmagne P *et al*: Analysis of Pollen and Nectar of *Arbutus undeo* as a Food Source for *Bombus terrestris* (Hymenoptera: Apidae). *J Econ Entomol* 2005, 98(3):656-663.
137. Thornburg RW: Molecular Biology of the Nicotiana Floral Nectary, Chapter 6 In Nectaries and Nectar, Nicolson S et al. (eds) 2007, Springer

Acknowledgement

First, I thank my wife, Darlene Martin, for her patient, tolerant, and accompaniment on my treks and travel. Further, I thank her for putting up with my humor and endless rambling about the beauty and marvelous aspects of the Madrona tree, particularly as I discovered and wrote about it. I could not have put together these pictures and writings without her patience and encouragement. Second, I thank my children (Troy, Paula, Timothy, and Gregory) and my grandchildren who have expressed enthusiasm and interest in my research and writings endeavors. Thirdly, I thank my two editors, Steve Conifer and Kathleen Kasa. First Steve for the hours he spent turning each section of my writing into smoother diction. His efforts were like taking large grit sandpaper to a very rough surface. Second, I thank Kathleen who looked at the total manuscript and suggested reorganization of some sections allowing the story to flow better, further polishing the text like using fine grit sandpaper on it. Fourthly, thanks go to Mike Prochoroff of Themadroneway, who is an *Arbutus* enthusiast and grower who regularly corresponded with me; further, he provided me with flowers, berries, and leaves of the *Arbutus xalapensis*. May his Texas Madrones keep sprouting and growing. Fifth, I thank our friends, Denny and Claudia Doneen who also have put up with my overindulging discussions about the tree and were kind enough to go on a Arbutus boating adventures with us. May there be many more boating voyages ahead.

Finally, I thank: Lorena Babcock Moore for the *Arbutus arizonica* photographs she provided me, Randy Baldwin of San Marcos Growers for his very helpful information and the blossoms he sent me; Daniel Mount for his guidance in locating some *Arbutus unedo f. rubra* trees and blossoms; James Causton for his insights; Professor Paul Sorenson of Northern Illinois University for his enlightenment, Professors Kosta Bersouklis and Marie Papafotiou of the Agriculture University of Athens for sharing their knowledge. I thank the University of Washington, Seattle, WA for the library support they provide for retired professors. Most of all I thank the Great Creator who made this beautiful and intriguing *Arbutus* tree for us to all enjoy.

About the Author

Roy W Martin, Ph.D. is an electrical engineer, bioengineer, inventor, researcher, photographer, author, and retired professor from the University of Washington. He has spent over 30 years in research in bioengineering bringing engineering experience to medical problems. He began when bioengineering was a budding field and out of necessity had to self-learn medical language and understanding of specific medical problems. In the same way after retirement, he became intrigued with the *Arbutus* genus. He is self-trained in the botany of this beautiful and mysterious tree and has become proficient in it. He lives with his wife on Fidalgo Island, a launching point to cruise the San Juan and Gulf Islands in the Salish Sea one the havens for the *Arbutus*. They have explored this in their boat, *Sea Overture*, and have traveled all over the world to observe and photograph these gorgeous trees.

Index

T

U

V

W

X

Y

Z

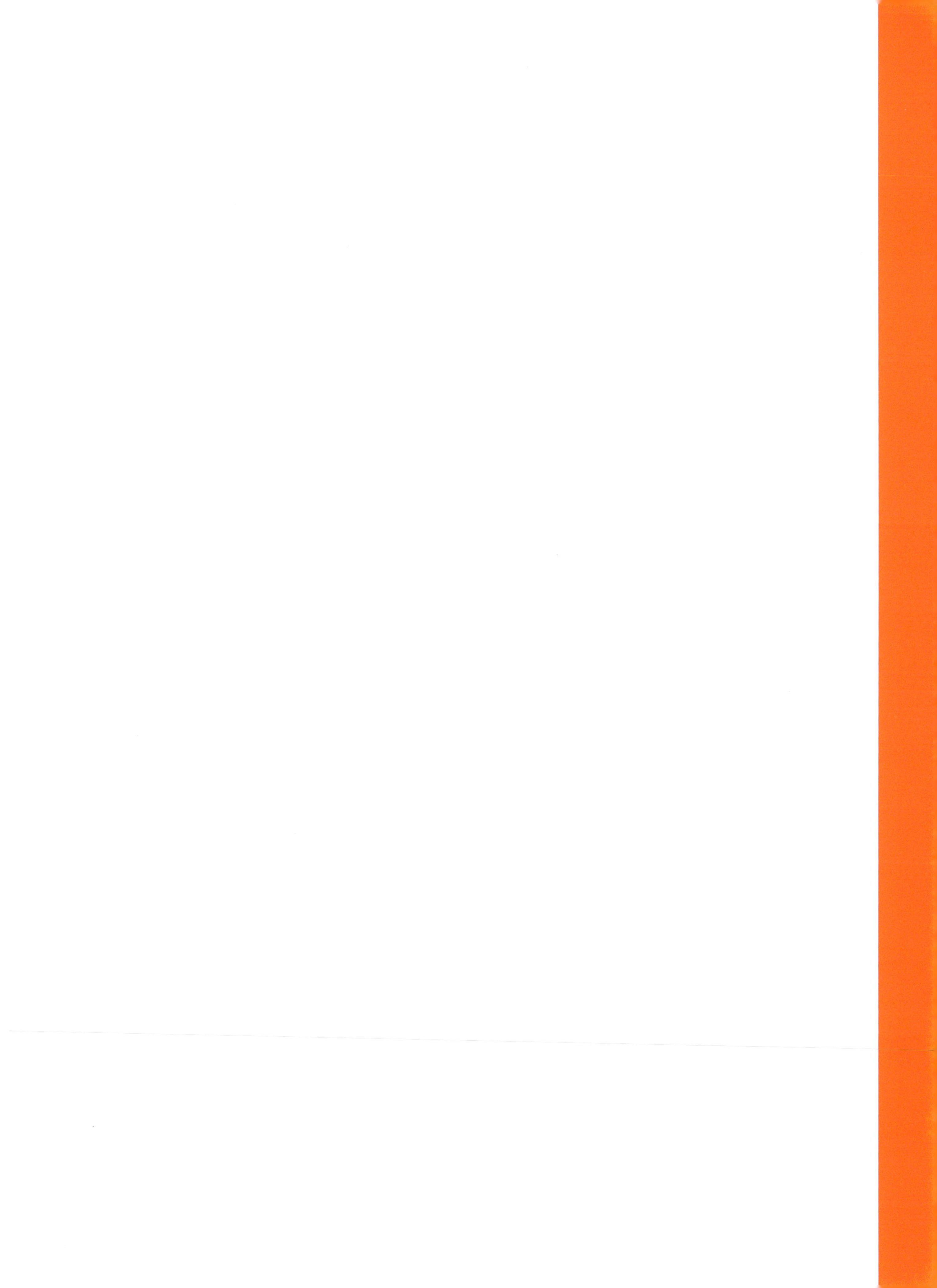

CPSIA information can be obtained
at www.ICGtesting.com
Printed in the USA
BVHW020916110422
633958BV00002B/11